CROOKED ALLEYS

SORAYA LENNIE

Crooked Alleys

Deliverance and Despair in Iran

HURST & COMPANY, LONDON

First published in the United Kingdom in 2021 by
C. Hurst & Co. (Publishers) Ltd.,
83 Torbay Road, London NW6 7DT
© Soraya Lennie, 2021
All rights reserved.

The right of Soraya Lennie to be identified as the author of
this publication is asserted by her in accordance with the
Copyright, Designs and Patents Act, 1988.

Distributed in the United States, Canada and Latin America
by Oxford University Press, 198 Madison Avenue, New York,
NY 10016, United States of America.

A Cataloguing-in-Publication data record for this book
is available from the British Library.

ISBN: 9781787384668

This book is printed using paper from registered sustainable
and managed sources.

www.hurstpublishers.com

Printed in Great Britain by Bell and Bain Ltd, Glasgow

For my mother

In this crooked, twisting dead-end chill,
they feed the fire
with the kindling of song and poetry.
Do not risk a thought.
These are strange times, beloved.

Ahmad Shamlou, *Dar In Bonbast*, 22 July 1979*

* Translated from Persian by Soraya Lennie.

CONTENTS

Map of Iranian Provinces

LIST OF ILLUSTRATIONS

1. From left to right: Ahmad Khomeini, Ali Khamenei and Ayatollah Ruhollah Khomeini, c. 1979. Source: Khamenei.ir, licensed under Attribution 4.0 International (CC BY 4.0).
2. Four presidents of the Islamic Republic: Hashemi Rafsanjani (far left), Ali Khamenei, Mohammad Khatami and Mahmoud Ahmadinejad (far right). Above them hangs a portrait of Ayatollah Khomeini, 3 Aug. 2005. Source: Khamenei.ir via Wikimedia Commons, licensed under Attribution 4.0 International (CC BY 4.0).
3. Grand Ayatollah Montazeri with Mohsen Kadivar, 30 Jan. 2003. Courtesy of Mohsen Kadivar.
4. Mugshots of Ali Khamenei and Hashemi Rafsanjani on the wall of Towhid Prison, Tehran, 2014. Photograph by Soraya Lennie.
5. The disappearing Lake Urumiyeh, 2014. Photograph by Soraya Lennie.
6. Coffins carrying the newly returned remains of Iranian soldiers killed in the Iran–Iraq War are lifted through a crowd at Imam Hossein Square, Tehran, 2014. Photograph by Soraya Lennie.
7. US Secretary of State John Kerry shakes hands with Iranian Foreign Minister Mohammad Javad Zarif at the end of

PREFACE

It was the summer of 2013, and thousands of Iranians had packed into Tehran's Shiroudi Stadium in a hot, sweaty cacophony to hear Hassan Rouhani speak. The cleric was running for president at a time when most Iranians felt a sense of great despair.

Since 2005, the presidency of Mahmoud Ahmadinejad had turned Iran into a veritable tinder box. Most of the country was ravaged by drought and water shortages, and the economy had collapsed under the weight of corruption and mismanagement, compounded by the imposition of the United States' unprecedented sanctions regime and a European oil embargo. The threat of war between the US and Iran had never been higher.

Internally, the rifts between Iran's elite had spilled out into the open, as President Ahmadinejad continued to antagonise not only the US, but also Iran's Supreme Leader, Ayatollah Ali Khamenei—the Islamic Republic's head of state and highest religious and political authority. Bitter divides emerged between hardliners and moderates, even between friends. Tensions flared, polite conversations strained, people snapped. In Tehran, it was as if the streets had become narrower, the buildings taller, the dirty air thicker. For most, there was no way out. The nation was suffocating. Iran was not just at war with the West. It was also at war with itself.

Rouhani's campaign—indeed, his election as president—came as a deep breath of fresh air, representing a revival of the moderates, the triumph of pragmatism over tired, old sloganeering, and a rejection of hardline policies and politicians. And it was the people of Iran, first and foremost, who chose that path.

But at the ballot box in 2013, no one could have predicted the confluence of catastrophe that would hit Rouhani's presidency like a biblical plague: natural disasters, a pandemic, terrorism. And back then, no one could have predicted the election of Donald Trump as president of the United States just three years later. Pulling out of a much-lauded multilateral nuclear deal— the Joint Comprehensive Plan of Action (JCPOA)—and the chance to end four decades of US–Iran hostility, the Trump administration attempted to collapse not only the Iranian economy, but the entire country. Perhaps worst of all, it attempted to deprive Iranians of their most important commodity: hope.

The US had attempted to close every avenue for opportunity, development and progress in Iran, denying Iranians the chance to reform their own country on their own terms and according to their own wishes. President Trump demonised Iranians simply because of their nationality, emboldening hardline saboteurs— both inside Iran and abroad, including sanctions-supporting diaspora—and granting radicals relevance, their greatest gift in a decade. A blanket of strangulation had thus been cast over a people who have survived for millennia. Ostensibly this was because four decades ago, in the Iranian Revolution of 1979, Iranians had overthrown a dictator, who was chosen to lead Iran not by its own people, but by foreigners. The 'strangling of Persia' thus did not begin and end with Trump, or Obama—it was very much the experience of generations.

* * *

Even before US President Donald Trump abandoned the Iran nuclear deal and re-imposed economic sanctions, back before

Hassan Rouhani became president, Iran was already in crisis. The Iranian rial was plummeting while inflation skyrocketed, and with it unemployment. Beyond the economy, the re-election of Mahmoud Ahmadinejad as president in 2009 had left the country traumatised and polarised. The vote that returned him to power was widely believed to have been rigged and triggered large-scale nationwide protests, dubbed 'the Green Movement'. Opposition leaders Mir Hossein Mousavi and Mehdi Karroubi were put under house arrest, thousands of students and academics were barred from university for being so-called 'seditionists', newspapers were shut down, and journalists were jailed.

While Iranians dealt with domestic dilemmas, the international crisis surrounding Iran's nuclear programme began to spiral out of control. From 2006, when the International Atomic Energy Agency (IAEA) referred Iran's nuclear file to the United Nations Security Council, to 2010, the UN passed six resolutions on the country, four of which imposed increasingly expansive sanctions.[1] Meanwhile, the US and its allies set out to cultivate suspicion, leading a campaign of accusations claiming that Iran's stated peaceful nuclear efforts were a guise for a clandestine atomic bomb programme. It made no difference that, despite its UN Security Council referral, the IAEA—as the sole agency responsible for inspections—had not found concrete evidence of nefarious activity.[2] The campaign didn't stop at the UN, but also included the Stuxnet malware sabotage of Iran's Natanz uranium facility in 2009–10; the suspected Israeli assassinations of at least four Iranian scientists in Tehran between 2010 and 2012; and a series of mysterious explosions at key oil, gas, and military facilities in 2010–11.[3] And, of course, an unprecedented multilateral sanctions regime, designed by the Obama administration, targeted everything from Iranian banks to shipping lines and oil.

Ahmadinejad described the sanctions as pieces of 'worthless paper'.[4] The Iranian president did not prioritise resolution through diplomatic engagement. Rather, in the words of Anoushiravan Ehteshami and Mahjoob Zweiri, he turned a 'twenty-first-century energy strategy into a populist cause'.[5] Perhaps even more alarmingly for the Iranian people, former nuclear negotiator Seyed Hossein Mousavian said that Ahmadinejad 'welcomed' sanctions, as he thought it would make the country 'more independent and self-sufficient'.[6] It was, Mousavian contended, 'the most radical position I had ever heard from an Iranian politician since the revolution'.

By the time Rouhani stood for election in 2013—as domestic stresses increased, and economic sanctions coalesced with the threats of an Israeli or US military strike—many Iranians had reached breaking point.

DAR IN BONBAST (IN THIS DEAD-END)

It was late 2012. The man's full moustache was peppered with streaks of white, and his eyes somehow smiled despite the agony and dreariness that accompanied his current predicament. Mahmoud Gomari had seen much in his life: an eight-year war with Iraq that threatened to drag Iran down into the depths of hell, bringing breadlines around the block and shortages of basic staples, such as sugar, flour, baby formula. Government-imposed rations had forced him to line up for hours, identity card in hand, hoping to get to the start of the line before everything ran out, knowing full well he had a family that depended on him not to come home empty-handed.

On many occasions, as the air raid sirens blasted through Tehran, Gomari would hurry through the small streets hoping luck was on his side, that his life would not be lost for the hot newspaper-wrapped *sangak* shoved under his arm.

The war was a pitiful misery, imposed on a population still wide-eyed with jubilation and horror in the wake of the impossible revolution in 1979. Saddam Hussein's invasion of Iran in September 1980 ushered in rivers of bloodletting and the quicksand of political struggle for the Islamic Republic's infant system, where it seemed no one knew what was going on, or what would happen.

Gomari had struggled his whole life to make ends meet, taking on odd jobs—sometimes illegal ones—for a few rial; anything was better than nothing and surely one day it would all work out. But that day never came, and Mahmoud, now in his late sixties, could only look around him and wonder about all the paths not taken, and how long it would take him to die.

A soft whirr emanated from the big blue machine keeping him alive, a few beeps here and there, numbers on its four panels. Lots of tubes came and went, some filled with a deep maroon-coloured blood. Gomari was hooked up to dialysis. His kidneys were failing, and without it, he would certainly die. Because of his age, the chances of a transplant were slim, and Gomari had neither the money nor the position in society that could curry favour to push him up the list or allow him to travel abroad for help. The machine was his lifeline.

His eyes were deeply creased in the corners, and he was bald, save for the short Friar Tuck ring above his ears. He spoke softly and was quite matter-of-fact: 'I'm almost sixty-nine years old. I've been coming here three times a week for the past year. If I do not, my body parts start to swell up. My kidneys don't work.'[1]

As Gomari lay in a hospital bed, his rolled up grey sleeves exposed a tattooed arm—a seemingly sporadic mix of ink; a cross, a woman, *eshgh*, or love. All faded like his hopes of redemption, of a new life, of a second chance. And so, this was his lot: a thin, crepe sheet–covered bed, boredom, silence, the collective agony of his fellow patients stuck in a hospital ward, five beds to a side.

In a normal country, in a normal situation, this would be as bad as it gets. As though kidney failure was not terrible enough. As though the prospect of a slow death was not shattering. As though the pain was not torturous.

But in Tehran, war loomed. Outside these hospital walls, in a fitful autumn of haze, clouds and brief rays of sun, the Iranian nuclear crisis had reached its peak. Though Iran had gone back to the negotiating table, there was no progress and little hope of a breakthrough. The country's president, Mahmoud Ahmadinejad, in the death throes of a final term, continued to antagonise both at home and abroad, seemingly oblivious to the rising chance of war or a military strike on Iran. But the tense atmosphere did not escape everyone's notice; in Tehran, foreign embassy officials had started going over protocols and test evacuations in case of war, while Iranians themselves started thinking about whether to stay or, if they had the means and possibility, to go.

The United States under Barack Obama, who was heading for re-election in November 2012, had already issued eleven orders sanctioning Iran for various sins, including its nuclear programme. Sanctions compounded an already troubling situation: the Iranian rial was in a death spiral, having lost 60 per cent of its value against the US dollar in just two weeks.

It was just about as bad as it could get. And this was well before anyone had even considered the possibility that, four years later, Hillary Clinton would lose the so-called unlosable election and Donald Trump would take a seat in the Oval Office, where he would wage his own, very special, 'tremendous' war on Iran's economy.[2]

In the midst of the Obama-era chaos, crisis and uncertainty, Gomari had come in for yet another dialysis treatment—the third that week—feeling deeply anxious and under immense pressure. He was also alone, with no one except his fellow patients to keep him company. 'Only God knows how long I'll have to keep coming here,' he quietly wondered, giving voice to the crippling nervousness of uncertainty. Knowing he probably would not get a donor. Not knowing if he would survive. Not knowing what would happen to his country. His primary concern, like that of the other patients in the room, was dialysis and survival, but the nuclear crisis too and the hovering threat of war had seeped into this place and poisoned any last well of optimism.

The nuclear standoff meant that these patients, as miserable as they were, as ordinary as they were, had been thrust into the middle of an international struggle of wills. And make no mistake: for many Iranians this struggle was—and continues to be—one of life and death.

For dialysis patients, survival was dependent on a $7 plastic filter. Although Iran had become increasingly self-reliant, including medically, the government estimated that imports accounted for 5 per cent of its medical supplies—including those cylinder-like filters, which were made in Germany. Known as an F70 dialyser, the filter is unexceptional-looking—about thirty centimetres long and encased in clear plastic. Inside, white hollow fibres run its length to filter the blood and dialysis fluids before they are returned to the patient.

Under normal circumstances—whatever they once were—buying these parts would not be an issue. In fact, they are available to patients on home dialysis the same way they are available to hospitals. But under sanctions, life in Iran was no longer normal.

And yet, it did continue. Under the worst multilateral sanctions regime in Iran's modern history, patients like Mahmoud had no choice but to come in for their scheduled treatments. But the stock of medical equipment was depleting at the hospital, one of the many branches of the Charity Foundation for Special Diseases, as it tried to keep up. According to the foundation's chairwoman, Fatemeh Hashemi Rafsanjani—daughter of former president Ayatollah Ali Akbar Hashemi Rafsanjani—they had been stockpiling as much as they could for almost a year, preparing for the worst. But, like other importers and buyers of foreign medicine, Hashemi had recently noticed a sharp increase in prices. Suddenly, the $7 filter became a $14 filter, then jumped to $21 apiece.

It has been widely assumed that nefarious price gouging and corruption—typical in Iran during times of economic crisis, and rampant during the presidency of Mahmoud Ahmadinejad[3]—had a significant impact on the sudden price increases under sanctions. That may be true of other types of goods, but there was another factor contributing to the rising costs of medicine and equipment. At the same time that the Charity Foundation for Special Diseases was trying to stockpile medicine and equipment, European exporters specifically targeted the Iranian market, raising prices. The trend began in early 2010, just as the Obama administration, the EU and the UN started to ramp up sanctions. The same period shows no such increase in price to other similar export markets, namely Russia, Turkey and Pakistan.[4]

The price hike continued into 2011, when on December 31, in the dying hours of the Georgian year, the Obama administration issued sanctions to target the Central Bank of Iran. The legislation specifically stated, 'The President may not impose sanctions under paragraph (1) with respect to any person for conducting or facilitating a transaction for the sale of agricultural commodities, food, medicine, or medical devices to Iran.'[5]

It was useless now to omit medical sanctions when traders with Iran were already hyperventilating in fear of US punishment. The European price hike had already created critical shortages inside Iran, disproportionately affecting people with rare or special diseases, as special medications made up a large proportion of imports. Customs data shows that by Norooz (Iranian New Year) on 21 March, the price of European medical exports to Iran in 2012 was €10,167.13 per 100 kilograms—a 40 per cent price increase compared to the same pre-sanctions period in March 2010.[6]

The stress of treating patients with rare diseases is high, but the added pressure of not knowing if you can continue to find the medicine and supplies, or if you can even afford to provide those services anymore, was palpable. The doctor overseeing the dialysis patients had had enough. Mentally, he had checked out. He had not shaved, his dark hair was matted, and his thin eyes were tired and dejected. 'We do our best to supply the needed medications and materials despite the increasing prices,' began Dr Ali Reza Fallah, who even spoke with a defeated air. 'We have to do it at any cost. If the medication is not supplied, it can lead to death. There is no other way to solve this problem. Even if one part of this equipment doesn't work, it's useless.'

The doctor walked through the ward, casually checking charts and monitors, making a few notes. He explained that his patients had nowhere else to go. True, Gomari might not get a kidney. He was in his seventh decade of life, and his physicians had determined that he was not an ideal candidate. But there were others in beds near him that might. A teacher, a mother, a wife. But that is only if they could get to that point, if the machines kept them alive for long enough, if Iran could keep buying foreign filters, even though the price was astronomical and it took all kinds of deals to get it done.

Gomari was caught in a situation over which he had no control: international politics. The Obama administration, like some in the Trump administration that followed, made a point of distinguishing Iran's leadership and institutions from its people—at least in speech. US Secretary of State Hillary Clinton stated, 'Our goal is to pressure the Iranian government, particularly the Revolutionary Guard elements, without contributing to the suffering of the ordinary [Iranians], who deserve better than what they currently are receiving.'[7] Some went even further, like Obama-era Treasury spokesman John Sullivan, who said Iran was to blame for its own problems: 'If there is in fact a shortage of some medicines in Iran, it is due to choices made by the Iranian government, not the US government.'[8]

A few short years later, the Trump administration followed the same script, with Secretary of State Mike Pompeo insisting that sanctions were directed at the Iranian regime, 'point blank', and 'not at the Iranian people'.[9]

It was a point of bitter frustration on the streets of Tehran—indeed, across the country; very clearly, sanctions were and are impacting average people, despite all the high-minded statements coming out of Washington. At the pop-up Mahak Charity bazaar for Norooz in the capital's suburb of Shahrak-e Gharb, one young volunteer described the US sanctions stance as 'someone holding your head underwater while telling you you're not drowning'.[10] At organisations like Foundation for Special Diseases, and Mahak, which supports children with cancer, the frustration was arguably heightened, as their patients have specialised needs because of their illnesses and rely on charity for treatment and assistance. For many, there is no other option but benevolence. Even that had become difficult. Because of EU sanctions that disconnected Iranian banks from the SWIFT bank service, charities could not buy foreign medicine through traditional avenues, and Iranians abroad could not transfer money home to help either.

But there is another side to this story: a government that empowered cartels, traded in nepotism and seemed to be more concerned with the promotion of excessive religious traditionalism than economic policy.[11] Economists had been warning Ahmadinejad for years—in writing—that his policies were devastating, but the president saw this as a 'challenge' rather than advice, and refused to listen.[12] And even as the price of oil reached record highs and Iran, before the oil embargo, was making more money from black gold than at any time in the republic's history, there was little to show for it. The administration had already drained the Oil Stabilization Fund, set up in 2000 by former president Mohammad Khatami, which according to its rules was to hold 85.5 per cent of oil and gas earnings in excess of the amount earmarked for the national budget. Some of the money went to fund one of Ahmadinejad's pet projects, the Imam Reza Love Fund, which he had set up to help newlyweds.[13]

By the time the Obama administration and its allies began imposing the worst of their sanctions regime, the country was already in deep economic trouble. Again, economists—including Saeed Laylaz—predicted that, if not handled correctly, the wave of sanctions would be a deathblow. But again, the president ignored them, focusing his efforts on resistance abroad and promoting his version of Iranian values at home. It was as though the president and his men thought sheer stubbornness could circumvent an international coalition that was cutting off all the country's financial lifelines.

Laylaz, seated in the corner of his lounge, described the negative effect of sanctions as a result of 'stupid policies by the government, rather than exclusively the fault of the West'.[14] Coming from an Ahmadinejad critic, Laylaz's views were not a surprise. He had been sentenced to nine years in jail in 2009 after repeatedly accusing the country's leaders, in both Iranian and foreign media, of rigging the election in favour of incumbent President Ahmadinejad.[15]

The economist, identifiably sporting his trademark large black-rimmed glasses, dark moustache and permanent salt-and-pepper stubble, served as an economic advisor to reformist President Mohammad Khatami. He also holds close ties to imprisoned Green Movement leader Mir Hossein Mousavi, for whom he worked during the 2009 election, and whose original artwork hangs on Laylaz's wall.

According to Laylaz, Ahmadinejad's handling of the subsidies crisis was also to blame for the country's situation. The administration, cheered on by the International Monetary Fund (IMF), had planned to phase out the Shah-era subsidies for basic staples like fuel, bread and rice, which drained an estimated US$100 billion annually from the budget.[16] But Ahmadinejad began handing out cash to counterbalance the reduction of some subsidies. And when there was no cash left, he ordered the Central Bank to issue more. Thus, said Laylaz, the wanton disregard for economic realities caused crippling inflation and the sudden devaluation of the rial.

Working-class suburbs, like Khorasan in downtown Tehran, were hit hard. And these had been the sorts of suburbs that had previously supported Ahmadinejad and his populist policies. Shopkeeper Hossein Arooni had been opening up his corner store at 5 a.m. for almost fifty years. In that time he had watched Iran change—through political upheaval, revolution and war. Until the economic crisis, profits from the little store were enough for Arooni to support his wife and their ten children, but he conceded, 'aside from the war, I've never seen things this bad'. He explained how the number of customers had decreased by 50 per cent, but his costs, 'like water, electricity and gas' had increased. 'People's incomes are not enough,' he said, 'and the tax we have to pay is not fair. The electricity, for example. This fridge, I can't turn it off—it should always be on, otherwise everything will go bad. There is a lot of pressure on us.'[17] Arooni didn't need an economics degree to figure out why. 'The biggest reason for increasing prices could be sanctions, but possibly it's also because of the government's management. I can't say it hasn't had an impact. If you have a good manager, things work well.'

But the president's response to criticism and pressure was 'go to hell'.[18] This directive also applied to members of his own cabinet, including Marzieh Vahid Dastjerdi, the health minister, whom he sacked for publicly complaining that her department had only been given a quarter of the almost $2 billion that the government had budgeted for medical imports. Dastjerdi told Iranian media: 'The Central Bank has not allocated any exchange for the import of drugs and medical equipment. ... We need $2.5 billion in foreign exchange to meet the needs of the medical sector for the year, but only $650 million has been earmarked.'[19]

Given that the Central Bank of Iran, or Bank-e Markazi, acts as banker to the Iranian government, is mandated to keep government accounts, and controls Iran's gold and foreign exchange reserves, it was a rather critical comment.[20] Dastjerdi's interview was also a key example of how, in the post-2009 election fiasco, as the Obama administration continued to pile on the pressure and turn the screws with its sanctions regime, once surreptitious and often venomous factional infighting had spilled out into the open. The fractures within Iran's ruling elite became more pronounced— including in the hardline camp, some of whom, like Dastjerdi, became exasperated with Ahmadinejad's mismanagement.

From behind her all-encasing, tightly closed black chador, Dastjerdi also raised another point, telling state TV: 'I have heard that luxury cars have been imported with subsidised dollars, but I don't know what happened to the dollars that were supposed to be allocated for importing medicine.'[21] In effect, the health minister was accusing the Central Bank and her own government of not only mismanagement, but also possible misuse of the subsidised currency scheme. While the medical industry was in crisis and Iranians were dying because they couldn't access or afford proper care, the government allegedly withheld money for medical imports and continued to allow the use of its precious little subsidised foreign currency for luxury goods—which, as Dastjerdi stated, included foreign cars.

Iran's own customs data corroborated the health minister's claims. Between March and November 2012, over 617 million dollars' worth of subsidised foreign currency reserves were used to import more than 5,000 cars—even though Ahmadinejad denied it was happening.[22] Those subsidised dollars are controlled by the Central Bank, which during that period was headed by Mahmoud Bahmani.[23] Bahmani has been accused of corruption and facilitating economically ruinous spending during the Ahmadinejad era.[24] He denies both.

Although the president had fired the health minister in part because she had aired the government's dirty laundry in public, none of this was a secret. In fact, while millions of Iranians stressed about how to pay for medication, and others watched the value of their savings disintegrate, more and more luxury cars hit the streets, zipping around North Tehran, or racing up the Tehran–Qom highway like it was *The Fast and the Furious*. Luxury car dealerships near Shariati Street continued to do a roaring trade, as rich Iranians, cocooned by wealth and seemingly oblivious to the plight of many of their countrymen, bought glittering Porsches and Maseratis straight out of showrooms, enraptured by the status they seemed to exude. Meanwhile, passengers on the beat-up Shariati Street bus, who paid 250 toman (about 5 US cents) for a ticket to and from Tajrish Square, would glance out the window as they passed, privately wondering how anyone could still afford such an expense. No one could really fault a person for wanting the best, or indeed for succeeding, but during a time of dire economic crisis, such obscene displays of wealth—often flouted by the young post-revolutionary *nouveau riche*, or *aghazadeh*s, not just in the streets but also on Instagram—were quickly becoming very unpopular.[25]

Dastjerdi had also touched on something else, although it's unclear whether she intended to or not: the racket of subsidised dollars. This was how, according to Laylaz, a particular group of Iranians had gone from laymen, merchants or clerics to millionaires—from special access to cheaper greenbacks. Years earlier, Laylaz had described it as 'exchange-rate fraud', estimating that Iran had lost '$3 billion to $5 billion annually ... and the lion's share of that went to about fifty families.'[26]

It works fairly simply—if a person had the right connections to get an import licence, they could use the licence to access foreign currency at a subsidised rate (through the Central Bank). At the height of the sanctions crisis in 2012, the government was selling greenbacks at about 12,260 rials to the dollar. After the Ahmadinejad-era currency crash, the resale value on the open market fluctuated between 35,000 and 40,000 rial, drawing a profit of about 200%.

If in the post-revolutionary chaos some select Iranian families had become immensely wealthy through such fraud, there is evidence that decades later, in the midst of crippling sanctions, the racket still continued. But this time, the effect on ordinary Iranians was arguably far worse.

* * *

It was telling that in years gone by, Iran's growing middle class had earmarked places like Dubai as favourite holiday destinations. With the rise and development of the United Arab Emirates from desert villages to glittering petro-kingdoms, a trip across the warm waters of the Persian Gulf had suddenly become a lot more alluring. As well as the estimated 450,000 Iranians who lived in the Emirates, mostly in Dubai, on average close to 400,000 Iranians visited the city each year.[27]

But as the pressure of international sanctions increased, the nature of many of those trips changed. While before the recession Iranians had returned with suitcases filled with clothes, handbags and shoes, some of those same suitcases were now full of medication.

If some patients relied on benevolence, many others relied on their personal networks. Indeed, those who could afford it were going to Dubai, or even Istanbul, with long lists of medicines, while others secured the services of friends or relatives to do it for them.

It was on this type of transaction that Narges Tehrani was counting.[28] At the market in the capital's inner western suburb of Gisha, she walked slowly between stalls, pulling her empty canvas shopping trolley behind her. Dressed in a colourful scarf and cream manteau, she stopped to inspect some tomatoes, which according to the handwritten sign were selling for 20,000 rial per kilo. The price had doubled in the last month. With a confidence held solely by middle-aged mothers, she berated the vendor over the price. He shifted from foot to foot and shrugged. 'Sanctions', he told her.

Clearly, tomatoes were not on the US sanctions list. And though they are a key ingredient in many Iranian dishes, as far as anyone can tell, they are not needed in the nuclear bomb-making process. But with Iran's economy in ruins, the domino effect of 'sanctions' had become the go-to explanation for just about everything.

Tehrani's annoyance over her groceries could be brushed aside, as more or less all shoppers were in the same boat. More pressingly, the fifty-something-year-old had breast cancer. The limited income she had as a teacher was stretched beyond measure, since the drugs she needed to save her life were in very short supply. In fact, of the seventy-three medications that researchers identified as subject to shortage in Iran in 2016, 23 per cent were used in cancer treatment.[29] So, Tehrani had gone from pharmacy to pharmacy, even frequenting the black-market drug sellers on Nasser Khosrow Street, close to Tehran's Grand Bazaar. While just up the street the traditional bazaars were hawking all kinds of wares—gold, textiles, carpets—the pill sellers were taking orders and filling prescriptions like back-alley pharmacists.

As a study in *The Lancet* concluded, 'delays in delivery of medical supplies to patients with cancer can be life-threatening, [and] even those who can access their daily required medicines are not guaranteed affordable prices'.[30] It was a seller's market.

The street pharmacists in downtown Tehran had sprung back to life as sanctions hit, peddling foreign drugs based on a type of tier system. American and European drugs were of course top tier, explained one such seller, which was reflected in the prices—often five times higher than before Obama-era sanctions. Turkish pharmaceuticals, less available and usually less in demand, were cheaper, followed by medications from India and China. The latter had started to make up most of the shortfall caused by the dwindling imports of often patented American and European drugs, forcing Iran to rely on poorer-quality medicines, even 'in cases where it had previously deemed them unsuitable'.[31] Obviously, no one was going to Nasser Khosrow with the express wish of buying medication made in India or China, but many patients and their families were faced with a stark choice: settle, or walk away empty-handed.

However, the one benefit of sanctions and international isolation since the establishment of the Islamic Republic had been Iran's push for self-reliance (which Ahmadinejad himself had mentioned to nuclear negotiator Seyed Hossein Mousavian). This drive translated to many manufacturing sectors, including medicine. Iranian-American businessman Siamak Namazi estimated Iran's medical industry, which included domestic manufacturing, to be worth $3 billion.[32] It had grown considerably since the revolution, when Iran imported an estimated 70 to 80 per cent of its pharmaceutical goods.[33] Since then, Iran has made use of its highly educated population and its penchant for the sciences, to the point that by 2018, Akbar Barandegi, head of Iran's Food and Drug Administration, estimated that Iran was producing around 97 per cent of drugs and vaccines itself.

However, Barandegi also estimated that 25 per cent of the raw materials were still imported.[34] Deputy Health Minister Mohsen Asadi Lari said the number was even higher, at 40 per cent.[35] And just as sanctions impact Iran's ability to import finished patented drugs, it also affects whether the country can import raw chemicals to make generic versions. In the growing absence of European and American raw goods, Iran had again increasingly relied on India and China. Medical researchers reached the same conclusion regarding the quality of these imports as they had with the finished products—they weren't good enough and, in some cases, were actually dangerous. Doctors had even started warning patients about usually reliable over-the-counter cold-and-flu medications made in Iran, after reports that several people had fallen seriously ill after taking them.[36]

So, failing to find the drugs needed at various pharmacies, and not willing to pay the extortionist prices at Nasser Khosrow for Indian- or Chinese-made pills, cancer patient Narges Tehrani was hoping a relative could come to the rescue.

Leaning on her shopping cart slightly, she explained that an in-law was at that moment in Dubai sourcing European-made drugs for the first round of her treatment. Tehrani, though, was nervous. Even though the quality was assured (compared to what she might be able to find on the street), the medicine would cost five times what it once had under 'normal' circumstances—not because of price gouging, but because the rial was now worthless, and she didn't have the luxury of buying the drugs at the government's lower exchange rate. Then there was still a worry about whether her in-law could get a suitcase full of medicine through customs. But realistically, what other choice did she have? The short answer, as far as she could tell, was death.

Back in 2012, and still in 2021, there were three scenarios that more or less every Iranian had in common, no matter their background or ideology. Everyone knows someone who was killed in the Iran–Iraq War. Everyone knows someone under the age of thirty-five who is unemployed. And now, everyone knows someone struggling to find or pay for medication because of sanctions.

There have been two periods in post-war Iran when stories like Narges Tehrani's became all too familiar—2010–15, while Obama was US president, and 2018 onwards, during the Trump and Biden years. That makes two periods of medical catastrophe induced by economic warfare in less than a decade. Yet both US administrations repeatedly reminded Iranians that sanctions 'do not target civilians'.

Back at the Charity Foundation for Special Diseases, Fatemeh Hashemi Rafsanjani was visibly annoyed. As a trained medical doctor, she had established the foundation with her father in 1995 as a philanthropic move. They were not short of funds to do so; Forbes Magazine once dubbed Fatemeh's father a 'Millionaire Mullah', who oversaw a family empire worth $1 billion.[37] During the Obama era, Ayatollah Rafsanjani, one of the founding members of the Islamic Republic and arguably Iran's most important and most powerful political kingmaker, had found himself under attack from the country's 'hardliners'. What's more, at least three of his children, including Fatemeh, had been sentenced at various points to jail time for so-called anti-government activities or, in the case of Mehdi Hashemi Rafsanjani, alleged corruption.[38] However, it was not the family's fluctuating fortunes that occupied the chairwoman's mind. It was what to do about the patients hooked up to machines in the nearby ward.

Wrapped in her traditional black chador, Fatemeh directed her anger at those in the Obama administration, including Secretary of State Hillary Clinton. 'Any person, any group, any organisation, that says sanctions don't target people is childish,' she said. 'They are well aware sanctions put people under pressure, not the government.' Though Fatemeh is typically polite and friendly, she bitterly reeled off the problems the charity was facing as a result of the nuclear crisis. They included shortages of equipment, such as the dialysis filter, of drugs needed for the treatment of blood diseases like thalassemia and haemophilia, and of chemotherapy drugs like Doxorubicin and Fluorouracil, both of which are on the World Health Organization's Essential Medicines List.[39]

Fatemeh estimated the sanctions had put the lives of six million patients across Iran at risk. If the foundation failed in its duties, she said, some of her patients could start dying in a matter of days rather than weeks. And because the Ahmadinejad government had failed to stop the referral of the Iranian nuclear dossier to the UN Security Council in 2006, it was not just the US or EU turning the screws; since then, the UNSC had passed six resolutions related to the nuclear issue, including a ban on Iranian shipping.[40] In Fatemeh's view, 'Global public opinion should take a position against them [sanctions], especially at the UN. While it should be defending people's rights, it's moving in the exact opposite direction. It's a human rights issue.'[41]

In September 2012, while his country was in crisis, Ahmadinejad travelled to New York to deliver his last address to the UN General Assembly. He was met with the usual protests, walk-outs and boycotts. Back home, many Iranians hung their heads in anticipation of a new level of shame.

However, the consternation was not really warranted. Where in previous years the president had delivered controversy, offence and defiance, for this last address, Ahmadinejad turned philosophical. He discussed the awaited return of Jesus Christ and the Hidden Imam, or Mahdi, his vision for a harmonious global utopia, and the injustice of the world and its imbalance of power, which he surmised was due to 'the self-proclaimed centres of power who have entrusted themselves to the Devil'.[42] Yet nowhere in his speech did he mention sanctions, the nuclear crisis or the suffering of the Iranian people. And it was that same month that the first reports about patients dying because of medical shortages started to emerge.[43]

Nor did the Iranian president directly address Obama, who warned Iran from the same podium the day prior that time to solve the nuclear standoff 'is not unlimited', and the United States 'will do what we must to prevent Iran from obtaining a nuclear weapon'.[44] Though Ahmadinejad's appearance at the UN was an embarrassment for many at home, it only emphasised just how out of touch the so-called populist had become. Very few people in Iran, save for the president's dwindling supporters, actually bothered watching.[45]

Ahmadinejad's administration had overseen the harshest crackdown on the press since the revolution, had banned thousands of students and academics from universities for alleged participation in the 2009 election protests, caused severe economic suffering through mismanagement and corruption, worsened the already battered reputation of Iranians around the world through Holocaust denial, and at home further empowered the Islamic Revolutionary Guard Corps (IRGC).

What's more, he continued to insist that sanctions were not having a dire effect on the country, despite all evidence to the contrary. And though many state actors were keen to use the sanctions crisis as a stick with which to beat the West, some were not actually all that happy with the publicity. A paradox emerged in the Iranian system, where one official would release data showing how sanctions had affected different sectors, while another would try to stop everyone from discussing it.

One of Iran's most seasoned pilots found that out the hard way. In late 2011, Hooshang Shahbazi had become a household name after pulling off a so-called miracle landing on approach to Tehran. It was the type of situation that senior pilots would never find themselves in, even in a career as long as the captain's.

His journey began back in the 1970s. After university, Shahbazi first took up a job as a safety investigator in Iran's Civil Aviation Organization. But by the mid-1980s, the thirty-year-old was chasing his dreams at Iran Air, which he joined as a flight engineer. Decades later he still remembered how proud he was to wear the Iran Air uniform, watching as the glimmering fleet came and went at Mehrabad Airport.

'That time, everything was new. We were extremely happy. We used to buy the best airplanes in the world,' he beamed.[46] After seven years as a flight engineer, then fifteen years as a first officer, the gold captains' wings were finally pinned to his broad chest and a fourth gold bar emblazoned on his shoulder epaulets. The Boeing 727 would be his chariot. It was one of the proudest moments in the captain's life.

Almost five years later, on 18 October 2011, Iran Air Flight 742 lumbered through the sky with all the grace of an old bird. The Boeing 727–200 had performed well since making its debut in Tehran in 1974. Back then, there were grand plans for Iran's aviation industry, specifically its national carrier, which boasted dozens of European routes and a non-stop flight to New York. The 727–200 was an integral part of that plan, proudly taking to the skies with the freshly painted mythical bird, *Homa*, on its tail.

But much had changed since 1974. The monarchy was long gone. In the West, the word 'Iran' no longer conjured up images of Orientalist fantasy; rather, for many, it conjured up stereotypes of Oriental fanatics. The reputation of Iranian aviation had also suffered, plagued by a long list of crashes and safety incidents due to the US ban on the sale of new aircraft or new parts to Iran, which the Clinton administration had put in place in 1995.[47]

By 2011, the 727–200 was thirty-seven years old and well past its prime in the world of aviation. Still, that year 21 million people flew on Iranian-flagged planes just like it, which, according to the International Civil Aviation Organization, are five and a half times deadlier than those of the rest of the world, accounting for more than 1,700 deaths since 1979.[48] Although the navy-blue *Homa* had been painted and repainted, it could not cover up the fact that the aircraft had seen better days. And if US sanctions on the Islamic Republic's aviation industry prevented it from updating its fleet, a paint job was the best the *Homa* could expect.

On the morning that the captain would end up at the centre of an international political crisis, he was watching a dirty grey fog lift over Moscow. Shahbazi was in the cockpit and had set the plane on its usual Tuesday course from Sheremetyevo International Airport to Tehran.

For the next three and a half hours, IRI 742 heaved its way towards Iranian airspace. Ahead, in the Iranian capital, save for the unusually warm weather, there was nothing extraordinary for the ground crew to note. Clear skies, patchy clouds and a slight breeze: ideal conditions for the captain and his 113 passengers and crew, and a welcome relief from the biting cold of Moscow in October.

Shahbazi, a veteran pilot with more than 15,000 hours of flight experience, and his two other flight crew members, including a flight engineer, were probably the only people on board who understood the veritable miracles of mechanical ingenuity that had kept the plane in the air for almost four decades. But as the plane approached Tehran's main international airport, Imam Khomeini International Airport (IKA), those engineering miracles ran out.

Twenty-five nautical miles out, the crew hit the switches to deploy the landing gear. Two lights on the instrument panel flickered to green, indicating both rear wheels had deployed and locked. But the third, for the nose gear, stayed red. They tried a second and a third time. No change. The landing gear appeared to be stuck. With time on their side, they radioed IKA air traffic control to say they would try a low flyover for ground staff to sight whether the indicators were correct. From the runway, it was clear; the plane had a problem.

Unbeknownst to the crew, inside the wheel well, a small part had become so worn that it had dislodged, blocking the extension of the wheels that were needed to prop up the aircraft's nose on landing. And in a holding pattern 9,000 feet in the air, there was little to be done about it.

The three-man crew ran through their very limited options and decided the best of their bad possibilities would be a controlled landing, which employed a complex mix of controls, speeds and angles. In these conditions, this was something that none of the crew had ever even practiced before, let alone executed with a plane full of passengers. There was a very real fear it would not work and that the plane could crash or break apart as it hit the ground and burst into flames. So, the crew decided to land at Mehrabad Airport, in the city's west, instead of IKA. Since the opening of Imam Khomeini on Tehran's southwestern outskirts in 2004, Mehrabad had been relegated to the city's second airport, although it was still the busiest, serving domestic flights. However, according to Shahbazi, it had better firefighting and safety management facilities than the newer, shinier international airport. The airport's ground crews were also considered much more experienced in a crisis. Later, the pilot would tell reformist newspaper *E'temad* that a crash at Mehrabad would also be less likely to cause as much embarrassment for the country's leadership as one at Imam Khomeini Airport, which bore the name of the founder of the Republic, and at which a major accident would have been 'a disaster ... politically'.[49]

The crew circled three times, burning off as much fuel as possible to make the plane lighter on impact, as well as to decrease the chance of an explosion. Video footage captured the moment the heaving plane approached the runway. Engineers and firefighters, standing by on the ground, held their breath. Inside the plane, the crew had told passengers to brace for impact. But with barely a jolt, the plane touched down on its back wheels alone, screaming down the runway with its nose in the air. Arguably one of aviation's most precarious balancing acts, it lasted for less than thirty seconds. As the plane quickly lost speed, its nose dropped and finally slid along the ground, coming to a sudden, rather unceremonious stop. Inside the plane, passengers stood up and cheered. No one was injured, and even the old plane, which only suffered a small amount of damage to its skin, had fared remarkably well.

However, once the jubilation had subsided, a torrent of questions—how and why—began.

The 727–200 plane that Shahbazi had safely landed was built at the Boeing Renton Factory on the shores of Lake Washington in 1974, and was delivered to Iran that same year. Though it wasn't until 2012 that the US Office of Foreign Assets Control (OFAC) added the aircraft to its Specially Designated Nationals sanctions list, blanket bans on the sale of aircraft parts and US-made planes had been in place since 1995.[50] Those bans also prevented the resale of spare parts, or any piece of equipment containing more than 10 per cent US-made components, without special permission from the US Department of Treasury. That meant Iran could not directly buy spare parts without OFAC's permission, which was incredibly difficult to obtain.

Back on firm ground, Shahbazi shuffled through papers on his desk, pointing out numbers and costs. He was a slightly portly man with a middle-aged paunch that stretched out his black-collared shirt, buttoned tightly under a black jacket. Balding, with a round face, he had a moustache and goatee. Without his captain's hat, he looked every bit the bureaucrat. He explained, 'We don't have original parts. We must buy fake parts from places like Korea, India, Pakistan or the black market. They're not safe and they are also much more expensive. For that reason, the safety of planes is in danger.' Tehran-based Iranian aviation analyst Ali Mohammad Khan Mohammadi agreed, saying that while 'airlines can supply parts through different markets ... sanctions have made it difficult.'

In a further illustration of how unsafe the situation had become, at the time of the incident, most of the Iran Air fleet was banned from flying to the European Union. The ban was instituted in 2010, after almost two years of warnings and an investigation that found 'significant deficiencies in the management of airworthiness and maintenance', and covered all triple-engine Boeing 727s, the Fokker 100, Airbus A320, Boeing 747–100, Boeing 747–200 and Boeing 747SPs. In short, Iran Air 742 should not have been in the air.[51]

The second issue the incident raised had to do with the government's drive to control its own narrative. After the near miss, the captain who had saved the lives of 113 people became Iran's most vocal critic against aviation sanctions, and he had widespread public support. Shahbazi was so incensed that he started an online petition, which garnered more than 100,000 signatures, to persuade the Obama administration to remove aviation bans. Travelling to Geneva to participate in the nineteenth session of the UN Human Rights Council, he argued sanctions were a breach of Article Two of the Universal Declaration of Human Rights, which states: 'Everyone is entitled to all the rights and freedoms set forth in this Declaration, without distinction of any kind, such as ... political or other opinion, national or social origin.'[52]

Ahead of the 2012 UN General Assembly, where Ahmadinejad delivered his final address, the captain recorded his own message to the US and posted it on his YouTube channel.[53] In accented English, the balding captain told the world: 'The biggest aviation threat and concern in my country is to fly airliners which have sixty-year-old technology and are technically worn out.' Shahbazi also directly addressed the American president, asking, 'Mr Obama, how am I supposed to believe you are sincere when you send a message of fraternity and friendship to the Iranian people on the eve of Persian New Year, Norooz, yet the next day move to endanger the lives of my countrymen by extending sanctions on civilian airplane spare parts?'

Shahbazi had become an Iranian hero. His story had drawn parallels to that of US Airways Captain Chesley 'Sully' Sullenberger, who two years prior had made an emergency landing on New York's Hudson River after both engines failed after hitting a flock of geese. The American captain had managed to land the Airbus A320 and save the lives of its 155 passengers and crew. And, like Shahbazi's effort, the landing was caught on camera. The so-called 'Miracle on the Hudson' was turned into a Hollywood movie starring Tom Hanks as the captain. Accolades and recognition followed: *Time* magazine named Sullenberger one of its 100 Most Influential Heroes and Icons; New York gave him the keys to the city; President George W. Bush personally called him to thank him for his actions, while then President-Elect Barack Obama invited the captain to his upcoming inauguration.

However, in Iran things were different. Although there was nothing Shahbazi had said that others in Iran had not, many in the Iranian government preferred the narrative that sanctions did not have such devastating effects. Officials at Iran Air, the national carrier, similarly were not thrilled that Shahbazi's statements (including to English-language foreign media) highlighted just how unsafe Iranian aviation had become.

Shahbazi had joined Iran Air in 1983 and at the time of the incident, at the age of fifty-six, had another nine years left before mandated retirement. However, following the incident, he was first banned from flying for two months, pending the outcome of an investigation, and then forced into early retirement. According to the former captain, who still proudly wears his gold wings on his blazer, his activism—including his trip to Geneva—had angered officials. They asked him to stop wearing his uniform when campaigning against sanctions, and then to stop talking about the effects of sanctions in general. The pilot refused, arguing that it was his duty as a captain to advocate for the safety of his passengers and his fellow Iranians. For his troubles, he received a belated thanks and ten gold coins—and lost his job.

Controversy aside, the third issue the emergency landing raised was the question of alternatives: what were they? For years, Iran had relied on its ageing fleet of Boeings and Airbuses, but in the absence of new planes it had also bought the Dutch-made Fokker 100 and Russian-made Tupolev to service its routes. The problem was that the Tupolev, specifically the 154, had a habit of falling out of the sky. In just ten years, between 2000 and 2010, at least four Iranian-registered Tupolev 154s had crashed, killing at least 315 people. Iran was forced to permanently ground the fleet in 2011.[54]

The post-revolutionary leadership still believed that the country had been hindered by its reliance on imports, and so Iran emphasised self-sufficiency. This translated to different areas, from food production to medicine to mechanical engineering. Aviation analyst Mohammadi surmised, 'Our engineering sector has been under pressure for thirty years and forced us to be creative. So, this has caused domestic engineering advancements.' But with various degrees of success.

For Iran, becoming an aerospace-manufacturing country in the face of international sanctions would be quite the achievement and a defiant point of pride. Back in 1995, the same year that the US first imposed aviation sanctions on Iran, the Iranian conglomerate Defense Industries Organization (DIO) put out a tender for licenced production of a fifty-seater turboprop. Respectable industry names participated, including Franco-Italian aircraft manufacturer ATR and Sweden's Saab, but due to the Clinton-era sanctions, political pressure and cost (Iran's economy was recovering from prolonged war with Iraq), Iran opted for the Ukrainian-designed Antonov 140.[55]

The rebranded IrAn-140, built from knockdown kits in Iran, became the centrepiece of Iran's domestic aviation achievements, which the government held aloft to prove that international sanctions, particularly the US ban on the sale of aircraft parts, had no effect on progress.[56] The Iran Aircraft Manufacturing Industrial Company (HESA), which assembled the kits at its Shahin Shahr complex in Esfahan, described the IrAn-140 passenger airplane as 'the fruit of expertise and commitment'.[57] As the first domestically made plane left the assembly line, the minister of defence, Admiral Ali Shamkhani, called them a 'gift presented to the heroic nation of Iran', while the minister of roads and transport, Mahmoud Hojjati, described the day as 'a source of pride which marks a milestone in Iran's aviation history'. When the IrAn-140 took its maiden flight on 7 February 2001, even the Ukrainian prime minister and later president Viktor Yushchenko attended.

Shahbazi saw this differently. 'They only built one workshop in Esfahan; they came, they showed off, but they didn't even give us the technology to actually build the planes. They didn't even give us the technical books.'

Despite this, by the end of 2010, HESA had built fourteen IrAn-140 planes, the first six of which entered commercial service in February the following year to replace the banned Tupolev.[58] However, there were several major problems. These only became publicly known in 2014 after Sepahan Airlines Flight 5915 crashed, just minutes after take-off in west Tehran, killing forty of the forty-eight passengers and crew on board. Plane parts—and people—literally fell out of the sky. The tail, painted blue and emblazoned with the airline's yellow dolphin logo, ended up in the middle of Azadi Boulevard. The landing gear, still extended, rested against a nearby wall. Meanwhile, the tops of trees were shorn clean off by the banking right wing, leaving a short yet horrific trail of breadcrumbs to a wooded area of an industrial complex where the plane had hit the ground and exploded. The pilot's last words, captured on the flight recorder, were, 'Oh, shit.'[59]

Following the disaster the new president, Hassan Rouhani, ordered the entire fleet to be grounded pending the outcome of an investigation—an unusual move given that Iranian air crashes were not uncommon. Iran's Civil Aviation Organization, tasked with investigating the crash, concluded that human error, atmospheric conditions and mechanical failure were to blame. First, the plane was overloaded with 500kg more fuel than was necessary and 190kg of extra luggage. The investigation also revealed that several mechanical faults caused engine failure immediately upon take-off, and found design flaws and a history of known engine problems, including an in-flight shutdown the year before. Antonov, the company that originally designed the plane, also knew the engines were too weak for their intended purpose and had identified the Pratt & Whitney Canada PW127A as a replacement engine for its own aircraft—but because of sanctions, it could not provide these to HESA in Iran to swap out. Further, engineers also pointed out the plane was known to struggle in the hot and humid Tehran summer heat (the temperature was 36°C on the day of the crash), but it continued to be used nonetheless.[60]

Ultimately, the findings were damning. Not only was the aircraft poorly designed, but, as Shahbazi later emphasised, 'because of the geography of Iran, the climate and high temperatures, this is happening a lot. The performance of these planes is really poor, and they just don't have the capability to carry people.' In short, he said, the aircraft, designed for the much colder regions of Ukraine and Russia, was not even suited to Iran's climate and should never have been commissioned in the first place. HESA's own statement after IrAn-140's maiden flight more than a decade earlier alludes to that fact, saying: 'tests indicated that for greater efficiency and full compliance of the airplane specifications with harsh climatic conditions of Iran, several changes had to be made. ... For this purpose, Iranian and Ukrainian experts took executive measures.'[61]

Engineers and aviation experts have concluded those measures were insufficient, but without the ability to buy more suitable planes—or even to swap the engines—Iran was desperate.

And in the end, dozens of Iranian pilots and civilians have paid with their lives.

2

THE WAR WITHIN

At the intersection of rising problems created by man and problems created by God, there was a veritable collision of misfortune. And during that time of escalation, a sudden catastrophe in Iran's north compounded the pain.

It was the summer of 2012. Some 700km northwest of Tehran, Behnam Sayfi was still dressed in his military camouflage uniform, despite the fact he was no longer on base.[1] He had the shaven head of a soldier and the rosy cheeks of youth, but his tall black boots, usually polished to a high shine, were filthy with dust. He knew that as a recruit only months into his compulsory two-year military service, the condition of his boots would raise his commander's ire. But he was no longer at training, or at his post.

His bright eyes were full of tears as he stood in the ruins of his family village, overwhelmed by the scene in front of him.

Two earthquakes had struck in just eleven minutes on 11 August, transforming northwestern Iran. Of the 600 villages in the impact zone, including Daman Abad, more than half were damaged or destroyed, leaving a disaster zone that stretched right through the mountains and valleys of East Azerbaijan Province. The young soldier had been away at training, carrying out his duties for his homeland, when the earth had rumbled without warning.

Sayfi's voice quivered and cracked as he spoke, almost in a whisper. His whole body shook with shock as he tried to explain how he had rushed home to find his village of only 300 people reduced to rubble, his parents and neighbours stunned as they sat in the middle of a quickly expanding cemetery.

The army had given him temporary leave, but he had to report back to base the following day. 'My family is all in the hospital... my brothers. I don't know what to do if I go. I can't concentrate, speak,' he said.[2]

In the mess, someone had managed to save his motorbike—a sturdy 125cc that was more valuable in such remote places than a car. Sayfi quietly dusted its seat and pushed it to a spot next to his fallen house, as though imagining the walls and pathways were still there.

The Red Crescent had just reached the village and was setting up white tents. 'We have nothing here... no water, nothing. Just me, I'm alone. I don't know what we should do,' the young soldier whispered. Nearby, a few women of the village watched the young man. They stood beside a cot, loaded with the few possessions they had managed to rescue earlier. Their faces were blank.

Back in the capital, news of the earthquake had spread. But the state broadcaster, known as Seda va Sima (literally 'voice and vision'), barely made mention of it for almost two days, despite the fact that its reporters and cameramen had immediate access to the disaster zone. Whilst foreign media and others awaited official permission to travel from the Ministry of Culture and Islamic Guidance, known simply as Ershad (guidance), the best images that Seda va Sima could come up with were a few cracks on buildings in Tabriz and Ahar.

Younis Asadi, parliamentary representative for Meshkin Shahr in neighbouring Ardabil Province, pointed out that on the night after the earthquake, state television was showing a comedy: 'Officials at Seda va Sima should be ashamed. Over there, people have lost their lives, but here, they're showing *Laughter Bazaar*. Foreigners are expressing sympathy with us, but not Seda va Sima.'[3]

Another MP, hardliner Nadir Ghazipour from neighbouring West Azerbaijan Province, criticised state TV for its lack of coverage and the president for not immediately announcing a period of national mourning, asking, 'Are our Azerbaijanis not dear?'

It was a similar story for government-owned newspapers. On his Facebook page, satirical Iranian poet Mohammad Reza Ali Payam, also known by the pen name 'Haloo', posted the images of four newspapers the day after the quakes. They all made mention of Syria, including in headlines, but there was no news from Iran's East Azerbaijan Province. Beside the pictures, Payam posted a short verse:

Who says we are an indolent government?
We are thinking of the plight of Arab people
Stop saying there was an earthquake in Ahar
For now, we are preoccupied with Damascus and Aleppo.[4]

Two days later, authorities arrested Payam and took him for questioning to Evin Prison, where he remained until his release on bail three weeks later.

Payam was not alone in his views. The lack of news coverage of the earthquakes and the government's seeming focus on foreign events further compounded the feeling of many Iranians, which had become rife since the election, protests and state crackdown of 2009, that their leadership had abandoned them.

Indeed, as the young Sayfi wandered about his ruined village in a daze, President Ahmadinejad left the country for Mecca, Saudi Arabia, to attend the Fourth Extraordinary Session of the

Organisation of Islamic Cooperation (OIC). Before boarding the Iran Air flight, he told reporters, 'The world today is in a very sensitive situation. ... I hope that the summit will focus on increasing unity and lowering antagonism.'[5]

This was not a reference to Iran's own predicaments, like the nuclear crisis, but rather to Syria. On the eve of the meeting, the OIC had moved to suspend Syria's membership, citing Bashar al-Assad's government's escalating human rights violations against protesters in demonstrations sweeping the country. The country's fate was top of the summit's agenda; the suspension required support of two thirds of the fifty-seven-member bloc to be implemented. With Assad facing isolation from both his Arab and his Islamic neighbours, the Syrian crisis had led members of the OIC very clearly to choose sides. While Saudi Arabia and its Persian Gulf Arab allies advocated arming the opposition, Tehran was firmly in Assad's corner, and the Iranian delegation, led by the president, was travelling to Mecca to make that known. One of Iran's key calculations was that during the Iran–Iraq War, Syria had been one of only two countries in the Middle East, the other being Gaddafi's Libya, to publicly stand with Iran. That support during the most traumatic period in modern Iranian history had not been forgotten, and the Iranian leadership—even a large percentage of the public, at least in the early years of the Syrian Civil War—contended that Iran should repay the favour.

But before he left for Saudi Arabia, Ahmadinejad ordered rebuilding of the ruined villages in Iran to begin at once—20,000 new homes in two and a half months, to beat the onset of a predictably bitter winter. In Tehran, a journalist at the reformist newspaper *Shargh* could not believe it. 'People are still being pulled out of the rubble! Why are they talking about rebuilding?'

And yet only twenty-four hours after the earthquakes, the Red Crescent had downgraded its rescue efforts to recovery, despite not having yet reached some of the affected areas. Asghar

Rasouli, a local Red Crescent official who was overseeing relief efforts in one of the small villages, explained the rationale: 'Most of the villages are not crowded. Everyone knows each other and knows who is there and who is not. Everyone was accounted for on the first night.'[6]

Nearby, in the provincial city of Ahar, where forty-five people had been killed, a protest was brewing outside the governor's office. Under the beating sun, dozens of men walked up and down the small street, asking guards to let them inside.

According to the government's initial estimate, 16,000 people had been made homeless. But that figure seemingly did not take into consideration the thousands of people, like the protesters, whose homes were damaged but still standing. Many had pitched colourful tents—the type they would usually take to the beach or on picnics—in a dusty park opposite the governor's office. They were too afraid to sleep indoors.

Tensions were also running high because it was Ramadan. Many people were fasting, which meant no eating or drinking from sun-up till sundown. Just like everyone else, the protesters were emotionally spent, exhausted and struggling in the heat. They claimed the government had abandoned them to their misery. Some, like a middle-aged man named Ali, questioned the decision to call off rescue efforts so soon: 'They say they know what they are doing. I am from here, and even I, who know those villages and areas, cannot get in. So how can anyone else?'[7]

A day later, two more survivors were pulled from the rubble of a remote village.

Not far away in Dehdeghan, farmer Reyhani was covered in dust. His once black shirt and blue pants had turned brown, his face caked so thickly that even his eyelashes were dirty. A pair of thin plastic slippers were all that protected the soles of his feet from the sharp metal of his shovel, as he stomped it angrily into the ground, over and over again, lifting up splinters of wood, roof and crumbled walls. He was digging at the dirt that had killed his sister.

When the first earthquake hit, Reyhani had been in a nearby field, carrying that same shovel across his shoulder and watching his dozen sheep as they grazed the short, withered grass. Though August in the north was much more bearable than in the rest of the country, the sun beat down with ferocity, and there was not a cloud in the sky to hide its afternoon rays. It had so far been an uneventful summer, and the farmers considered themselves lucky that the drought and water shortages that had ravaged much of Iran were not as bad here as in the country's centre.

The men of the village had been out since dawn prayers and had only stopped for a siesta at noon, before heading out again to finish the day's chores. It was just before 5 p.m., and their thoughts were drifting back to the village—to washing off the day's grime and sweat with the cool well water, and sitting in the shade with a bowl of fruit to break the Ramadan fast. Another quiet evening among the high, mudbrick walls of home. It was then, without warning, that the earth shook with such vengeance, such anger, that the farmers were thrown to the ground. In the distance, the little village began to crack. The sounds of screams punctured the angry roar of the earth. Houses shuddered and heaved, then disappeared in a cloud of dust.

Beneath the rubble were mostly women and children, who were home at that time of day. Those mudbrick walls, whose shade had calmed so many hot summer days, gave out and spilt sideways into the narrow alleyways, clogging the maze-like streets so no machines could get through—and none could get out.

Reyhani raced to the village, running in his plastic slippers through the alleys, climbing over rubble and broken wooden beams to his sister's house. When he had seen her last, earlier that afternoon, she had been watching TV with her two young children. As he dug with his bare hands through the wreckage, he could hear their cries for help. Minutes passed. Only minutes. The earth shook again. More screams filled the village as survivors held on to what they could, and the dust rose once again. When it settled, the house's giant wooden ceiling beams were sticking up out of the rubble like pieces of a skeleton. The farmer managed to pull out his niece and nephew—hurt, but alive. But next to them, their mother was dead, bound to the earth under a mountain of mudbrick. Reyhani dug her out with his hands and buried her himself.

Three days after the quake, the searing summer heat continued unabated. Still, a heartbroken Reyhani continued to shovel dirt. There was nothing left but to clear the debris and try to save anything left of the family's meagre possessions. His neighbours were doing the same. When his shovel clanged against something hard, he would bend down to see what it was—mostly wooden beams, split and shattered underfoot. He felt helpless. There had been no machines, no police, no rescue services around to help retrieve the bodies. Stopping to catch his breath, Reyhani kicked the dirt about with his feet, staring at it absent-mindedly. He had done all he could to save his sister, but in the end, it was useless.

'If we had had help,' he started in a thick northern Azeri accent, 'she would have survived.' He leaned the weight of his tired body against his shovel, 'I myself had to pull her out.'[8]

One of the men had managed to commandeer a little red tractor that had escaped the destruction. It was the only useable machine in this part of the village and still, debris blocked it from driving any further.

There were still no rescue services here. Admittedly, the operation was a monumental task. The destruction zone, stretching across East Azerbaijan Province, was the size of Switzerland. According to a Red Crescent official report, which came two weeks later, the twin quakes affected five cities and hundreds of villages, of which forty-six were destroyed and 356 damaged by between 30 and 100 per cent. Further, 11,908 homes throughout the region were found to be more than 60 per cent damaged. All this left 157,000 people homeless.[9]

However, aside from shock and grief, what upset survivors the most was that earthquakes in Iran are routine. The Arabian and Eurasian tectonic plates converge in Iran—their collision even created the formidable Zagros mountain range—yet the government was still unprepared for the consequences. Many of the villagers felt abandoned to their fate, with no one to rely on but each other.

'All the people were relatives, and if not, there is no difference. My neighbour was dearer to me than my own brother,' said Javad Behjat, sitting on a metal chest he had managed to pull from the wreckage.[10] He had been in Tehran visiting family when the quake hit. And although he had to drive eight hours from the capital back here to the ruins of his family house, he had still beat rescue teams to the village. With no officials to help, Behjat and his neighbours had put together their own list of ninety dead, which included Behjat's aunt. They had also dug the graves, performed the funeral rites and buried the dead themselves.

As all this was happening, some 2,600 kilometres away in Mecca, Mahmoud Ahmadinejad was having a personal victory of sorts. He was standing shoulder to shoulder with Saudi King Abdullah bin Abdulaziz al-Saud to greet guests as they arrived at the OIC meeting. Abdullah had personally invited the Iranian president to the summit and positioned him at his left hand in an effort to placate Tehran over the OIC's position against Syria.[11]

Though the meeting served a predictable blow to Tehran's Syria policy, the optics were striking: the Iranian president, the blacksmith's son from Aradan, standing shoulder to shoulder with the world's most powerful petro-monarch, in the place of the Kingdom's traditional Gulf Cooperation Council (GCC) allies like Bahrain's King Hamad bin Isa al-Khalifa, greeting OIC members, including Iran's—and Ahmadinejad's—adversaries.

It was an important gesture of unity as Saudi–Iran relations were strained, and not just because of Syria. Just two years earlier, Wikileaks had revealed, in a dump of thousands of US diplomatic cables, that King Abdullah had personally lobbied the US to bomb Iran's nuclear facilities, insisting the US 'cut off the head of the snake' before it was too late.[12] Other OIC members, including Bahrain and the UAE, had supported Abdullah's efforts. Abu Dhabi's crown prince, Mohammed bin Zayed al-Nahyan, even likened Ahmadinejad to Hitler.[13] Although the Iranian president had dismissed the revelations, the very public airing of such undiplomatic commentary was nonetheless embarrassing.

Though the summit's agenda had regional implications, much of the importance was lost on the Iranian public—not because they didn't understand its significance, but because they had their own problems to worry about. It would continue to be a familiar theme as the nuclear crisis and Iran's domestic economic ruin escalated.

Even members of parliament criticised both the president's decision to travel at a time of crisis and the government's response. Abbas Fallah Babajan, a parliamentary representative for Ahar and Heris in East Azerbaijan Province, exclaimed, 'We have not received any help from outside our region. ... Our villages desperately need help. Please, dear Iranians hear this cry, the people need your help.'[14] He went on to make an extraordinary observation about the ongoing relief efforts: 'The Red Crescent are wrecking it. They [Iranians] should come themselves. They can reach the areas by car. I ask people to bring their donations in person as volunteer groups to the survivors.'

Babajan didn't need to push very hard. Thousands of Iranians had already headed to their nearest blood banks to donate.

Others had loaded up cars and trucks, boot to roof, with blankets, clothes, mattresses and food. Motorways into the province were clogged with convoys from across the country. Turks too had also come across the border, some 190 kilometres away, to bring what they could to help the mostly Azeri-Iranians in need.

In one of the villages, as the wind blew and dust whirled in the air, cries of sorrow floated from under the nearby trees—the only shade left in the great expanse of rubble. Beneath their branches a group of women had gathered, wrapped tightly in flowery chadors. They sat in a circle and cried loudly, slapping their faces and throwing dirt on themselves. As was tradition, the official period of mourning would last forty days. But certainly, the shadow of tragedy would follow these small communities for much longer.

As well as grief, there was fear. In the ten days after the twin quakes, there had been at least 1,400 aftershocks and an earthquake of magnitude 5.1, which violently shook the buildings that were still standing and sent thousands of people, including the dozens of journalists who were covering the disaster, running for their lives.

After the Mecca meeting, Ahmadinejad returned to a sullen population—and one not at all impressed that he had left the country in the middle of a crisis. However, the government didn't seem all that bothered by the negative reaction. In fact, it had another distraction on its radar: the last Friday of Ramadan and the annual Quds Day rallies, which were engineered to express support for the Palestinians and oppose Zionism. Only six days after the earthquakes, thousands of die-hard supporters of the Islamic Republic, including the president himself, took to public squares in cities around the country, burning Uncle Sam effigies and US and Israeli flags. One Iranian journalist described it as 'a competition of fanaticism'. And, like in years gone by, most Iranians ignored the events.

It took Ahmadinejad thirteen days to visit East Azerbaijan, despite having appointed its governor and the fact that, according to official results, the quake-stricken province had helped to deliver him the presidency on two occasions.[15] In this climate, with so many focused on outside events and ideological causes, one would be forgiven for thinking that aside from a natural disaster, there wasn't much else to worry about within Iran. But that of course was not the case, for only one month earlier, the European oil embargo had come into effect.[16]

The embargo, which the Council of the European Union had announced six months in advance in order to give fragile economies like Greece time to find new suppliers, banned new European contracts for Iranian crude oil, insurance for Iranian exports and investment in the Iranian petrochemical industry, and ordered the end of all existing oil and petrochemical deals by 1 July 2012.[17] Sanctions also froze the assets of Iran's Central Bank within the EU and banned European businesses and banks from trading gold, precious metals or diamonds with Iran. These measures added to an already critical move by the EU in March to sever Iranian banks' access to the Belgian-based Society for Worldwide Interbank Financial Telecommunication, or SWIFT, which most of the world's banks use to facilitate financial transactions.[18] Its CEO, Lázaro Campos, called the decision 'an extraordinary and unprecedented step'.[19]

The sanctions also meant that any state attempting to purchase embargoed Iranian petrochemicals could not do so through traditional means. Prior to the embargo, the EU was the second-largest importer of Iranian crude and condensate. Iran exported 2.6 million barrels of crude and condensate per day, of which 600,000 barrels went to Europe. But by the time the embargo came into effect in July, Iranian exports had halved.[20] Energy experts had correctly identified that the oil sector was Iran's Achilles heel. As Volker Blandow from the

Association for the Study of Peak Oil and Gas told *Deutsche Welle*, 'the Iranian government is caught in a double bind. They urgently need the revenue from oil sales. And at the same time, the price of goods from abroad has risen sharply because of the currency depreciation.'[21] The Obama administration had also issued an executive order banning any business or entity from purchasing Iranian oil or doing business with the National Iranian Oil Company (NIOC).[22]

Ahmadinejad, never one to mince words, stated that oil embargoes against an oil-producing nation were senseless and 'among the most ridiculous behaviours of a bunch of political retards.'[23] But even though soaring oil prices helped the Iranian government to make up for export losses in the short term, Iranians were feeling the pressure. One businessman in Tehran acknowledged the first month of sanctions was one of the worst he could remember: 'It wasn't without effect. Both internal and external pressure played a role. Especially if you weigh the impact on the economy, it was something else.'[24]

Tehran-based political analyst Foad Izadi said the impact on average people was partly due to government 'mismanagement' in terms of preparedness. He noted that Iran had been able to skirt sanctions in the past, which made it clear that 'sanctioning a country, especially a big country like Iran, is quite difficult'.[25]

The international sanctions coalition against Iran made it appear that the nation of 80 million people was adrift, all alone, a pariah without friends or connections. 'Isolation' became the go-to word at the US State Department, in the EU and at the UK Foreign Office. But that was not quite true.

In the midst of Iran's so-called 'isolation', Tehran was hosting the Sixteenth Summit of the Non-Aligned Movement (NAM). At the event, Egypt's new president, Mohammad Morsi—the first Egyptian leader to visit Iran since the 1979 Revolution—was to officially hand the NAM presidency to Ahmadinejad.

With 120 world leaders expected, Tehran was being scrubbed to a shine. Parts of the Tehran–Qom road, along which the Imam Khomeini International Airport is located, were being cleaned, trash picked up, sidewalk barriers re-painted, and colourful flowers planted on roadsides and in city squares. New posters and billboards had gone up, promoting Iran and announcing its grand welcome to delegates. Some Tehranis watched on with pride, while others harboured a mix of feelings—amusement that the city had suddenly sprung into action, as its employees milled about carrying broomsticks and plants from pillar to post, coupled with disappointment that so much money was being spent on cosmetic fix-ups to impress foreigners. 'The city looks so beautiful these days,' remarked one young Iranian half-sarcastically, as she drove her dark grey Peugeot 206 on the Chamran Highway. 'Pity it's not for us.'[26]

Meanwhile, state TV wedded itself to a type of self-induced hysteria. In rolling coverage of the arrivals at Imam Khomeini Airport, reporters asked delegates cringeworthy questions about Iranian hospitality and provided self-aggrandising commentary of the pending summit, as though God himself would attend.

Hosting the NAM—the world's second-largest political bloc after the United Nations—was a key opportunity, not just for the president and his government, but for the Islamic Republic to show that actually, it was not isolated at all. Importantly, NAM represented the same values as revolutionary Iran: independence and anti-colonialism. According to NAM, its bloc's actions had been 'a key factor in the decolonisation process, which led later to the attainment of freedom and independence by many countries and peoples'.[27] In fact Iran, which had been aligned with the United States before 1979, only joined the movement after the Iranian Revolution, as its eighty-eighth member.[28]

According to Tehran-based analyst and political scientist Sadegh Zibakalam, since Iran was facing a 'difficult time in its struggle with the United States and the West ... the gathering in Tehran was terribly important for Iranian leaders, because they demonstrated to the United States, to the West, to enemies of Iran that they have not succeeded.'[29] Zibakalam acknowledged that people would have attended the summit as part of their membership obligations 'even if the gathering had been conducted on the moon', but pointed out that the US 'specifically put pressure on countries not to go to Tehran'. Even so, those countries did not only send representatives—they sent senior representatives, including 'heads of state, presidents, kings, prime ministers ... so Iran can justifiably say it has scored some points against the United States and Israel'.

But for all the hysteria, the summit did not go according to plan. The Syrian crisis exposed deep divisions within NAM, as Morsi used part of his speech, which was broadcast live, to criticise Assad. This caused the Syrian delegation to walk out and prompted an awkward moment when the interpreter suddenly stopped translating his speech from Arabic to Persian. As Mehdi Khalaji from the Washington Institute for Near East Policy surmised, for Iranian leaders, 'the image of reality is much more important than reality itself'.[30]

It was the same point detractors made after the earthquakes, when state TV had initially refused to show the extent of the damage. And it was a point that would be made time and again, including a decade later, when in 2020 a Seda va Sima reporter claimed authorities had extinguished fires that had ripped through five provinces in the Zagros Mountains, although just a few metres away, out of the camera frame, local villagers armed only with tree branches and buckets were still desperately trying to quell the flames—alone.[31]

Despite all of Iran's internal maladies, the external pressure on the country and its psychological toll had created an atmosphere where hearts were hardening. And it was not what

Western analysts had predicted. Increased nuclear sanctions did not lead to Iranian capitulation, or even compromise; instead the Iranian government had dug its heels in. 'You take up arms against the nation of Iran and say, "negotiate, or we fire". But you should know that pressure and negotiations are not compatible, and our nation will not be intimidated by these actions,' said Supreme Leader Ayatollah Ali Khamenei.[32] For once, that stance reflected the mood of the country, regardless of whether someone was a reformist, moderate or hardliner. And it was not simply sanctions; every US or Israeli threat of military action added fuel to the fire.

In inner Tehran, teacher Mina Heydari watched the reporting of these comments, repeated by various US officials including Defense Secretary Leon Panetta and President Obama, with a look of bitterness on her face.[33] 'If a US soldier sets foot on this soil, I will make it his graveyard,' she spat, perhaps accidentally sounding like one of the country's military leaders. The thirty-year-old was in no way a hardliner, or even a conservative. She partied and drank alcohol, opposed compulsory hijab and said she did not believe in God. If before the nuclear crisis most of her disgust was directed towards her own government, particularly after the presidential elections and protests she had witnessed in 2009, she had since begun to exhibit quite a bit of venom for the US and its allies. And the young Tehrani was not alone. At a late-night gathering with colleagues and friends, who included writers and at least one Iranian born and raised in Europe, it was an almost unanimous position. With their drinks of black tea and homemade *aragh sagi* (an Iranian distilled spirit, usually made from raisins) in hand, they offered to take up arms in the event of any foreign invasions.

But popular support, including from young secular Iranians, for the Republic's position against imperialism and bullying did not equate to support for Ahmadinejad, or for his individual policies. Nor did it extend to support for the Supreme Leader, or for the system, or for any other current politician. Rather, it was simply a position of resistance based on the long-held grievances Iranians felt towards the West. And that list was long.

'The historical effect [of Western foreign policy] on the Iranian psyche cannot be underestimated,' noted an Iranian diplomat based in the region, 'The West fails to understand this. They just don't understand Iranians and how this history, no matter how far off, is very much alive in our minds.'[34]

Many of the grievances felt by this young crowd were a century old and had been the same grievances that drew millions—including some of their parents—to overthrow the Shah in 1979. Of the pre-revolutionary complaints, one in particular would always stand out: the 1953 overthrow of populist Prime Minister Mohammed Mossadegh.

Mossadegh led the charge to nationalise the Iranian oil industry in 1951.[35] It was a deeply unpopular move for Britain, which had held sway over Iran's most precious natural resource since 1901, when businessman William Knox D'Arcy, with the backing of the British government, had reached an oil concession deal with the Iranian Qajar monarchy, giving him exclusive rights to prospect for oil in the kingdom then known as Persia.[36] Under the deal, Iran would receive only 16 per cent of net profits from any oil discovered on its territory.[37] In 1914, the British government bought the D'Arcy concession and established the Anglo–Persian Oil Company (APOC), which was later renamed the Anglo–Iranian Oil Company (AIOC) and in 1954 became British Petroleum, or BP. From the outset this was an unpopular arrangement amongst the Iranian public. Whilst Iranian oil paid for British lifestyles and powered its warships, the vast majority of Iranians—including those working at the refineries—were destitute.[38]

In 1932 the new monarch, Reza Shah Pahlavi, who had overthrown the weak Qajar dynasty in 1921, ripped up the D'Arcy concession, noting that Iran had only been given £11 million from £171 million in profits between 1906 and 1932.[39] But Reza Shah's much-lauded new agreement was not much of an improvement. Among Iran's new gains was a promise that the AIOC would treat its Iranian workers better, while Iran would now receive 20 per cent of dividends, distributed between regular shareholders, along with an additional four shillings per tonne of oil.[40] Yet at the same time, the agreement also extended the concession for another thirty-two years, from 1961 to 1993. Anti-British sentiment in Iran worsened even further in 1941, when Britain and its allies, nervous over Reza Shah's cordial ties with Nazi Germany, invaded Iran and forced Reza Shah to abdicate the throne in favour of his son, Mohammad Reza. The invasion also served to secure an uninterrupted supply of almost free Iranian oil for British battleships beyond World War Two.

The war too had only intensified the appalling conditions in the country. In his memoirs, the Shah's oil advisor Manucher Farmanfarmaian describes a visit to Abadan, the city with the country's largest oil refinery, in 1945:

The workers lived in a shantytown called Kaghazabad, or Paper City, without running water or electricity, let alone such luxuries as iceboxes or fans. In winter, the earth flooded and became a flat, perspiring lake. The mud in town was knee-deep, and canoes ran alongside the roadways for transport. When the rains subsided, clouds of nipping, small-winged flies rose from the stagnant waters to fill the nostrils, collecting in black mounds along the rims of cooking pots and jamming the fans at the refinery with an unctuous glue.

Summer was worst. It descended suddenly without a gasp of spring. The heat was torrid, the worst I've ever known—sticky and unrelenting—while the wind and sandstorms whipped off the desert as hot as a blower. The dwellings of Kaghazabad, cobbled together from rusted oil drums hammered flat, turned into sweltering ovens.[41]

Farmanfarmaian, who hailed from one of Iran's most noble families and was himself a prince, noted the contrast between how the Iranian workers in Abadan lived, compared to those in the British section, who had 'lawns, rose beds, tennis courts, swimming pool and clubs'.[42]

By the late 1940s, Iranian oil had become the symbol of nationalism and independence. It was a cause promoted vociferously by members of the Iranian parliament, aligned with the newly elected Prime Minister Mohammad Mossadegh, who successfully introduced a nationalisation bill to parliament, which the young Shah signed into law on 1 May 1951. Nationalisation cancelled the British oil concession and allowed Iran to seize the AIOC's assets.[43]

When Iranians lowered the symbol of the AIOC at its headquarters in Khorramshahr and triumphantly raised the Iranian flag in its place, British paratroopers had amassed in neighbouring Iraq, while London had positioned nine warships off the coast of Abadan. For many in Iran, nationalisation 'showed the world that the country had finally gained true independence', but for Britain, it marked an unacceptable 'step in the dissolution of the Empire'.[44]

In response to Iranian nationalisation, British warships blockaded the Abadan Refinery, while the British cabinet imposed economic sanctions, banned the export of key British commodities, such as sugar and steel, and blocked Iran's access to its hard currency accounts in British banks.[45] Millions of barrels of Iranian oil sat in the Persian Gulf to rust.

Tremendous British pressure led the Shah to fire Mossadegh, but then rehire him in the face of a popular nationalist revolt. Britain, unable to reverse the concession decision, asked the US for help. In his 2003 book *All The Shah's Men*, Stephen Kinzer details how in March 1953, US Secretary of State John Foster Dulles directed the Central Intelligence Agency to plan a coup, code-named Operation Ajax in the US, and Operation Boot in the UK. Kermit Roosevelt Jr, the grandson of US President

Theodore Roosevelt, was sent to Tehran to direct it. CIA documents, declassified just two weeks after Hassan Rouhani was sworn in as president sixty years later in 2013, offer first-hand evidence of the foreign-orchestrated plot.[46]

Under guidance from Roosevelt, CIA operative Donald Wilber, and MI6, the Shah dismissed Mossadegh and appointed General Fazlollah Zahedi as his replacement. The move caused widespread revolts, which left 300 people dead and forced the Shah to flee to Rome, yet the CIA and Zahedi managed to wrest back control of the country through propaganda, paid thugs and eventually the military. Mossadegh was arrested amid violent upheaval, and the Shah returned from his brief exile.[47]

Images of Mossadegh on trial are seared into the collective memories of Iranians. The country's nationalist hero—a patriot already in his seventies and in ill health—shackled in the dock of a kangaroo court, brought down not just by a corrupt Iranian monarch, but by two foreign governments.

That coup and its aftermath consolidated the Shah's already immense powers and delivered the supposed constitutional monarch absolute rule. The Shah would never forget how power almost slipped from his grasp, nor how the public had risen against him. The coup would have lasting impacts that would lead to both the 1979 Revolution and, according to countless historians, the Iran hostage crisis.

The fact that the overthrow of Mossadegh also coincided with the British oil blockade and economic warfare, perhaps in part explains why generations later the US and EU oil embargoes struck such a nerve. It offered proof to Iranians that no matter what they did or what government they had—a monarchy, a democratically elected prime minister, or an Islamic Republic—imperial powers would not allow the country's independence.

'This is an issue of self-determination,' concluded Seyed Mohammad Marandi, professor of North American studies at the University of Tehran. The US-born Iranian, son of the much-lauded former health minister Ali Reza Marandi, saw significant correlation between the events of the early 1950s and those in the 2010s. 'These are the same anti-Iran policies that Iranians have seen for generations. It does not surprise anyone,' he said.[48]

It was not bluster or hardline theories—just as in the 1950s, Iranian oil was sitting in rusting barrels in the Persian Gulf. Off the coast of Bandar Abbas, a key maritime port, Iranian troubles were clear to see. At least three giant Iranian tankers were moored, bobbing in the gentle warm, blue waters. And they were going nowhere. As the embargo hit, Iran was still pumping oil, but with inland storage space limited, and until that point largely unnecessary, it had begun storing millions of barrels on oil tankers along the coast. Speaking to *The New York Times*, one smuggler relayed that he had 'never seen so many just waiting around'.[49]

It was a bitter pill to swallow for anyone who heard the news. The only lesson learned from 1953 was that oil was Iran's Achilles heel, and not simply in monetary terms; oil was still a symbol of Iranian independence.

In the decade leading up to the East Azerbaijan earthquakes, Iranian petrochemical exports—oil and gas—accounted for roughly 70 per cent of the annual budget.[50] Thus, exports were necessary to fund everything from the military to roads to hospitals, including those damaged in the quakes. The fact that the country's real GDP shrank by 6.6 per cent in 2012, according to the World Bank, made plain the dire straits facing the country.[51] It meant that there was less money for investment, industry and, of course, rebuilding after sudden natural disasters.

Just before the onset of winter, a light snow fell across East Azerbaijan, dusting its rolling mountains and valleys, fields and cities, rubble and broken things, and the tents and shelters in which thousands of survivors had been living for four months. The air was crisp, but it had enveloped the little villages in a thick, bitter, cold mist that even swallowed the mountain tops. Though the geography was beautiful, it was an unforgiving region.

In the middle of the small village of Hiagh, Mohammad Hamiat wiped the tears from his old eyes, exposing a hand that was so swollen from labouring in the cold that his skin had split, forcing the farmer to bandage several fingers.[52]

It was unusual for Hamiat, hardened by a life of toil and unlucky circumstance, to show such emotion, but he was overwhelmed. For four months he and his wife had been living in a tent donated by the Red Crescent. They, like the other three hundred or so people who lived in the village, had lost their home in the twin earthquakes.

Just metres away, bricks had been piled up and a few laid for the foundation of Hamiat's new home. But that was all. For the pair, it was frustrating waking up every morning in a valley that was so familiar yet so transformed, and even more frustrating waiting for someone to finish building their house. The couple had blankets, a few plastic dishes, a gas heater and the clothes on their backs, but not much more. When it rained, the tent leaked, and it was only getting worse as winter approached.

'We wear three jackets when we sleep. We are freezing. Even animals cannot tolerate the cold, let alone us,' Hamiat said in his thin white tent. 'Who is to help us? We have no life. No water, no bathroom, no money, no clothes, no food.'

Beside him, his wife displayed the soles of her dirty, deeply creviced feet. The reason for their rough condition, she said, was that there was no hot water to wash properly. On a little gas samovar, she prepared tea to go with apples and pomegranates, grown from their own few trees down in the valley. Life in this tent offered a stark contrast to that of the materialistic affluence of North Tehran, some 650 kilometres away.

Most people here were impoverished farmers who survived by working the land, but their livelihoods, which were already meagre, had been altered by the quakes, as one man explained from his temporary home—a metal shipping container. 'We sold our animals—we can't farm because of the problems with the land after what happened. In this season we used to plant wheat, but no one has done it,' he said.

It was no surprise that thousands of people were still living this way. The promise to rebuild in two and a half months was ambitious to say the least. At the time, the government floated the idea of moving entire villages as a shortcut to rebuilding, not understanding that farmers were tied to their land and therefore could not go anywhere. So, the government had offered loans, damage payments and the promise to set up essential services such as gas and electricity, free of charge.

Nearby, engineering supervisor Ali Gheshlaghi explained that it took two months alone just to clear rubble. 'We've finished ten to thirty-five houses,' he said, but the project was so large that they couldn't find enough workers and contractors. 'There's also an issue of getting material. It's not the season for construction, but because of the earthquake we have to do it.'

Back in his tent, Hamiat could barely hide his anger. 'They lie. They work better for anyone who pays them off. Our construction is going so slowly. The engineers told us if we pay them, they'll work better, but I have no money,' he complained.

Some officials have also cited financial mismanagement as a reason for the lack of progress. Allahverdi Dehghani, a lawmaker from the region, told Iran's parliament that after three months, only 15 per cent of people affected by the quakes had been resettled. 'Mismanagement has meant that people in sixty-three villages still live in tents though the snow and cold has already arrived,' Dehghani told the *Vatan Emrooz* daily.

The governor of the province, Ahmad Ali Reza Beigi, an associate of President Ahmadinejad, politely refuted the claims, saying people had unrealistic expectations. 'The affected area covers 5,000 square kilometres. It's a complicated project,' Beigi said from his office. 'Most of the problems are related to people who only live in the villages in spring and summer—our priority is permanent residents. But they think if we don't build the houses now, they won't ever be built.'

Iran's economic crisis had been a contributing factor in the plight of the quake victims, with the value of the rial tanking and inflation, already at 30 per cent, steadily rising, making basic goods and raw materials much more expensive.[53] And for people who were already poor before the disaster, it meant they had even fewer avenues to turn to.

In another little village, children ran around barefoot, seemingly oblivious to the snow on the ground and chill in the air. Their mothers stood in a narrow dirt street with their colourful flowery chadors wrapped around them and looked out at where the temporary met the permanent. Some houses had survived, some had not. One woman whispered that no one had helped them. And it was all the fault of local government representatives.

She explained that the government had appointed local councils, where people could go and make their complaints and claims. But according to the woman, and, it turned out, many others, they were corrupt. As thousands struggled to deal with the bad luck that had befallen them, local representatives were lining their pockets, doing favours for friends or for those who could pay. Everyone else was literally left out in the cold.

In that particular village, there was only one toilet. The portaloo made of flimsy plastic walls sat in the middle of a small dirt lot, perched about half a metre in the air. Inside, it was no more than a metre by a metre. There was one hook on the wall, ostensibly for clothes or towels, as the box also doubled as a shower. About twenty villagers had been bathing with a wash bucket in the tiny plastic room for four months. And it was freezing.

Nearby a new house, which consisted of only one large room, with a gas stove in the corner for cooking, a television in the other and a carpet weaving loom against one wall, had been built. Next to the stove, between neatly stacked pots and pans, women crouched to make tea—expertly and with speed. It was not unusual that in a traditional village the house had no bedrooms. It was warm and its concrete floor was covered with a huge carpet. It was also spotlessly clean.

Inside, the man of the house explained why his house had been built, while others' had not. The state had put up the cost for the basics as promised: gas, electricity and water. But even to get the house built, forty-something Ali had to do it himself. There were no contractors, builders or engineers. So, the village men had banded together. Together, they knew enough about construction, piping and wiring to have completed it in three months. 'We,' he explained, gesturing to his elderly mother and three sisters nearby, 'would have frozen if we [the men] hadn't done it ourselves.'

The earthquake, just like the failing economy, inflation and subsidies problems, highlighted a glaring issue for government detractors: not only was corruption rife, but the government had based many of its policies on the advice of loyalists, rather than experts. The president, however well intentioned, had issued sweeping promises without bothering to consult anyone qualified on the topic of mass rebuilding or managing a crisis in such a geographically challenging place. And even if he had consulted one of his relevant ministers, there was a good chance that parliament had found them unqualified for their jobs, nepotistic or corrupt, as the startling number of impeachment attempts was proving.[54] And as the villagers knew, corruption had very real implications in everyday life.

While the farmers continued to struggle with their predicaments and winter came with predicted ferocity, the president himself was in parliament, trying to defend yet another member of his cabinet. Labour Minister Abdul Reza Sheikholeslami was there to answer allegations that he had illegally appointed a man accused of murder and torture as the head of Iran's social security fund.[55]

That man was Saeed Mortazavi, the former deputy prosecutor general. What a former prosecutor was doing as the head of a social security fund posed another glaring question, but the allegations of abuse were much more serious than those of nepotism and a lack of relevant experience.[56]

For years Mortazavi had faced allegations of brutality, including overseeing the brutal 2003 torture, rape and death of detained Iranian-Canadian photographer Zahra Kazemi.[57] In 2010, a parliamentary commission found him complicit in the torture and deaths of three protesters—Mohsen Rouholamini, Mohammad Kamrani and Amir Javadifar—who had been arrested during the 2009 protests. The report revealed the three were amongst 147 others who were held in a 70-square-metre cell in Kahrizak Detention Center for four days.[58] Rouholamini was the twenty-five-year-old son of a conservative politician and close associate of former Islamic Revolutionary Guards Corps (IRGC) commander Mohsen Rezaee. Though Mortazavi claimed the three protesters died of meningitis, the parliamentary report found a 'limitation of space ... heat, lack of ventilation and ... physical attacks' had killed them.[59]

But whilst the head of the judiciary, Sadegh Larijani, brother to Speaker of Parliament Ali Larijani, suspended Mortazavi from office, the president rewarded him with political postings, first to an anti-smuggling taskforce in an attempt to protect him from prosecution, and later, with Sheikholeslami, to the top position at the country's Social Security Organization. That was why Sheikholeslami had been dragged before parliament.

As if accusations of murder and torture were not enough, the impeachment proceedings provided a dramatic escalation in the dispute between ruling conservatives. In front of a packed chamber, Ali Larijani in the speaker's chair accused Ahmadinejad of trying to blackmail him: 'Ahmadinejad's deputy came to me this morning saying, "I have an urgent message from the president." He said if this impeachment is not solved, he has a tape about one of my relatives and will play it. He threatened me.'[60] But Larijani told the deputy to go ahead and play the tape. 'The difference between you and I,' Larijani told the president, 'is that you have gathered people around yourself who have charges against them in court,' alluding to Mortazavi, 'and you insist on keeping them and giving them positions, while I say if any one of my relatives has a legal problem, we must investigate it, even if the person is my brother.'[61]

Ahmadinejad had brought the tape in question with him to the proceedings. Amid scenes of outrage and accusations that the blacksmith's son was defiling the office of president, the DVD played on a big screen monitor for all—including Ali Larijani—to see. Although it was largely inaudible, it showed another Larijani brother, Fazel, talking to Mortazavi. It was clear from the angle that the video had been surreptitiously recorded. Allegedly, Fazel Larijani told Mortazavi that he used his family's status for economic gain and could do so by striking a deal with him.

It was one of the most explosive political exchanges in parliament in decades, and it revealed just how deep the schism between conservatives really was. It also exposed a new layer in the corruption and nepotism allegations that had become rife in Ahmadinejad's Iran. It was no wonder then, as parliament dismissed Ahmadinejad's ninth minister with raucous cheers and claps, that accusations of wrongdoing and incompetence dominated conversations hundreds of kilometres away in villages in the middle of nowhere.

Although supposedly under investigation for what had happened at Kahrizak in 2009, Mortazavi was only arrested in

February 2013, the day after Ahmadinejad threatened Larijani in parliament.[62] He was released after twenty-four hours but faced court three weeks later on charges of ordering employees to falsify death certificates of the Kahrizak detainees, conducting illegal arrests and being an accessory to murder.[63]

It was a spectacle. And although the allegations were unsurprisingly severe—Mortazavi had been accused of crimes, human rights abuses and waging war against the press for a decade—very few people ever expected anything to come of it. 'No matter what the result, or the verdict, the very fact that he's on trial is very significant,' said political analyst Sadegh Zibakalam in Tehran, choosing his words carefully. He also pointed out that this was arguably the first time in Iran's recent history that someone so powerful had faced criminal charges.

It took another two years for a court to ban Mortazavi from political and judicial positions for life, and it was not until 2018 that the former prosecutor was sent to prison for two years for Rouholamini's death.[64] He was acquitted of involvement in the deaths of both Kamrani and Javadifar.[65] Kamrani's father criticised the outcome, wondering aloud how the verdicts could be so different, given the similarities of the cases.[66] Onlookers pointed out the fact that only one of the dead detainees' fathers, that of Rouholamini, had connections.

3

ROMANTIC REVOLUTIONARIES

If the bitter politicking proved anything, it was that the Republic is no monolith. Naturally a nation of more than 81 million souls is not exempt from the regularities of the human condition, its fractures, fissures and laments. Nor is it a demographic equation, fought between the majority of the population born after 1979, who had no say in the critical events of that year, and their parents and grandparents, who did.

The struggle over narratives exists within factions, within distinct generations, within the many layers of society itself. It is no surprise that as those struggles became more pronounced, some of the very men and women who created the Islamic Republic in the first place—revolutionaries and clerics—became its fiercest critics. These were people who risked their lives—and many did indeed pay with blood—to build the Islamic Republic, only to find that not even impeccable revolutionary or religious credentials offered protection against radicals, hellbent on setting the direction of a country and controlling its story.

In the West, the hostage crisis of 1979 is the defining moment in Iran's modern history. In public consciousness, especially in the United States, little else registers. Images of US servicemen, diplomats and yes, even spies, blindfolded, handcuffed and paraded in front of the US embassy are seared into the collective memory of US politicians and the public. It has formed the baseline of American perceptions of Iran for four decades.

According to Gary Sick, the principal White House Iran aide at the time of the crisis: 'One generation after another has passed that image along ... and it has complicated politics. The Iranians have sort of moved on. Once a year, they remember the event and then they go on to do other things. In America, it really has never been forgotten, and Iran ended up paying a truly enormous price for that.'[1]

Outside the US embassy on the thirty-fourth anniversary of that day, thousands of Iranians rallied—only a few compared to the tens of thousands who used to gather in the 1980s.[2] There were a lot of school children, bussed in for what is considered an excursion. And certainly, there were die-hard supporters of the establishment, including war veteran turned politician Saeed Jalili, who spoke in his usual demure tone against imperialism and US hegemony, eliciting tepid cheers and claps from the audience. Although days like the anniversary of the embassy takeover provide hardliners with the opportunity to promote their own ideologies, it was startlingly clear that they had become the minority.

Behind barricades, women wrapped themselves tightly in black chadors, holding up bright yellow signs reading 'Down with USA' in English, and 'Death to America' in Persian. There were of course the usual jarring expressions of creativity, including a cardboard effigy of Benyamin Netanyahu dressed as a two-horned Uncle Sam and the US flag spliced with a hidden Star of David. Others held aloft images of the Supreme Leader Khamenei bearing one of his more famous catchphrases: 'America can't do a damned thing'. A short distance away, cameras filmed as a group of men tried to burn American and Israeli flags. Most people looked on with mild amusement. Flag burning was becoming harder these days. Not because instigators cared that the wider public thought it crass, but because new fire-retardant materials made it almost impossible to set a flag on fire, without dousing it in diesel or some such fuel beforehand.

Nonetheless, television sets across the world would beam those images of supposedly unhinged Iranians into the homes of ordinary people and politicians alike. And although only a couple of thousand people showed up, many of them children, the media gave the perception that the rally was a rippling sea of people representing the whole Iranian nation. In fact, it was clear from the general mood of the country that Iranians had overwhelmingly concluded it was time to move on. But the rallies, however small, continued to prove there were still people who hated the US government—and even Obama. Just as many had been moved to act three and a half decades earlier, today there were those who had been moved to carry signs and chant slogans outside the American embassy, which was empty of everything but its ghosts.

But in this battle over narratives and direction, those who had actually created that day of infamy in 1979 were today notably absent. Instead of rallying and chanting, they were at home, quietly turning over the moment when they had scaled the embassy walls, unsure of what awaited beyond. To their frustration, their action, which they had legitimately believed was an attempt to stop a counterrevolution and the repetition of history, had now become the basis for propaganda, hijacked by hardline ideologues. Those outside the embassy had little relation to what had happened here three and a half decades prior. And they had certainly not been part of the core group of students who engineered what is considered to be one of America's great political humiliations.

On 4 November 1979, a scene was playing out that very few people in Washington had predicted or might have believed, even if they had seen it with their own eyes. A young man was inside the walls of the embassy in Tehran, sitting behind a wooden office desk and holding up a sniper rifle that until only hours before had belonged to a US Marine. Its light-coloured wooden stock felt smooth in his hands. The black barrel and scope shone under the harsh overhead lights. Classmates at the prestigious Ariamehr Industrial University (later renamed Sharif University of Technology) often remarked that the man's face, bearing a thin black moustache, stubble beard and perpetual frown, always looked serious and deep in thought. Holding a gun made it seem much more so.

But Ebrahim Asgharzadeh was no hardened fighter, or even at that time a military man. In fact, he probably could not have hit a target 10 metres away. But in the autumn of 1979, the twenty-four-year-old leader of Iran's most important post-revolutionary student union—the Islamist-leaning Office for Strengthening Unity (OSU), founded that year by Ayatollah Mohammad Beheshti to counter the spread of Marxist and communist ideology amongst students—was enraptured by revolutionary fervour, and his marksman skills didn't matter. From his plastic yellow chair, he commanded the room with the naïve conviction of youth.

Ten months earlier, Asgharzadeh had been just one of millions on the streets of Tehran who had helped to overthrow the Shah. Now, he was sitting inside the US embassy, dressed in a collared shirt and cardigan, making sure the deposed king did not return. So far, everything had gone to plan. Hundreds of thousands of protesters had begun marching that morning to commemorate the one-year anniversary of an attack on Tehran University, in which the Shah's military had killed five students.[3] Asgharzadeh had joined the march, but there was something only he and three other people, all members of the OSU, knew—the goal was not simply to commemorate the deaths of those students, but to lead the protest to the US embassy and take it over. Just two weeks prior, the Carter administration had allowed the deposed Shah into the United States for cancer treatment,[4] but the students feared it was a guise for a counterrevolution to reinstall the Shah on the throne, as had happened in 1953.[5] Only one in that group of four disagreed: Mahmoud Ahmadinejad, who was then an engineering student at Elm-o-Sanat University in East Tehran, reportedly argued that communism was actually the greatest threat to post-revolutionary Iran and their efforts should be directed two blocks away, at the embassy of the Soviet Union. Though Ahmadinejad was overruled, he did not betray the group's plans.

It had taken about two hours for the students to break into the embassy on Taleghani Street, which had only recently been renamed from Takht-e Jamshid. Amongst the thousands of protesters, Ebrahim Asgharzadeh, Mohsen Mirdamadi and Habibollah Bitaraf had led a group of dozens of students to the gates and, with little to no resistance, had taken over the compound in downtown Tehran.[6] Witnesses say the students were unarmed, save for a couple who had sticks. Even the guns they held aloft later at the press conference were not theirs; they belonged to the US Marines who had surrendered in the face of the angry crowd. For an event that would go down in infamy and cause a catastrophic rupture in US–Iran relations—and taint every relevant policy decision vis-à-vis the two countries—it all started in a rather orderly fashion.

The core group of students, who called themselves Muslim Student Followers of the Imam's Line, even had the presence of mind and courtesy to announce their intentions on signs, which they held up in front of the embassy before they walked in. The signs announced they had no plans to harm any of the American staff and that they were merely there for a sit-in, which according to Asgharzadeh was to last a couple of days. Maybe three. The number 444 had never crossed his mind, neither then nor any time earlier while the takeover was being planned. On that first day, in those first hours, 444 was not even a whisper in the chilly November air.

Inside, the student leaders had hurriedly wandered through the main building, past desks that had been hastily abandoned, through a document processing room filled with application forms and passport-sized photos of smiling Americans, and into another room filled with metal filing cabinets and carpeted in a plush yellow shag. The choice of carpet gave the otherwise dull office-like room a luxurious feel that was out of place in a diplomatic mission; in the eyes of the more radical students, it was a sign of American excess. Not far away in a light blue room, locked behind two vault doors, the bin of an industrial paper shredder overflowed with the documents that diplomats and their local staff had desperately tried to destroy. In the weeks that would follow, the students would set up a production line of sorts to painstakingly piece the slivers of paper back together. And as if the students did not have proof enough that this was the scene of nefarious intentions, they had managed after much effort to gain access to the communications station on the second floor. It was a metal room within a room, outfitted with all kinds of equipment. One device—or rather the words written on it— caught the students' attention; on a black metal TSEC/HW-28 encryption device, with strange green and red keys, the words 'National Security Agency' stood out in bold white print. The centre point for America's Middle East presence had suddenly become the Den of Spies.

When Asgharzadeh, Mirdamadi and Bitaraf convened a haphazard press conference in front of a throng of journalists and cameramen, they had no doubt American spies were up to no good. They also had no doubt that there were CIA operatives among the dozens of American staff the students had detained that day. Behind them, printed pictures of Ayatollah Khomeini had been hastily taped to a wooden partition, unmissable to any camera snapping away at the young revolutionaries. As Asgharzadeh steadfastly explained his motivations for the embassy takeover, he had no idea that he and his colleagues had just changed the course of history.

Many years later, on another bitterly cold day, the older and greyer revolutionary would remark dryly that they had been 'romantic students. Romanticism in the sense that we could change the world.'[7] And they did. But not in the way they had envisioned.

Of course, that temporary sit-in became the famous Iran hostage crisis. The students were told not to release the hostages after a few days as they had planned; the revolutionary leadership instead commandeered the enterprise to settle scores both against the US and within the Iranian post-revolution leadership, specifically to topple the president, Sayyed Abolhassan Banisadr. Looking back, Asgharzadeh remarked, 'We were not afraid of anything. We thought if we did something, afterwards we would be able to make a paradise for sure, a very ideal society.'

But today there is a great divide amongst those men and women who marched, fought and shed blood to create a revolution. Mohsen Kadivar, a prominent progressive Islamic scholar and former student and confidant of Grand Ayatollah Hussein Ali Montazeri, explained: 'In the time of revolution, there were two approaches among the revolutionaries. Some were followers for example of [revolutionary ideologue] Dr Ali Shariati, as I was, and later we changed our minds and became liberals. The other revolutionaries became hardliners and conservatives. All of us were revolutionaries. But all of us did not remain revolutionaries.'[8]

Kadivar, who fought to topple the Shah as a student in Shiraz, said that for him, the revolution ended with the overthrow of the monarchy and the establishment of a new regime. 'I was a revolutionary at the time of revolution,' he laughed. 'That means I haven't called myself a revolutionary in forty or so years. After 1979, the term "revolutionary" is meaningless.' Most of the men and women who fought for the revolution have no regrets about ridding the country of the Shah. 'If I was in the same position again,' Kadivar continued, 'I'd make the same decision. I advocate, even today, the aims of 1979. Freedom and liberty, independence and sovereignty and justice.' But many of them accuse today's hardliners, including a new generation who were barely in their teens in 1979, of hijacking the revolution to serve their own interests. To many of the original revolutionaries like Kadivar and Asgharzadeh, the current situation in Iran is not what they had in mind.

Asgharzadeh is an example of a predicament described by French journalist Jacques Mallet du Pan in 1793: 'like Saturn, the Revolution devours its children.' In many ways, he has found himself an enemy of the very state he fought to create and later served. In the infancy of the Islamic Republic and through the dark days of the Iran–Iraq War, he worked diligently with Mohammad Khatami, who was editor of the state mouthpiece *Kayhan*, then minister of Culture and Islamic Guidance. Asgharzadeh himself also went on to serve in parliament and in the Tehran city council for eight years. Both men are examples of how yesterday's radicals are today's reformists. Indeed, the two were architects of the reformist movement that enabled Khatami to win the presidency in a landslide in 1997 and re-election in 2001.

But those who criticise the Republic—even if they have impeccable revolutionary credentials—are under immense pressure. In and out of prison, and barred from running for parliament at least once since his first term, Asgharzadeh spoke circumspectly, tabling his arrests from one system of government to the next: 'I was arrested once [before 1979]; however, I was also arrested after the revolution. And I will probably be arrested if there is another regime in the future.' Mohsen Mirdamadi, another of the student organisers of the hostage crisis, also went on to become a key reformist politician. He was arrested, put in solitary confinement for 110 days and jailed for six years as part of the 2009 election crackdown.[9] In 2004, he had also led a sit-in on the floor of parliament after many reformist politicians were banned by the Guardian Council from running in that year's election.[10]

Along with the former hostage takers, dozens of senior and well-known revolutionaries ended up as pariahs of the state, in prison, under house arrest or, like Kadivar, abroad. The list was extensive and included the leaders of the Green Movement— Mehdi Karroubi and Mir Hossein Mousavi, the latter of whom was a post-revolutionary prime minister (the last before a constitutional amendment reformed the Republic into a presidential system)—and Khatami, who is barred from appearing on state television and is often threatened by hardliners for his reformist principles.

Even the families of the Republic's founding fathers, Ruhollah Khomeini and Ali Akbar Hashemi Rafsanjani, are not spared. Hassan Khomeini, grandson of the late Ayatollah Khomeini, is reviled by today's hardliners, who consider him a traitor and have gone so far as to attack him. The cleric, who like his grandfather wears the black turban of a *sayyed*, or direct descendent of the Prophet Mohammad, has been barred from running for a position in the Assembly of Experts.[11] He has close ties to reformists, including Mousavi and Khatami, and also to moderate president Hassan Rouhani. Despite his troubles, some reformists have floated him as a possible candidate for president.

As for Rafsanjani's children, Faezeh Hashemi Rafsanjani is perhaps the most outspoken. Amongst her most stinging observations, as quoted by the Iranian daily *Mostaghel*, is that 'although the Islamic Republic is deep-rooted, it owes its strength mainly to intimidation and terror.'[12] Imprisoned in 2012, Faezeh learned under the Islamic Republic what revolutionaries like Asgharzadeh learned decades earlier under the Shah: at some point intimidation and terror do not work. As Asgharzadeh explained, 'Back then at university, I was arrested in a student demonstration and was put behind bars. But the number of these arrests increased so much that it lost its effect and the fear was gone.' Kadivar recounted that when he was jailed as a student in Shiraz in Adelabad Prison (whose name he points out ironically means 'place of justice'), he thought it was a boon. 'I thought, OK, when and if I return to university,' his voice cracked with laughter, 'I will let all my classmates know I was in prison. Prison was honour! Being in one of Shah's prisons was an honour!'

Just as prison did not intimidate many people then, it has not necessarily worked now. Even though Faezeh has already been sentenced to jail twice and has been threatened with arrest on more occasions, she has continued speaking. On the fortieth anniversary of the revolution, she even went so far as to tell the Spanish news service EFE that 'religion and politics do not work together'[13]—the antithesis of the concept on which her father and others had established the Islamic Republic. As her sister Fatemeh noted with a hint of pride while Faezeh was behind bars, 'Faezeh is doing well in prison and doing her duty.'

It's not just those so-called pillars of the revolution and their offspring who have lost faith in their own creation. The revolution was made by foot soldiers and average men who protested day after day for months, who risked being shot by the Shah's soldiers or were thrown into jails like Adelabad or Towhid in the middle of the night, hoping dawn would not find them at the end of the hangman's noose like their friends. It was also made by women who defied threats from fathers, brothers and even husbands to lead protests in front of tanks and snipers, demanding a representative system of government and an end to 2,500 years of imperial rule. In Tehran's inner east, Hossein Amiri worked as a taxi driver to pay the bills. Now in his late seventies, he had retired as an architect almost twenty years prior, with a cake and gilded framed painting from his colleagues, thinking that was that. But now the once radical student follower of Ayatollah Khomeini sat behind the well-worn wheel of his old Paykan, the one he had refused to get rid of, despite complaints from both his overbearing wife and the government, ferrying passengers around. With a glint of nostalgia in his old eyes, deeply creased at the corners, he casually pointed to the army base across the street: 'We took the guns from there.' His mind was back in 1979, and the time when, as a younger man full of revolutionary fervour, he and a small group of fellow Khomeinists had raided the base and taken to the streets. They were determined that the Shah who had fled Iran would stay gone for good. Amiri fell silent for a while, focused on the road ahead. The heaving traffic had brought him back to the present. 'They are all sheep.'

As a young man, in the early 1960s Amiri was so devout he travelled to Qom to hear Ayatollah Khomeini speak. He had even considered staying to join the seminary, until his mother talked him out of it. Instead, like many of his friends, he put himself in the service of Khomeini, who was sent into exile in 1964 due to his opposition to Shah Mohammad Reza's 'White Revolution' reforms. This did not dampen the young Amiri's devotion; in fact it strengthened it. In the early sixties, Amiri secretly furrowed himself away in the attic of his family's home to copy Khomeini's grainy taped sermons, which had been smuggled in from Turkey, and later Iraq. He would spend his nights skulking through the streets, plastering anti-Shah posters on walls, emboldened by the same type of suicidal confidence and conviction that would lead Asgharzadeh to the embassy fifteen years later.

But it was a dangerous time. In 1957, under the direction of the CIA, the Shah had established a new security branch, which even six decades on still invokes a shudder in those who remember it: Sazeman-e Ettela'at va Amniyat-e Keshvar, or the National Organization for Security and Intelligence, better known by its acronym SAVAK. Although officially the organisation had an estimated 5,000 employees, it was known to have a network of thousands of informants across the country, who spied on their fellow citizens, from the armed forces to the universities, to root out any anti-Shah dissidents. It is unknown exactly how many people SAVAK killed and tortured before it was disbanded in 1979, but most estimates, including by former members, put the number in the low thousands.

Amiri's luck ran out late one night as he shoved a pamphlet through the metal bars of a shop window. Before he knew it, two men had dragged him into an unmarked car and spirited him off to a police station. As he drove through the pollution-clogged streets of Tehran decades later, he explained how he had spent four months in prison before being released back to his family. 'I was lucky,' he concluded, thinking of all the people who never lived beyond the next dawn. 'My mother told me she wished I had just stayed in Qom.'

Among the brown brick facades and fading Qajar-era grandeur of old Tehran is a reminder of what revolutionaries faced, both before and after 1979. From the street, it is an unassuming building, recognisable only because of the green sign above the door: Ebrat Museum of Iran, the 'lesson' museum, more aptly known as the Tehran Torture Museum.[14]

In the 1970s, SAVAK and the police established the Anti-Sabotage Joint Committee to coordinate suppression of the Shah's opponents.[15] This prison was the centre of that operation and housed the highest-profile agitators. It was here that SAVAK agents put prisoners through various methods of torture to obtain information, and, according to some former inmates, just for fun.

ROMANTIC REVOLUTIONARIES

The building itself was designed by Nazi German architects in 1937 at the request of Reza Shah for maximum miserable effect. It is four stories tall and shaped like a cylinder, with dark passageways and corridors branching out from its centre. In the middle, ringed by four floors of prison bars with little 'S' shapes twisted in the middle, a circular courtyard and pond are exposed to the elements. Throughout the complex, mannequins have been staged in various positions of torture, death and woe to imitate some of the pre-revolutionary conditions. At the edge of the pond, a guard holds a prisoner's head under the icy water. Above them, another hangs by his feet, while on the second-floor landing, a similarly grotesque mannequin screams in agony, his arms and legs chained to the prison bars.

The grey-haired guide who shows visitors around tells them he was once a prisoner here, though not for long. Following the bloody footsteps painted on the concrete ground in a not-so-subtle show of brutal navigation, he explained the structure was designed with the Tehran elements in mind; in winter the concrete building is an icebox, while in summer its little cells become unbearably hot. 'So hot,' he said, 'the concrete floor would burn underneath you.'

Interrogators were rather imaginative in their drive for misery. Their repertoire of grim tools to use included:

> nail extractions; snakes (favored for use with women); electrical shocks with cattle prods, often into the rectum; cigarette burns; sitting on hot grills; acid dripped into nostrils; near-drownings; mock executions; and an electric chair with a large metal mask to muffle screams while amplifying them for the victim. This latter contraption was dubbed the Apollo—an allusion to the American space capsules.[16]

One long corridor is lined with prisoner mugshots; among the black-and-white photographs are some very recognisable faces. A who's who of revolutionaries and leaders: Hashemi

Rafsanjani, former president Mohammad Ali Rajai, Ayatollah Ruhollah Khomeini and Ayatollah Ali Khamenei, the latter having been jailed six times under the Shah. Red tulip stickers are affixed to the images of those who have since died, including Rajai, who along with post-revolutionary prime minister Mohamad Javad Bahonar was killed in a 1981 bombing blamed on the Mujahedin-e Khalq (MEK) far-left opposition group.[17] Before he was killed, Rajai blamed a damaged foot on the torture he sustained during two prison stints here, famously showing off the bare sole of his right foot at a UN press conference to prove it.

Missing from the Ebrat Museum is any acknowledgement of the fact that this torture chamber, renamed Towhid Prison after the revolution, continued to operate after 1979 until scrutiny forced its closure. If the Islamic Republic claims SAVAK and the Shah defined the concepts of injustice—arguably the main 'lesson' drawn from Ebrat—the former monarchy certainly did not monopolise it. Indeed, the stories of torture and ill treatment that followed the 2009 uprisings, particularly under Tehran's then Chief Prosecutor Saeed Mortazavi, are just as hair-raising as anything done by the Shah's henchmen. Perhaps under the Shah, SAVAK's tower of torture elicited the most fear, but under the Islamic Republic, other prisons, such as Evin or Kahrizak, took its place.

There is a sign at Towhid that reads, 'The governments of oppression never learn from history.' Its message would certainly seem apt to disillusioned revolutionaries like Amiri, their generation's activist children, like Faezeh Hashemi Rafsanjani, or revolutionaries turned reformists like Kadivar, Asgharzadeh and economist and journalist Saeed Laylaz.

Today Laylaz is still a vociferous supporter of Khomeini, the founder of the Islamic Republic. Back in his sitting room, a framed grainy photo of the two men was positioned pride of place beside him on a table. But Laylaz too had since fallen out of favour with the establishment, today contending that this Republic was not the one Khomeini had envisioned. It was this sentiment that led him to declare, after the interior ministry made the shock announcement that Ahmadinejad had won the 2009 election, that Khomeini's heir, Supreme Leader Khamenei, had rigged the results.[18] Laylaz had been a key adviser to the campaign of Green Movement leader Mir Hossein Mousavi. Like millions of other Iranians, he could not believe the claim that Ahmadinejad had won—and had apparently done so by such a large margin, taking 62.63 per cent of the vote while runner-up Mousavi managed only 33.75 per cent.[19] Speaking to *The Guardian* at the time, Laylaz stated:

> The regime is making a decision to shape the direction of Iran for the next decade. I am sure they didn't even count the votes. I do not accept this result. It is false. It should be the opposite. If Ahmadinejad is president again Iran will be more isolated and more aggressive. But he is the choice of the regime.

Like Faezeh Hashemi Rafsanjani, Laylaz considered his prison time a type of civil service. 'I had been in jail for more or less one year,' he said, in accented English, 'but personally, I have no complaints, because it has been a cost which I should pay for my nation and for my country.'[20]

Discord is not limited to laymen. Indeed, there is disagreement in Iran's theological centre. Around 140 kilometres south of Tehran, the sporadic minarets of Qom rise as though from the sweeping desert plains. Qom is arguably Iran's most conservative city, where women, regardless of where they fall on the scale of religiosity, almost exclusively wear the enveloping black chador as they go about their business in public. Certainly, in areas closest to holy sites, such as the Hazrat-e Masoumeh Shrine, it is rare to find any woman not wearing a chador. And naturally, as Qom is home to the country's seminaries, men in robes and turbans seem to outnumber men in trousers and shirts.

It was in Qom that 'Khomeinism' was born. Historian Ervand Abrahamian describes it as a 'flexible political movement expressing socio-economic grievances, not simply as a religious crusade obsessed with scriptural texts, spiritual purity, and theological dogma'.[21] Ruhollah Khomeini, the late Grand Ayatollah and father of the Islamic Republic, was not just the typical cleric. He was a revolutionary, but well before anyone in the West had ever heard of him. Arguably, perhaps even before the Shah's intelligence units had heard of him.

What Khomeini did was mix religion and politics, something that was not at all a traditional practice among Shia clerics, particularly the *marja*s, or Grand Ayatollahs. In fact, many of the Shia *ulema*, or clergy, including their most exalted leaders, found the concept of mixing man's ideas with God's work just short of heretic. According to Kadivar, 'Most of the clergy were quietists [apolitical]. There was distance between them and the political regime of the time.'

At the time, the separation of the *ulema* from the state was also a matter of self-preservation, as remained the case in following decades. Many senior members of the clergy decided it was better for them and their followers to stay apolitical, at least publicly, than to incur the iron fist of Reza Shah or later his son Mohammad Reza. Even Khomeini's first mentor from his earliest time in the seminary in Arak, Sheikh Abdul-Karim Ha'eri, was well known for his 'scrupulous avoidance of politics'.[22] When Ha'eri moved his seminary to Qom, around the early 1920s, the city became Iran's most prominent centre of theological study, overtaking the holy city of Mashhad, which is home to the shrine of Imam Reza, the eighth Imam of Twelver Shia Islam.

After Ha'eri's death in the late 1930s, Grand Ayatollah Sayyed Hossein Boroujerdi was given the high honour of becoming *marja*.[23] Like Ha'eri before him, he banned clerics from involvement in politics. Boroujerdi and Khomeini are believed to have enjoyed a close relationship, and for the most part, Khomeini followed Boroujerdi's rule forbidding political involvement—until the early 1960s. The decade would see the top-down 'White Revolution', in which the Shah instituted a series of sweeping yet contentious reforms, as well as Boroujerdi's death and Khomeini's subsequent ascension as Grand Ayatollah. Though not the most senior Ayatollah at the time, Khomeini seized the opportunity to become a leader of the *ulema* by going on the offensive against the monarchy and the Shah's reforms. It was particularly daring, but in doing so Khomeini quickly gathered followers, not just amongst younger clerics, but also amongst laymen. Many were disgruntled with life in the Shah's Iran, and the more conservative members of society did not approve of the lightning changes and developments under the White Revolution.

Khomeinism was not simply a way to show dissatisfaction with a system, as other clerics had been doing. Unlike the other *ulema*, Khomeini vociferously advocated a radical and public relationship between the state and religion. His activism, which drew in followers from not just Qom but across the country, like Amiri and future president Hassan Rouhani, became a thorn in the Shah's side, eventually leading to the cleric's arrest, imprisonment and exile. But Khomeini would not back down. From exile in Najaf, Iraq, he delivered a series of sermons in the 1970s elaborating the need for a political system of clerical rule. By that time, Khomeini had set himself apart from his contemporaries, at least in a political sense. And it was this legacy—the combination of religion and politics—that became the bedrock of the new republic's post-1979 constitution and that has impacted everything in Iran since.

If Khomeini rose to prominence merging politics and religion in pre-revolutionary Iran, others continued in his footsteps after the revolution. Yet it emerged that not everyone shared Khomeini's views for what an Islamic Republic should look like, nor how fused religion and politics should actually be.

Khomeini opened the floodgates for religious-political dissent, and so it is fitting that the most prominent dissident in Iran was someone very much like Khomeini himself: a leading revolutionary and a *marja*, Hussein Ali Montazeri. The theologian was respected by both revolutionaries and ordinary people because of 'his down-to-earth style, constant criticism of injustices [and] corruption ... as well as his tolerant approach to moderate opposition leaders'.[24] According to Kadivar, who was a student of the *marja*, Montazeri was such a staunch ally of Khomeini that he was 'the second copy of Khomeini's political thought. There was absolutely no difference. He even believed that Iran didn't need a president, just a Supreme Leader.'

Between 1985 and 1989, Montazeri was Khomeini's deputy and chosen successor, whom Khomeini 'habitually referred to as "the fruit of my life".'[25] But Montazeri, who was not just one of the most senior Shia clerics in the world, but one of the most respected, was fired just three months before Khomeini's death in June 1989.

'Montazeri had plans for the future of Iran,' recalled Kadivar. 'He would have supported a liberal as president, like Ezzatollah Sahabi.[26] He had good ties to [Mehdi] Bazargan too, but Khomeini didn't like it. They thought he was too liberal.'

While Montazeri did not criticise Khomeini's decisions in public, he did so privately. One criticism of a key moment in post-revolutionary Iran would be his downfall. During the dying days of the Iran–Iraq War, Khomeini ordered the establishment of a special tribunal to try members of the Mujahedin-e Khalq (MEK) and other leftist groups.[27] After the revolution, thousands of MEK members had fled into neighbouring Iraq, setting up a military base there and working, very literally, with the enemy. Saddam Hussein provided them safe haven and weapons including tanks, which they then used in a failed invasion of Iran. Those already in Iranian prisons of course could not have participated, but according to the Commission, they were guilty by association.

Mass executions were carefully orchestrated and occurred largely in secret. Nonetheless, Montazeri lambasted Khomeini in a series of letters, writing, 'this is not what we fought for'.[28] He accused the Special Commission, which some referred to as the 'death commission', of 'violating Islam by executing repenters and minor offenders who in a proper court of law would have received a mere reprimand.'[29]

The Commission included Ebrahim Raisi, who unsuccessfully challenged Rouhani for the presidency in 2017 but was later appointed Iran's chief prosecutor, and Mostafa Pourmohammadi, who served as Ahmadinejad's interior minister during his first term and Rouhani's justice minister during his first term. An audiotape, leaked almost three decades later by Montazeri's son Ahmad, captures Montazeri telling Raisi, Pourmohammadi and the other two members of the Commission—the then Tehran Prosecutor Morteza Eshraghi and Judge Hossein-Ali Nayeri—that 'the biggest crime in the Islamic Republic, for which history will condemn us, has been committed at your hands, and they'll write your names as criminals in history.' That meeting took place on 15 August 1988—one month after the executions began in earnest, according to witnesses.[30] In his own memoirs, Montazeri estimated that between 2,800 and 3,800 prisoners had been executed.

Montazeri lost his position as Khomeini's designated heir and was stripped of his title of Grand Ayatollah—something almost unheard of. He had been one of the two most senior religious figures amongst the Shia *ulema*, the other being Grand Ayatollah Sayyid Abu al-Qasem al-Musawi al-Khoei in Najaf. Further, his photos were removed from public spaces and a hardline campaign was enacted to tarnish not only his impeccable revolutionary credentials but also, rather impossibly, his religious ones.

'I attended one of his classes in Qom in about 1986 or 1987,' recounted Kadivar, a cleric himself. 'It was so crowded. All three salons were full. ... Many of the so-called students had come from Tehran, not to gain religious knowledge—that was clear from their unacademic questions—but ... trying to gain Montazeri's favour for future jobs. I didn't return until the day after he was fired. Suddenly 1,000 students had become 300.'

From Qom, Montazeri became more critical of the regime, and in 1997 he questioned Ali Khamenei's qualifications as Supreme Leader. In response, his religious school was closed, streets bearing his name were changed and he himself was put under house arrest.

Kadivar recalled the 'evolution' of Montazeri's views towards the system he created, which were influenced not least by his own mistreatment by the Republic. At the time, Kadivar himself had been sentenced to eighteen months in jail. 'I was in Evin [Prison] and after three months was allowed to make my first phone call. So, I called *Ostad* (Professor). Just think: the student was in prison and the teacher was under house arrest.'

Kadivar's close bond with Montazeri continued after his release from Evin. He used his freedom to go to the house of Ahmad Montazeri, the cleric's son, to call his ailing teacher who lived next door. They spoke on an iPhone, and sometimes Kadivar would call from the roof of Ahmad's house, looking over the fence at the elderly cleric as he sat in his backyard. It was this relationship that would lead to Montazeri's last act of defiance before he died.

After the Green Movement protests swept Iran in summer 2009, Montazeri issued a *fatwa* in response to a letter from Kadivar that asked questions about whether Khamenei was fit to rule after the disputed election. Montazeri stated: 'Injustice is the intentional opposition to the teachings of religion, the foundations of reasonableness and rationality, and the national accords and consensus that have become the laws of the land. The ruler who opposes these is no longer qualified to rule.'[31] But he went even further in response to a question about whether the political system of the Islamic Republic should be preserved at all costs, decreeing:

> A political system based on force, oppression, changing people's votes, killing, closure [of organs of civil society], arresting [people] and using Stalinist and medieval torture, creating repression, censorship of newspapers, interruption of the means of mass communications, jailing the enlightened and the elite of society for false reasons, and forcing them to make false confessions in jail, is condemned and illegitimate.[32]

Montazeri died only a few months later. Seda va Sima did not use his Grand Ayatollah title in its broadcasts and instead called him the 'clerical figure of rioters', in reference to his support of the Green Movement.[33] The Supreme Leader issued a loose condolence, adding that he hoped Montazeri would be shown 'God's lenience' because he had failed a 'test' by disagreeing with Khomeini.

In a further display of just how respected he was amongst the wider Iranian population, Montazeri had become a patron of sorts for the reformist movement. Protesters in 2009, who had not even been born in 1979, chanted his name in the street. Others wondered aloud what might have become of the Republic had Montazeri succeeded Khomeini as was originally planned. Even the retired Amiri said that he had an old black-and-white picture of Montazeri in his house, tucked away for safekeeping amongst his family photos.

But clerical dissent did not die with Montazeri. In fact, most senior Qom clerics refused to congratulate Ahmadinejad on his supposed re-election in 2009. Others, such as Grand Ayatollah Yusuf Saanei and Grand Ayatollah Asadollah Bayat-Zanjani, even supported the opposition. In response, radicals attacked their offices and blocked their websites. Another Grand Ayatollah, Ali Mohammad Dastgheib, called on the Assembly of Experts, of which he is a member, to exercise its constitutional responsibility to review the performance of the Supreme Leader Khamenei. Dastgheib, who studied under Khomeini, came under violent attack, including at 'my home in which my wife and children live ... on my seminary, the Ghoba Mosque [in Shiraz, where Dastgheib conducts Friday prayers], and my seminary students.'[34]

Dastgheib refused to attend the Assembly for at least two years after, saying he feared for his safety. In letters to its chairman, Ayatollah Mohammad Reza Mahdavi Kani, he provided probably the most scathing criticism of the Supreme Leader since Montazeri, noting: 'It is strange that protecting Islam has been reduced to protecting one man [Khamenei].' He further made sweeping accusations that core branches of the Islamic Republic, including the Assembly of Experts, the Guardian Council and the Islamic Revolutionary Guards Corps (IRGC), were trying to 'eliminate [from the political system] those who were and still are linked to the Imam [Ayatollah Ruhollah Khomeini].'[35] Dastgheib was referring to Hashemi Rafsanjani, who spent the last decade of his life under attack from both Ahmadinejad supporters and radicals, and whose destruction he believed 'was the destruction of the clerics.' Dastgheib was not alone in his criticism; even one of Iran's most radical post-revolutionary clerics, Hojjat al-Islam Hadi Ghaffari, the founder of Iranian Hezbollah, accused Khamenei and some radicals of 'turning religion into lying.'[36]

In the end, there are revolutionaries who became reformists. Others are in exile, jail and even enveloped in the dirt of their beloved country. But perhaps even more prevalent amongst that section of society is apathy.

Even the once radical Amiri has lost his fervour. The last time the aging revolutionary went out to protest was outside Tehran

University in 1999, to denounce the closure of the reformist newspaper *Salam*, which was linked to Mohammad Khatami. But the protest turned violent when paramilitary Basij forces stormed the dormitories and threw several students off a balcony, forcing the staunch Khomeinist to hide in a nearby garden. It was not lost on him that those Basij militia members were not even born when he had been dodging SAVAK agents a lifetime earlier. It was also not lost on him that he was hiding from the very state he had helped to create.

A decade later, in 2009, as millions of others took to the streets to protest the disputed re-election of Ahmadinejad, Amiri stayed home. Protest was no longer his business. Instead, he sat in front of his television, chain smoking Bahman cigarettes. In front of him, an image of the re-elected president crossed the screen. Seda va Sima referred to the protesters as foreign-backed seditionists, troublemakers and vandals. The events of that summer confirmed to the old revolutionary and those like him, what they had long feared—they had accidentally replaced one brand of authoritarianism with another.

But just as there are thousands, maybe millions, of former revolutionaries who have lost faith in the current version of the Republic, it does not mean that they want to tear it down. Reformists like Mousavi in the Green Movement or former president Khatami advocate for change within the Islamic Republic, not its overthrow, and certainly not its destruction. Beyond that, there are millions more who do not advocate reform. They believe the Republic is fine the way it is and staunchly hold fast to the rule of the Supreme Leader.

In a little electric shop near Bagh-e Melli in Tehran, Agha Reza sat behind a glass counter, screwdriver in hand, peering into what looked like half an old radio.[37] Behind him, two pictures of Khamenei and Khomeini had been framed and hung on the wall. It is a common practice in most restaurants and shops in the country, regardless of what the owners might think. But Agha Reza was not a man of show—he was a true believer. In the days before Ahmadinejad fell afoul of the Supreme Leader, his picture was also displayed in the shop. Proudly, he said these pictures also hung in his living room at home.

Agha Reza was portly and pious, his forehead bearing the permanent bruise that was a common product of repeatedly pressing one's head to the clay tablet used by Shia Muslims in prayer. He said he was just a little too young to fight in the war, but his father, a member of the volunteer Basij militia, had done so and mercifully returned home (at least physically) unscathed.

Anyone who knew Agha Reza considered the shopkeeper kind, hardworking and generous to others, even though he was by no means well-off. And it was no surprise that politically, he was conservative. Although Iranian politics is not party-driven, Agha Reza said he was most in favour of Jebha-ye Paydari-e Enghelab-e Eslami, or Paydari as it's informally known, a right-wing faction of conservatives, which includes war veteran and former nuclear negotiator Saeed Jalili. According to the shopkeeper, those on the 'Imam's path are righteous'—and this certainly did not include reformists like Khatami and Mousavi, or moderates like Rouhani and Rafsanjani. Both Khatami and Mousavi were 'traitors', he stated, and anyone associated with Rafsanjani, like Rouhani, was not far off. He considered the two moderates unfaithful to the leader and the revolution and did not care about the religious credentials of either man. Though he recalled liking Rafsanjani as a younger man, he now believed that 'if it was up to him, we would be like the US—corrupt and faithless.'

In the face of sanctions and external pressure from Obama and later Trump, Agha Reza saw no issue slandering reformists, even clerics. According to him, there was no room for compromise, and anyone who did not hold fast against imperialism was a 'country seller'. The issues were black and white. The Islamic

Republic was the last holdout in the region against US hegemony, and that was why it was under such pressure.

Curiously, Agha Reza supported a nuclear agreement, but not direct talks with the US, citing regional issues. 'Anyone who trusts them is not intelligent. Look what they have done to Muslims, in Afghanistan, Iraq, Palestine. We should not talk to arrogant powers,' he said, sounding very much like a politician, not a shopkeeper.

Agha Reza was just one man, but he had an enthusiasm for politics which many others did not. He said he voted in every election, be it municipal, parliamentary or presidential, and considered this not just his civic duty but the best way to have his voice heard as an individual. And although he did not attend rallies often, like that celebrating the takeover of the US embassy, he did encourage others, particularly younger people, to go.

According to voting trends, Agha Reza was in the minority—hardliners lost control of the Tehran municipality in a reformist landslide in 2013, and in parliament in 2016. Nonetheless, they traditionally held sway over unelected offices, including the Guardian Council, and with the increase in external pressure, their voices, even in the minority, had become louder.

'They think they are justified,' said a Tehran-based journalist, 'because they can say, see, we told you.' The pressure didn't just work to keep Iran's foreign policy in a reactive state—it limited both the domestic avenues and tolerance for dissent, continued the journalist, who worked for a reformist-leaning paper.[38] 'It is as though we [Iranians] are in a constant state of war—that's the mentality. War against the outside, and war against anyone who does not stand with them. It's tiring.' She said the government and its supporters justified stifling reform on the basis of national security, as though division equalled weakness, and dissent equalled disloyalty. It was irrelevant that reformists like Asgharzadeh or Khatami considered themselves patriots and had, in one way or another, served their country and people for decades. It was a point that caused a lot of bitterness: that the men and women who fought for the revolution or who had been imprisoned by the Shah were now accused of being traitors, including by people who were not even born in 1979.

One thing that has helped to make it possible to challenge who controls revolutionary narratives is that the clergy no longer holds sway in the way it did in the years after the revolution. Certainly, clerics still control many key unelected institutions— including the highest office in the land—but they have lost power to conservative laymen elsewhere, including national security, intelligence and elected institutions like parliament. The rise of a new brand of hardliners, like Ahmadinejad, who had no religious credentials, challenged the post-revolutionary hierarchy that positioned men of God at the top. That hierarchy was based on the belief that in the Islamic Republic, the clergy were the sole representatives of God on earth. But a new brand of younger conservatives has effectively laid claim to the same moral standing to cultivate their own bases. Ahmadinejad and his aide Esfandiar Rahim Mashaei went the furthest, claiming the imminent return of the messianic Mahdi, or Hidden Imam.[39]

Most of the younger conservatives, including Ahmadinejad, have military backgrounds, not theological ones. They draw their legitimacy from the battlefield, not the seminary. And at least within conservative politics, it has been a winning strategy—so much so that two thirds of parliament's presidium, elected in 2020, have IRGC or Basij backgrounds. The most conservative propagate a hardline stance in domestic politics, which includes authoritarianism, the oppression of reformists as 'seditionists' and absolute loyalty to the Supreme Leader.

On an international level, radical hardliners object to talks with the US and vociferously espouse the idea of 'resistance'. While President Carter's aide Gary Sick suggests that Iranians have paid a high price for the continued acrimony between the US and Iran, including the States' refusal to move on from the past, it is clear that some Iranians don't think the price was too high. Resistance, in all its forms, is a duty not a cost.

4

HOPE RETURNS

By the end of the Ahmadinejad era, the lines between revolutionaries and radicals, reformists and regimists, had been well and truly drawn. And that decade had come at a great cost, both at home and abroad.

On an economic level, the Iranian currency had fallen from 8,200 rial to the US dollar on the open market in mid-2005, when Ahmadinejad took office, to 42,000 rial to the dollar when his presidency ended in mid-2013. According to the Central Bank of Iran, inflation too had skyrocketed; in August 2005 it listed Iran's inflation rate at 14.2 per cent, but by 2013, inflation was 39 per cent.

Almost every aspect of life in Iran had suffered from some type of trauma. And this set the scene for arguably the most important election in the country's post-revolutionary history.

Election season in Iran is short compared to countries like the United States, where campaigning is a never-ending process. So even six months before the election, it was still unclear who would end up in the race. With Ahmadinejad unable to run for a third consecutive term under the limits of the constitution, there were only two candidates that seemed, at least at the time, obvious—Ali Larijani, then speaker of Iran's parliament, and hardline politician Saeed Jalili, although neither had publicly declared intentions to run.

Larijani's very prominent personal position and family (all five Larijani brothers have held important political roles, and at the time two led branches of the state—Ali himself in parliament and Sadeq as head of the judiciary) had never translated into popular support. Though many parliamentarians, including some reformists, respected the way in which Larijani conducted himself, for many voters his anti-reformist activities and press censorship, particularly as former head of the state broadcaster, Seda va Sima, were troubling. And whether or not he had earned his position, the standing of the five Larijani brothers in Iranian politics had sparked accusations of nepotism.

As for foreign policy, Larijani had succeeded Hassan Rouhani in 2005 as secretary of the Supreme National Security Council (SNSC) and chief nuclear negotiator. Larijani had been quite vocal in his opposition to Rouhani's initiatives to solve the nuclear dispute, including the 2004 agreement in Paris to halt Iran's uranium enrichment programme, which he described as exchanging a 'pearl' for a 'bonbon'.[1] It did not matter that Rouhani and the nuclear team had the support of the Supreme Leader to go ahead with the agreement, or that the team had managed to prevent the International Atomic Energy Agency from referring Iran's nuclear dossier to the UN Security Council, which everyone knew would be a precursor to sanctions and escalation.

Although Larijani himself resigned after only eighteen months in the job, with Ahmadinejad spokesman Gholam-Hossein Elham revealing he 'had submitted his resignation many times before', he had shown support for at least one of the president's key policies—the so-called 'Look East' strategy. Through this policy, Ahmadinejad had tried to elicit support from Eastern and

Non-Aligned states for Iran's nuclear position. Predictably, the strategy failed, and not only was the Iranian nuclear dossier referred to the UNSC in 2006, but two years later, members of the Eastern bloc and the Non-Aligned Movement actually voted in favour of UNSC Resolution 1803, which required Iran to cease and desist from uranium enrichment.

Saeed Jalili, the other obvious runner in the presidential race, was a conservative like Larijani, but with several crucial differences. He did not come from a prominent family, nor was he connected to centres of power through the webs of marriage that had become a curious staple among Iran's elites. While Larijani participated in the Iran–Iraq War as a member of the elite Islamic Revolutionary Guards Corps (IRGC), Jalili fought in the war with the volunteer Basij militia. In 1986, Jalili was gravely wounded in battle and lost the lower part of his right leg, earning him the title 'living martyr'. In addition to support from other arch-conservatives, including Ayatollah Mohammad-Taqi Mesbah-Yazdi, it was no small thing that at election time, Jalili could count on his fellow members of the Basij, which numbered at least a quarter of a million, to go out and vote—and to rally others around their candidate.

Like Rouhani and Larijani, Jalili also served under Ahmadinejad as secretary of the SNSC and chief nuclear envoy, taking up the role in 2007 after Larijani's resignation. While both of his predecessors had been appointed by the Supreme Leader, and Rouhani had already held the post for sixteen years before Ahmadinejad took office, Jalili was chosen for the position by Ahmadinejad himself. His appointment was the first time a president had exercised, albeit through force, Article 176 of the constitution, which decreed it was the president's right to choose the Security Council secretary.

For most people, Jalili was far too extreme. Indeed, as a product of Iran's most conservative university, Imam Sadiq, which selects students in part on the basis of professed piety, he is thoroughly and unabashedly wedded to Islamic prescriptions and ideology. And though he spent a significant number of years in politics, including as Iran's chief nuclear negotiator, he gained very few, if any, diplomatic results. In fact, as nuclear chief, he oversaw a period in which the Iranian nuclear crisis escalated rapidly, along with Iran's own nuclear advancements, including the ability to enrich uranium to 20 per cent. Under Jalili and Ahmadinejad, the Republic had slid to its most precarious position since the end of the eight-year war with Iraq. And yet, Jalili would later emerge in the earliest polls as one of the top three candidates most likely to win.

But there was also another conservative candidate whose name was generating buzz: Mohammad Baqer Qalibaf, the mayor of Tehran. Like Larijani, Qalibaf had run—and lost—in the presidential race in 2005. Balding, bespectacled and barrel-chested, he was also a decorated war hero and looked very much the military man turned politician. His broad shoulders filled out his sharp suits, and he exuded a polish and confidence that many other conservatives lacked. Unlike Larijani or Jalili, he was quite popular with a broad section of the public, at least in the capital.

Although it was not public at the time, Qalibaf was already preparing to run. In a non-descript building opposite the former US embassy, he had set up his temporary campaign headquarters, run by Seyed Hosseini, a cleric and old friend from the war. The black-turbaned veteran had decorated the office with pictures of Qalibaf from their time in the trenches—faded photographs of a young smiling man sporting a neat, light-coloured beard, dressed in beige fatigues on some faraway battlefield. Beside the photos hung symbols of the Supreme Leader and the IRGC, including a keffiyeh—supposedly Qalibaf's own from the war—of white-and-black chequered embroidery, just like that worn by Khamenei.

Dressed in a brown, sweeping linen robe, Hosseini said he was supposed to be the international media advisor for the presidential campaign, though it was a rather ironic title given Qalibaf did not grant a single interview to foreign press from that point on. Nonetheless, the cleric was certain Qalibaf was the right man to lead the country. After all, he had already proven himself a natural leader as a soldier, who at the age of twenty, and barely a year into the war, was given command of his own brigade.

But the office, although temporary and hastily decorated, held a telling absence: there were no photos of Qalibaf as mayor. And to any observer, especially one from Tehran, that was odd. Qalibaf was serving in his eighth year in office and had achieved a great deal. In fact, ask most Tehranis old enough to remember the city before Qalibaf became mayor in 2005, and they would readily admit that he had transformed the capital. During the Ahmadinejad mayorship, Tehran had been a different place. Its parks, then fewer in number, had been bland, and many of its streets had been dirty and scattered with rubbish. Under Qalibaf, city beatification became a priority. Concrete sidewalks were paved, potholes filled, parks expanded and green spaces protected. City workers seemed to be all over town in their green overalls, sweeping streets, planting flowers and picking up trash. The mayor also set about trying to fix some of the traffic-choked capital's worst bottlenecks, which routinely led drivers, usually jammed between what felt like every car in the country, to spew the foulest of language. A second tier was added to the sprawling Sadr Expressway, which connects east and west Tehran, while the Niayesh Tunnel finally opened near Park-e Mellat, to the relief of anyone who had to work uptown. Meanwhile, construction on new lines of the Tehran Metro increased, and the delayed marble-encased Shahid Ghoddousi and Tajrish stops finally opened. So too did Pol-e Tabiat, or Nature Bridge, a 270-metre pedestrian overpass vaulting the Modarres Expressway between

Taleghani and Ab-o-Atash parks. With its greenery and views, the bridge became popular among both visitors and locals eager to enjoy a weekend stroll.

But there were also serious criticisms—bloated bureaucracy, unmitigated urbanisation, corruption, neglect of outlying poorer areas, and nepotistic tender awards. Qalibaf's detractors claimed he had embezzled money and that his family, including his son, were hiding funds abroad. This was not to mention the city's approval of the wanton destruction of historic buildings and homes in downtown Tehran to make way for new apartments and buildings.

While missing from his temporary office, it was all of this— his time and work as mayor—that Qalibaf was now most known for. After all, most Iranians were too young to remember his wartime heroics, even if there were many; aside from hardliners, no one pointed to his military experience as a reason why he would make a good president.

It didn't take long for Qalibaf to outrun Jalili and Larijani in the presumptive candidate stakes. Soon his name was everywhere. It was not just a given that he would run; in the absence of anyone stronger, there was a real chance he would win.

But one look at Qalibaf's campaign headquarters was enough to reveal several things about the direction the mayor's campaign would take—and where it would go wrong. Qalibaf wanted the conservative vote. He was not trying to win over the masses, nor students or anyone who prioritised social reform. Those early days also provided a glimpse into the Qalibaf ideology and scratch-paper attempts at building a brand, which foreshadowed the rise of a new generation of conservatives who would sweep to power years later, on the back of Trump's destruction of the nuclear deal.

* * *

Given what followed, it may come as a surprise that, until a few weeks before the four-day window to register for president, Hassan Rouhani's name was barely mentioned in the mill of speculation. But as summer approached, the bespectacled cleric, who grew up as Hassan Fereydoun in Sorkheh in northern Iran, became a household name.

Rouhani arrived at the interior ministry on Fatemi Street on 7 May 2013 with little fanfare. As he submitted his paperwork to register his candidacy and smiled for photographs, he told reporters, 'I have always been moderate' and had good relations with both 'moderate principlists [conservatives] and moderate reformists'. Indeed, the ability to work as a centrist was a hallmark of his time in various levels of office. Though it is true that political parties don't traditionally play a major role in the personality-driven world of Iranian politics, Rouhani was the official candidate of Hezb-e E'tedāl va Towse'eh, or the Moderation and Development Party, which he had founded in 1999. But while he was known for his ability to bridge political divides, the party had come under attack from arch-conservatives and hardliners for supporting Green Movement leader Mir Hossein Mousavi in the 2009 elections.

On 11 May, the last day of registration for the race, dozens of tightknit Iranian journalists milled about the courtyard of the interior ministry. The blazing sun beat down with a blinding ferocity. A few cameramen sipped on juice boxes, joking and chatting with each other, while journalists leaned against the tiled walls, or garden beds, waiting idly for something to happen.

Most obvious candidates had come and gone. Perennial candidate Mohsen Rezaee, an IRGC man from Khuzestan, registered again. So too did Jalili and Qalibaf. The Supreme Leader's foreign policy advisor, Ali Akbar Velayati, also put his name down, as did the conservative former parliamentary speaker Gholam Ali Haddad-Adel. Meanwhile, Ali Larijani, who had been an early favourite, never registered. One political commentator surmised that his political positions were too similar to Velayati's.

As for the reformists, there was only one standout: Khatami's former first vice president Mohammad Reza Aref. The Stanford-educated engineer had served in politics since the revolution and was known to favour social liberalisation and pragmatic foreign policy. As he put his name down amid a cacophony of clicks and flashing cameras, it was uncertain whether the Guardian Council would approve his candidacy, given his close links to the out-of-favour Khatami and the Green Movement.

Registration was due to close at 6 p.m. But even as the hours ticked by, and as journalists grew tired and red-faced from sunburn and the heat, no one dared to leave. In another part of the ministry, some political theatre was brewing. For years Ahmadinejad had been grooming a successor—his chief of staff and closest confidant, Esfandiar Rahim Mashaei. Many saw the incumbent president as trying to initiate a Putin–Medvedev leadership arrangement with Mashaei. Ahmadinejad himself had stated that 'Mashaei means Ahmadinejad and Ahmadinejad means Mashaei'.

But Mashaei had been accused of leading a so-called 'deviant current' and advocating what one journalist aptly described as his own odd mix of 'Shiite millennialism' and 'Persian nationalism', all with a tinge of anti-establishment sentiment.[2] Together, the pair were championing a new circle of elites, what they dubbed the 'Spring' movement, independent of the traditional factions rooted in the revolution and well and truly an annoyance to hardliners—including the Supreme Leader.

That afternoon, Mashaei emerged with the president by his side, flashing victory signs and a wide smile. Cameramen fell over themselves, catapulting chairs and clicking furiously as the pair made their way through the throng, while angry security officials berated the press for their lack of decorum.

But if the possibility of an Ahmadinejad–Mashaei spectacle had awakened bored journalists, something else jolted them to their feet. Hashemi Rafsanjani, the political kingmaker and revolutionary giant, was on his way. A pragmatist and founding father, Rafsanjani had even been characterised as a Gorbachev-like figure, who could bring Iran out of its cold war with the United States, and who might be the only man, aside from the Supreme Leader, powerful enough to offer a referendum on the future of the Republic.

When Rafsanjani emerged moments after the pair had departed, with all the grace of a man of his standing, the interior ministry exploded with frenetic energy. Dressed in dark-brown robes over a grey tunic and white shirt, Rafsanjani walked through the rippling crowd as though he was parting the sea. Unhurried, the white-turbaned cleric signed his name and posed for photographs, knowing full well he had just turned the race upside down.

It would take the Guardian Council two weeks to vet candidates, and it was no shock that Mashaei was disqualified. But so too was Hashemi Rafsanjani. At the time of the election, Rafsanjani was seventy-nine years old, and although he was generally considered in good health, the Guardian Council rejected his candidacy on the grounds that he was too 'feeble'. One political observer pointed out with incredulity: 'Hashemi can literally say, "I am the revolution, I am the Republic," and even that is not enough anymore.' Rumours swirled that his disqualification was payback from hardliners, part of the internal dispute that pitted Rafsanjani against Khamenei in a duel of influence that had worsened after 2009. Others said it was a balancing act to placate Ahmadinejad supporters—disqualifying Mashaei on one side meant disqualifying Rafsanjani on the other.

Without a candidate as well known as Rafsanjani, moderates and reformists only had three weeks to catch up to conservatives.

There were only two choices—Aref or Rouhani. A vote for the latter was seen as a vote for the continuation of Rafsanjani's pragmatic agenda, including in foreign policy. But that was not nearly enough.

Early buzz surrounded Qalibaf. And although the small headquarters provided a glimpse into the image some of his supporters were trying to nurture—a pious war veteran, dedicated to service—the campaign simultaneously tried to present a more polished image, as posters of the broad-chested man donning a navy suit popped up around town. Another juxtaposed a black-and-white photo of Qalibaf, gazing seriously into the distance, over the colours of the Iranian flag, with the words 'Qalibaf, truly selfless' scrawled underneath. Through the sharp and eye-catching posters, the mayor projected a confidence in his appearance that many other candidates lacked, including the reformist Aref, who, despite the obvious intelligence and conviction of his speech, showed up to a key televised debate clutching a briefcase, dressed in a tan suit and looking very much as though he were on his way to teach at university. As for Jalili's camp, which the Basij endorsed, it plodded along with pledges of adhering to the status quo, seemingly oblivious of the fact the country was on the brink of war and economic ruin.

Meanwhile, in Haft-e Tir, the heart of Tehran's Armenian district, the largest poster of Rouhani had been draped down the front of at least five floors of a cement-coloured building. Inside, the smiling, white-turbaned cleric had set up his campaign headquarters. There, workers milled about, answering calls, organising rallies and trying to create energy around Rouhani's campaign. It was a tough ask. In Tehran, Qalibaf had led in popularity since before he had even officially registered. There was a genuine buzz around his candidacy, and even some reformist-leaning voters had initially shown interest in what he might say. In one poll conducted in the first week of June, two weeks before election day, Qalibaf led the charge with decided voters. At least 35 per cent said that if the election were held that day, they would vote for the mayor. Compare that to just 15.2 per cent for Rezaee, 12.3 per cent for Jalili and just 7.4 per cent for Rouhani. There was also a very interesting rural–urban split among hardliners, with almost 40 per cent of urban voters favouring Qalibaf, whilst 42.9 per cent of rural voters voiced support for Mohsen Rezaee.

It was no surprise that conservative voters were most enthusiastic to vote. Apathy had riddled moderate and reformist politics since the 2009 fracas. As one poll suggested, almost 60 per cent of respondents said they either did not know who they would vote for or even whether they would vote at all. And inside Rouhani's campaign headquarters, this was a problem. Campaign manager Mohammed Reza Nematzadeh acknowledged that many Iranians, particularly the youth after 2009, had been 'battered' under the Ahmadinejad administration and had no faith in elections. Thus, he conceded, the biggest challenge was not getting voters to listen to their message; it was getting voters to the ballot box in the first place.

In Darband in the city's north, the sweet smell of blueberry-flavoured shisha smoke wafted gently through the air. For once on this stifling summer's day, there was no hint of a breeze—not even here, up the well-worn cobbled stones and steep, winding alleys. One of Tehran's most popular little villages, Darband is a place of great nostalgia, where thick, sticky *lavashak* and sour preserved fruit are still made as they were generations ago and sold in colourful little stalls that line the narrow paths. High mudbrick walls ring its many little alleys, some crumbling under the weight of age, of winter's heavy snows and neglect. And from behind them, the houses of a bygone era rise, their tin roofs darkened by the skies of the century since each piece was nailed by hand into place. As is common throughout

Tehran, countless historical buildings have been torn down to make way for new, uninspiring apartment blocks, usually finished with painted cement or marble facades, devoid of any charm or trace of the old city.

This once quiet village gets busy on a Friday afternoon, especially if the weather is good. Groups of Tehranis hike through the village up the mountain, bringing with them picnic lunches of flatbread, honey, cheese and cold *kotlet*, and sometimes homemade *aragh*, for a sip or two once they reach the top. Even on a burning summer's day, the weather is usually a little cooler the higher the ascent, making the trek just slightly more bearable, but only just.

Past the *lavashak* stalls, restaurants and tea houses spring up one after the other. The best-known meals here are traditional barbeque fares—coal-cooked *kabob*, *joojeh* marinated in yoghurt, saffron and lemon, ground-beef or lamb *koobideh*, and even liver, all served with a side of grilled tomato, basil and flat bread or buttery rice. Whilst *ghelyoon* (shisha) smoke wafts from tea houses, here the distinct scent of barbeque lingers in the air.

In a tea house just off the main street, past a little stand where walnuts bobbed in water-filled plastic containers, Mina Heydari casually drew smoke from a pipe. Her navy linen scarf draped precariously off the back of her head, revealing thick, black, curly hair, pulled loosely together in a bun. For her, life was moving slowly on this Friday, even if the rest of the city, plastered with political posters and campaign colours, was buzzing with activity. The election was only a week away. Mina pondered aloud, 'I don't think I'll vote. What for?'

Mina was a little petulant, stubborn and very rarely optimistic. Now a teacher, she was born into a working-class family from the border province of Khuzestan, only two years into the Iran–Iraq War. Her first memories were not of toys or picnics in the park, but of terrified parents, Iraqi bombs and air raid sirens.

A self-declared feminist, who paradoxically seemed to be in a constant state of heartbreak, Heydari was proudly vocal about many things. But not politics. At least not anymore. Like millions of other Iranians born after 1979, Heydari belonged to the generation who came of age under Mohammad Khatami, when the promise of reform swept the country and electrified universities and student organisations with a kind of 'anything is possible' attitude. That hope had been missing in the country since the days of the revolution—in the republic's first two decades, there was post-revolutionary score-settling, then war, then the slow march to salvage a broken country. As hardliners had imposed an austere environment on civil society, activists and journalists, many of whom were disappeared, murdered or jailed, it becomes clear why Khatami's presidency felt like a renewal. Those students were young and, unlike the generation that came of age in the traumatic 1980s and early 1990s, unburdened by many of the effects that revolutionary upheaval and war had wreaked on society.

But like millions of other Iranians, Heydari was burnt. Whilst Khatami provided almost a decade of relief, his reform movement inevitably failed. And though the president had tried to stand up and push back against hardliners and unelected establishment figures, he had folded. It was clear to many that ideals and youthful hope were useless in the face of a deeply entrenched system, where even a president—elected in a landslide—could not win. Add to that the Ahmadinejad years and the trauma of 2009, when Heydari had decided at the last minute to vote for Mousavi, and it is easy to see how dashed hopes had not been forgotten.

A decade and a half later, for Heydari and many like her, apathy and derision had replaced expectation. She sat on the carpet-covered raised platform, known as a *takht*, and reclined casually back on the colourful pillows, grey-socked feet tucked under her to one side. She inhaled from the *ghelyoon* deeply, as the water bubbled with a deep gurgle in its glass base. 'No,' she decided aloud, 'I'm not going to vote.'

For the rest of the afternoon, Heydari sat and smoked. Here and there she would pick the skin off the water-soaked walnuts, douse them in salt and nibble on them between puffs. She was in no hurry to go anywhere or join in any election debates. From up here by the trickling river, it seemed the young teacher had not a care in the world. But under the calm façade, the furrowed brow betrayed her. Her mind turned over and over with worry. About her life. Her job. The future. And, of course, the election.

Back in Rouhani's campaign headquarters a few days later, on the ground floor of the building in Haft-e Tir, plastic tables and chairs lined a little café selling a small assortment of *kabob*s and steaming hot tea in paper cups. Some volunteers had come downstairs to sit in the summer heat, which a small metal fan lazily moved back and forth. Some sipped on tea and puffed on cigarettes, gazing up at the small television perched above the counter. These days, state TV was filled with election campaigning, rather than its usual programming, which included football. The debates especially had captured the public's attention, with many tuning in even while refusing to vote. The televised specials, which included all candidates together at one time, were largely devoid of the theatrics of 2009, when Ahmadinejad had famously threatened Mousavi with a manila folder containing so-called secret, damaging documents.

Nematzadeh thought Rouhani had started to win over some of the dejected youth like Heydari. The television debates were helping. Each was themed, and in the second and third debates, Rouhani had scored points with young voters, as he attacked the crackdowns on students and the press, reiterating the point that the state was there to govern, not meddle in people's lives. Meanwhile, his mention of beloved traditional singer and composer Mohammad Reza Shajarian had also set social media alight.

The last debate also focused on foreign policy and gave a number of the candidates a platform to reveal their strengths, as Rouhani, Jalili, Aref and Velayati had all served in high government positions—Rouhani as the long-time head of the SNSC, Jalili as a former foreign minister, Aref as Khatami's first vice president and Velayati as the Supreme Leader's foreign policy advisor. But the debate also showcased some shortcomings; Qalibaf had never worked in the federal government, and although he promised to end the 'status quo', he seemed out of his depth. Velayati controversially stated that solving the nuclear crisis was easier than accepting the UN resolution that ended the Iran–Iraq War, to which an annoyed Qalibaf replied that this was easy for him to say, for while Qalibaf himself was being shot at on the front line, Velayati was 'having coffee' with French President Francois Mitterrand.

Meanwhile, Jalili claimed that Iran's foreign policy must be based on 'pure Islam' and offered no strategy to get the country out of its current quagmire. Velayati lambasted the war veteran over his handling of the nuclear dossier and contended that what Jalili was doing—rhetoric and more sanctions—was not diplomacy. Overlooked by many, it proved one of the most important comments of the campaign, and gave an indication that some hardliners, including the Supreme Leader's most important advisor, were more flexible and in favour of diplomacy than many had thought.

As for Rouhani, he postulated that the nuclear issue could only be solved through real negotiations by skilled, experienced people. He had linked the country's economic predicament to the removal of sanctions and argued throughout the campaign that any economic policy that ignored sanctions was pointless. He balanced his campaign on two promises—more social liberalisation at home and resolution of the nuclear crisis abroad.

And just as Nematzadeh hoped, the debates made a difference. 'Every day, more young people come here to see how they can help—it shows we are catching up,' he said. Suddenly the polls began to swing, and the campaign, which had never garnered much attention before, was surging. The election was no longer just a competition between hardliners.

It was most obvious just a few blocks away, as a sea of purple, Rouhani's official campaign colours, took over the Shahid Shiroudi sports complex. Rouhani supporters choked the foot-paths, bouncing with a type of excitement unseen at any other rally. As well as purple, some wore green wristbands, in a sign of support for the Green Movement and its detained leaders. Inside, a deafening cheer arose when Rouhani appeared on stage, bran-dishing a key—the so-called key to the country's problems. He spoke of freedom, hope and, crucially, ending the house arrest of the Green Movement leaders. The crowd chanted back: 'Greetings to Khatami, Mousavi, Karroubi.' For the first time since 2009, hope was alive, and the cleric holding the key had suddenly become its symbol.

Student Simin Siadat, who had tied purple ribbons around her wrists and around her head, commented afterwards: 'His speech, especially about the rights of students, the rights of women in society and security of women, was good. ... Rouhani supporters are super energetic. I know we are going to win.'[3]

But in the sea of hope, there was of course, reality. At an earlier and much smaller Rouhani appearance at Tehran's Jamkaran Mosque, supporters broke out into wild cheers for both Rouhani and the detained Mousavi. Nematzadeh later alleged police had detained several of them.

* * *

If voters were suddenly energised by the Rouhani campaign, it was not just happening in the city. The biggest swing in polls started in rural areas, where like in the cities conservatives were leading. Suddenly Rouhani's popularity surged from almost

5 per cent of rural voters to almost 20 per cent. Although there was still a week left in the campaign, the jump in numbers offered further proof that rural Iranians were not as politically conservative as many made out.

On the road out of Tehran to Esfahan, the city very quickly falls away into great expanses of farmland and open fields. Here and there crumbling mud brick walls demarcate lines between properties, jutting up as a reminder of old, long-forgotten times. In the summer, half-naked children, tanned a deep brown by a life outdoors, play in the cool water of the irrigation canals that run along the roadside, splashing and jumping and squealing while their parents tend the fields or sell watermelon and fruit from the back of little blue Saipa Zamyads. There is quite a stark contrast between an uncomplicated existence on the land and the intense ruckus of the smoggy city in the distance.

Past the small Hoz-e Soltan Salt Lake and the distant golden domes of Qom, the road stretches into an endless desert of brown peaks and rocks, before small patches of green suddenly spring forth in a sign of renewed life. Amid the hot dusty landscape, the historic city of Kashan appears. Many of its buildings tell the tale of hundreds of years of neglect, of a disastrous earthquake, and of a city in need of hope. But this little city of 320,000 people is also endowed with a caravanserai beauty, with dome-like buildings and old hamams. Tourists stop here for a quiet glass of tea or a stroll on the way to Esfahan, and Tehranis come for a weekend getaway to lose themselves in the narrow alleys and old-world charm.

Aside from agriculture and carpet weaving, tourism is a key source of income for locals. Kashan is famous not just for its architecture or even its baklava, but mostly for its herbal juices, teas and the quality of its rosewater. But in a growing city, indeed in a country with a highly educated young population, the tourist trade does not offer anything close to a secure future.

Many young people were struggling to find ways to establish their own lives and grow out from under their parents and the limited traditional jobs the little city offered, in universities, factories and industry.

Indeed, making a life and a living was a problem facing young people across Iran. According to government figures, at the time of the 2013 election, the national unemployment rate stood at around 12 per cent, but the unemployment rate for fifteen to twenty-four-year olds was more than double the average at 26.8 per cent. And this was official data, which considers a person over the age of ten to be employed if they have worked one hour in the past seven days. The statistics of course did not consider the number of young, educated Iranians who had been forced to leave the country to look for work abroad.

The predicament was not difficult to imagine, especially when one spoke to a student like Ali Moqaddasianfar. He was studying for a master's degree in mathematics, but really would have preferred to be working. In Kashan, education was not necessarily the key to success; in many cases, it was a tactic to delay the inevitability of looking for a rare professional job—especially, for Ali, one that might actually match his hard-earned qualifications.

When not at university, Ali could be found around town, studying or sitting in the back of his friend's blue truck. In the summer, his friend sold huge blocks of ice on the side of a dusty square, and Ali would sit there to pass the time. Ali had the very distinct look of a sensible young student. He was tall, thin and bespectacled, with carefully groomed hair and a freshly shaven face. His checked shirt and jeans were neatly pressed, and his light brown shoes polished and clean. Sitting in the back of a truck, he looked out of place.

Ali explained politely and with a certain shyness that it had been almost a year since he finished his bachelor's degree. 'I passed many employment tests,' he said, 'but no luck. If you have connections, finding a job is much easier, considering the current economic situation.'[4]

After leaving university the previous year, Ali had spent several months working in a textile factory, unable to find a professional job. He was not alone. In fact, he said, many of his former class-mates did the same thing. Some of them were still there, labour-ing away, degree or not. Ali explained that he thought going back to university and getting a master's degree might help him to get a better job. But even so, he did not sound very convinced. 'I can't picture myself with a bright future. Nor for anyone else my age.' Ali found himself stuck in Kashan, which, though beautiful with its dusty wide streets and relaxed charm, might as well have been a dead end.

Across the road, Javad Jamalpour and his friend Reza sat on Javad's beat-up motorcycle, watching the sporadic traffic slowly swing through the roundabout.[5] Javad was seventeen years old and just finishing high school. Two days before Iran's presidential election, he had gone to register for university. He wanted to study, find a job and live in the place where he was from. But even as a teenager and not yet quite old enough to vote, he knew there was a difficult road ahead. 'Many people in Kashan have to move out due to its lack of facilities and unemployment rate. ... There are many graduates who are still unemployed, or those who are not satisfied with their jobs,' he said.

Although Javad could not vote, he liked Rouhani, whose promises of economic improvement seemed to have struck a chord. 'I hope the future government will provide young people with more opportunities for employment,' he said, adding that he also agreed with Rouhani's comments that the state should limit its involvement in people's personal lives.

Not everyone has the chance to go to university. Masoud Rezakhani was just twenty years old, tanned and athletic. Born and raised in Kashan, he became a plumber here, following in the footsteps of his father. For him, getting to work and making money, even if it came to less than US$7 per day, was his best option. He said he wanted better opportunities, but financial realities, particularly in an economic crisis, meant university was off the table. Even so, he was optimistic and looked to the election for change and hope, not just for himself but also for his friends, 'Youth are the hope for the future in every country, so there must be special attention towards them so they can have a better future.'[6]

Unlike many well-to-do Iranians, these three young men did not have the means to go abroad to eke out a new life. In any case, they all conceded they wanted to stay not just in Iran but in Kashan. To them, the most important thing was to further their futures here, in their own country and their own city. All three could not underscore enough what it would mean to them to be given the chance to make lives for themselves in their hometown. They wanted an end to the political standoffs and international brinkmanship that were crushing their chances at a decent future. For Ali, in the back of the van, he faced life with a kind of exasperation. Far away, people were making decisions and imposing embargoes that smothered his very existence. Even closer, others were proselytising from podiums their own ideologies that offered absolutely no relevance or practicality to improving his day-to-day life. As for Masoud, he wanted to earn more money to help his family, and to one day start his own. And young Javad, not even out of his teens, just wanted to know that hard work could pay off.

Back towards the capital, on the very southern edge of Tehran Province, the little city of Varamin emerges without pomp or ceremony. It is not known for many modern splendours but was an important post during the Sasanian Empire. It is also believed to be the ancient city of Varena, mentioned in the Zoroastrian sacred text, the Avesta. Remnants of its former glory can be found on its outskirts, in particular the Qaleh Iraj, or Iraj Castle, which rises in the middle of a farming field like a ruinous mountain. The purpose is a point of contention for archaeologists, who suspect it was most likely a military fortress constructed to protect the city of Rey, which was at the heart of the vast Sasanian Empire and home to two important noble houses. Within Varamin, the charming thirteenth-century Jameh Mosque forms the central point of the city and still remains its most important congregation point. These days Varamin is a blue-collar city, with many of its citizens employed in little businesses or the factories scattered along the Tehran–Varamin road.

In the middle of town, Hamed Heydari was trying to stretch his sore back, which constantly ached as he bent over for much of the day to look under the hoods of cars. His hands were stained with oil, and no matter how much he washed them, he just could not clean out the little black lines stubbornly engraved in the cracks of his skin.

In his late twenties, the mechanic sported a thick head of black hair and was clean-shaven, save for an intentional patch under his lower lip. In his dark coveralls and broad frame, Hamed looked very much the blue-collar worker. He was also a proud newlywed. But instead of being filled with the euphoria of love and possibilities, he was overcome by anxiety. He worked hard, sometimes seven days a week, at his automotive business in the centre of town. It was only large enough to fit two cars at any one time, and with only two mechanics, they wouldn't be able to handle much more work. Despite all this effort, Heydari said he was not getting ahead.

'The dollar exchange rate has affected every service, especially imports. People cannot afford to buy things, especially in our industry. So, people are paying in instalments, but our purchasing costs are constantly increasing. Even hour by hour,' he explained.[7]

Just a few doors down, poultry butcher Bijan Ghorbani quickly hacked apart a chicken. His shop was small—just a front counter and some bench space in the back to do his work. Middle-aged with a wife and children, he wore a white butcher's coat, which somehow defied the reality of his job with its bright cleanliness. Unlike Heydari, Ghorbani's business didn't need imports or foreign parts, and the price of basic staples, which included chicken, was set by the government. So even as the Iranian rial crashed against the US dollar and sanctions choked the country, Ghorbani could continue with a steady customer base, because, as he put it, 'people need to eat.'[8]

But that did not mean he was exempt from the maladies of Iran's financial crisis. Inflation had affected everyone and almost everything, so even if his business purchases were price-controlled, his living costs were not. No matter how hard he worked, like Hamed Heydari, he could do nothing about the rocketing costs of daily life. For many of the residents of Varamin, one of its benefits had always been that it was cheaper than the capital, some two hours' drive away. Life here was supposed to be more affordable, more liveable. But sanctions and government mismanagement had caused such a deep economic slump that no corner of the country was exempt.

Although Varamin is technically located in Tehran province, it is generally considered a rural city. Being predominantly working class, it was exactly the type of place where Ahmadinejad drew his support base, and many people—including conservatives and some analysts—presumed it would continue to support hardline ideological politics. Indeed, Hossein Naghavi-Hosseini, who had represented Varamin in parliament since 2008, was a member of the rather extremist political party the Front of Islamic Revolution Stability, which considered the radical Ayatollah Mohammad-Taqi Mesbah-Yazdi to be its spiritual guide. Jalili was running as the party's presidential candidate, and it was widely assumed that he would poll strongly amongst locals. But on the eve of the election, just like everywhere else across the country, economics and sanctions were at the forefront of most people's minds, not personal conviction.

The internal pressures and crises within the country grew from the earliest stages of the Ahmadinejad presidency and reached fever pitch in the aftermath of 2009. But with the advent of Obama's sanctions regime, coupled with Ahmadinejad's economic mismanagement, a crushing desperation and hopelessness had ravaged the country like an epidemic. From the villages in the north, down to the busy capital and industrial cities like Varamin, along the caravanserai trails in Kashan and south to Bandar Abbas on the Persian Gulf, where millions of barrels of oil sat trapped by the oil embargo, nowhere was spared. Perhaps only a small minority of people was left unaffected, cocooned in immense wealth—or hardened ideology.

This small group did not just include those still buying uber expensive foreign cars; it could also be glimpsed outside Friday prayers at Tehran University.[9] Unlike those in many other Muslim-majority countries in the Middle East, or even in Turkey on the cusp of Europe, most Iranians do not pray at mosques, even on Fridays for *jumah*. Traditionally, even many conservative Iranians choose to perform their daily prayers at home, believing faith to be a private issue. But Friday prayers at Tehran University were different—and political. The vast hall, which separates men and women, was always full for *jumah*, and it was common to find politicians and other public figures sitting in the front rows. For some worshippers, who were not solely there for the business of God, it was the perfect place to bolster their loyalist credentials.

On the last Friday before the election, flyers and posters littered the streets. It would be a maddening clean-up for city workers, though it was nothing compared to the fervent campaigns of 2009, when campaign posters seemed to cover every square inch of public space.

As prayers ended, the crowd snaked out of the hall and back into the city streets. Dozens of downtown shopkeepers jumped on well-used motorbikes and zoomed off back to their lives. But one group of worshippers stayed to chant slogans. They were all men, and bore some tell-tale signs of conservatism, including short beards and untucked shirts. The most vocal were in their twenties and thirties and proudly declared that they would be voting for a smattering of conservative hardliners: Velayati, Jalili and Qalibaf.

Friday prayers at Tehran University were the traditional house of Iran's principlists—those loyal to the revolution, religion and ostensibly the clergy. But though Rouhani was the only cleric running, very few people here voiced any support for him. Despite very much being a man of God, Rouhani was not outwardly ideologically driven. This point of divergence became most evident under Ahmadinejad, with the ascent of a faction—including Ahmadinejad, Jalili and Qalibaf—that drew its support and ideology from the days of the Iran–Iraq War, rather than from the seminary or the revolution like older conservatives. Even though they had no religious training or qualifications, members of this camp were often publicly—and paradoxically—more conservative than many clerics. What is more, many of them had started to claim themselves as the true guardians of the Islamic Republic, even though they had played no role in its creation.

At the prayers one young man, who declared he was about to enter seminary school, said that he would not vote for Rouhani because he thought he was too liberal, although he respected him as a man of faith. Instead he would cast his vote for Jalili, because, he said, that was what the Supreme Leader wanted. Jalili followers would often chant, 'I vote for Jalili for the love of my leader!' It didn't matter that Khamenei had not in fact endorsed any candidate—not even Velayati, his closest advisor.

Another religious man, who identified himself as a member of the volunteer Basij militia, turned his nose up at Rouhani as well. He too favoured Jalili and did not care whether Rouhani was a cleric or not—his close ties to Rafsanjani were a problem. Many likeminded conservatives did not like Rafsanjani. They saw the revolutionary founding father as a threat to the Supreme Leader and far too liberal, especially given that he and members of his family had supported Mousavi in 2009, which to the most extreme hardliners was akin to treason. Until Rafsanjani's death in 2017, they would never forgive nor forget.

What also mattered little to some conservatives was that Rouhani was a revolutionary and a devout follower of Khomeini. In fact, before the revolution, he was credited as the first person ever to publicly refer to the exiled Khomeini as 'Imam', at a memorial service for Khomeini's oldest son Mostafa on 23 October 1977. It was this act that led Rouhani to flee Iran for Europe in order to escape persecution by the SAVAK.

Rouhani was also the ultimate insider, who held the confidence not only of Khomeini until his death, but also of his successor, Khamenei. Under the latter's leadership, he had been appointed to a number of sensitive positions in the Islamic Republic, including secretary of the Supreme National Security Council at its inception in 1989.

But hardline supporters dismissed these credentials as a thing of the past. In years to come, their criticisms of the pragmatic cleric would become much more vociferous, and sometimes violent. And Rouhani's opponents weren't all ordinary members of the public; he also had detractors in the state and security branches.

As the crowd at Tehran University dwindled and hardliners dispersed back into the city, one of the last to remain made an observation. With confidence, he stated that even if reformists had some support in the capital, it was foolish to think the picture outside Tehran was the same. Rural Iranians, the man said, did not care for so-called liberal policies. It would have then come as a great surprise, less than a week later, when Rouhani swept the election with 50.71 per cent of the vote. What's more, the moderate cleric won twenty-nine of Iran's thirty-one provinces, including one of the most conservative: Qalibaf's home province of Razavi Khorasan in the country's northeast. Rouhani also won quite comfortably in the supposedly conservative city of Varamin.

As it turned out, just three days in June—the last seventy-two hours before the election—were the most crucial in the whole race; former president Khatami had convinced his first vice president Aref, a reformist, to drop out of the race, and both he and Rafsanjani backed Rouhani. Despite being banned from Seda va Sima and shunned by the establishment, Khatami proved he was still a force to be reckoned with amongst those who mattered most: the public. His endorsement had spurred millions of apathetic Iranians not just to polling booths, but crucially into the camp of a fellow moderate cleric.

5

MR FEREYDOUN

'Our revolution was a revolution of light and morality, but today, where is morality in our society?'

Hassan Rouhani[1]

The morning after was quiet. Newsstands fluttered with rows of papers, held down by a rock or broken brick. One read, 'hope has returned'. Many people walked around still shocked. Others wore the heavy eyes of a sleepless night.

The late surge towards the Rouhani campaign carried through until the polls closed at 11 p.m.—five hours later than scheduled. The last-minute 'rush of voters', as Interior Minister Mostafa Mohammad-Najjar called it, had forced the ministry to extend polling hours as long as possible.[2]

Shortly after Mohammad-Najjar announced live on state television that Rouhani had won the election, the result and turnout were being compared to Mohammad Khatami's first presidential win in 1997.[3] That year, 79.92 per cent of eligible voters had participated and handed Khatami the type of landslide that had never been seen before or since.[4] According to official figures, in

2013, 72 per cent of eligible Iranians voted, in what the Supreme Leader labelled a 'political epic'.

Soon after the official announcement, Rouhani supporters began filling squares, streets and highways all over the country. In the capital's north-west, police tried to keep the buoyant crowds from blocking traffic, but it was a useless exercise, as even drivers got out of their cars to dance and celebrate in the middle of the road. Revellers screamed and cheered, yelling 'Ahmadi bye bye,' in a not-so-subtle message to the outgoing administration. One young voter could barely contain herself, as she stood out of the sunroof of a car, screaming, 'Victory, we were victorious!' while flashing peace signs. With a purple scarf wrapped around her head, she breathlessly revealed her sentiments: 'I am so happy I don't even know what to say. We made this victory and all I hope is that everything goes well, like we wish. I want us to be happy and to live in a way that we want.'[5]

Another young man and his friend said they were happy because it was 'their' victory. 'It was our votes, they counted our votes, it was our win, nobody else had a hand in it,' they said, alluding to the suspicious outcome of the 2009 election.

Although most of the revellers were voters in their twenties and thirties, the message of hope transcended age. One woman, Sima, had come out to celebrate by herself. As a mother of two, she had seen first-hand how the failed economy and Ahmadinejad's so-called 'third revolution' had affected her own children, both university graduates. 'The young people of this nation are so depressed. They [the government] must help them. They have no jobs, no prospects, nothing.'

Through the night, pro-reformist slogans arose through the country along with chants for the release of political prisoners. Others sang the praises of the man elected the country's seventh president. It was as though, on that summer night, anything was possible. As the paper suggested, hope had indeed returned.

But for some, happiness was tempered with the cautiousness of bitter experience. The Khatami years were transformative in many ways, and clearly, as Khatami's influence on the election proved, a large portion of society still greatly admired him. But those years taught his supporters that great expectations often lead to great disappointment. Though Khatami had been elected by popular mandate, parliament and unelected sectors of the establishment, like the Guardian Council, would block his attempts at reform, and he could not do very much to change that. While younger voters revelled, those old enough to remember the Khatami experiment had a warning for the new president-elect. A middle-aged man who had come out to celebrate put it simply: 'Mr Rouhani should do his job in a way that in four years, at this time, we will gather here again. Don't disappoint us.'

From her apartment near Borj-e Milad, the teacher Mina Heydari watched the results with little nostalgia or excitement.[6] She, like many others, had decided at the last minute to head out and vote, casting her ballot for Rouhani—not because she truly believed he could change things, she explained later, but to prevent the election of a hardliner, in particular Jalili. Even some members of Rouhani's camp conceded later that the fear of a hardline win contributed to the sudden mobilisation of reformist voters. Indeed, Rouhani himself, after casting his ballot in Tehran, told reporters, 'I have come to destroy extremism and when I see that these extremists are worried by my response and my vote, I am very happy.'[7]

It was a telling sign that the president had identified so-called 'extremists' as his opponents, in particular as that contest would present the greatest challenge and obstacle to change throughout his term in office. Speaking on state television after his win, Rouhani asked for help, saying:

> I'm proud that the great people of Iran, the honourable people, thought that I deserve this. They trusted me so that I can begin on

the path to serve the country, to enhance people's lives and welfare, and preserve national pride and national interests. I deeply feel that I need your assistance along this path. I need you to be there. I need your cooperation.[8]

* * *

Almost 200 kilometres east of Tehran, on the edge of the Dasht-e Kavir, or Great Desert, Mohammad Reza Salaami watched Rouhani's victory press conference with tears in his eyes. His heart was bursting with pride and happiness at the sight of his old childhood friend, who had just been elected president of Iran.

The oldest of five children, Hassan Rouhani was known in childhood by his birth name of Hassan Fereydoun. Salaami, who looked up to the slightly older Rouhani, had grown up in the same corner of Sorkheh, a town of only a few thousand, whose outskirts are dotted with the ruins of caravanserai on the ancient Silk Road from China. He told how their lives had diverged, influenced by those around them as well as the politics of the Shah's Iran. Whilst Rouhani had headed towards the seminary, Salaami had taken the path of science.[9]

The morning after Rouhani's victory, Salaami stood outside his little pharmacy on the corner of the dead-end alley, at the end of which stood the Fereydoun family home. If there was any doubt that the cleric was popular, all one needed to do was look around this town, starting with Salaami's shop windows. Rouhani posters, many bearing the campaign slogan of 'prudence and hope', covered almost every corner of spare space. In the days that followed the election, Salaami would replace them with a large poster of the smiling cleric, emblazoned with the words, 'The government of prudence and hope has arrived.' Outside the city's main mosque, a giant purple banner had been hung high across the narrow street: 'We have faith in your prudence and hope.'

Salaami was beaming. 'I'm so happy, I'm so happy because of this election! This city is blessed! For young people who study in our schools and go to class,' he said, pointing back to the centre of town, 'to see that one has grown up here and has become the president is such an honour! This will pull people up.'[10]

Like most of the establishment leaders, Rouhani—born in 1948—came from a conservative upbringing in rural Iran. Interestingly, he was not the only president to hail from Semnan Province; his predecessor Mahmoud Ahmadinejad was born eight years after Rouhani in the neighbouring village of Aradan. The two towns were similar, too—quiet and traditional, where people are friendly and sometimes curious of outsiders.

As Salaami alluded to, if anything set the young Hassan on the course to becoming a revolutionary, and eventually the president, it was life in Sorkheh. Rouhani also recounts life here in his memoirs, detailing how he learned to read at a school run by his grandmother, and in the summer break had often helped his father with farming and carpentry to pay for his education, which was important to his parents.[11] 'Those days were a little tough for me,' Rouhani explained during the election, 'but I soon realised how enjoyable it is to stand on your feet.'[12] Two days after the election, Sakineh Peivandi, Rouhani's elderly mother, recounted to *Shargh* newspaper that her eldest son was quiet and helpful and possessed a good memory, which allowed him to gain early acceptance to theology classes in Qom.[13] This had played an enormous role in setting the direction of Rouhani's life.

In Sorkheh, the summer wind blew dust off the streets, as old men whiled away the day sitting on stoops chatting, with their canes and prayer beads in hand, watching life around them pass by at a leisurely pace. Like many other towns or villages, the busiest place to be at noon was still the local mosque. As prayers ended and worshippers slowly filed out, some of the older men recounted the president-elect's early influences. Beyond life in Sorkheh, political upheaval under the Shah and religion, Rouhani's path in life had also been shaped by his father, the late Hajj Asadollah Fereydoun, who was, according to the men, a towering figure of piety and revolutionary zeal. One of the worshippers pointed across the street to a little shop on the corner, closed, some of its windows covered with cardboard. It was the little spice shop that Hajj Asadollah had run for decades until his death in 2011—just two years before his eldest son became president.

Asadollah had come from humble means; he was an orphan with little formal schooling, who had deserted the army after the British invasion of Iran in 1941 to return to Sorkheh. He had managed to marry into a well-to-do family of good religious standing and in 1958, through his connections and reputation for devotion, was appointed the *vakil*, or representative, in Sorkheh for Grand Ayatollah Sayyed Hossein Boroujerdi, one of the most revered Shia leaders in the world and Iran's most important religious figure until his death in 1961.[14] The appointment propelled Hajj Asadollah (as he became known after a pilgrimage to Mecca) into an important position. Travelling clerics and important contacts of Boroujerdi often stayed at his house. All the while, his eldest son was by his side.

In addition to being a man of faith, Hajj Asadollah was vehemently anti-Shah, and by the early 1960s, enraged by the White Revolution reforms and inspired by Khomeinism, Asadollah was actively agitating against the Shah's rule. In his memoirs, Rouhani writes that his father was arrested more than twenty times between 1962 and 1979.

It was no wonder then that Hassan Fereydoun from Sorkheh became Hassan Rouhani: cleric, revolutionary, politician.

After anti-Shah riots in Qom forced Khomeini into exile, Rouhani, like his father, joined the fray. In his memoirs, Rouhani recounts secretly distributing Khomeini's leaflets among fellow students and travelling around to villages preaching and denouncing the Shah.

But as prominent agitators like Hashemi Rafsanjani, Dr Ali Shariati and Ayatollah Ali Khamenei were moving through the fortress-like Towhid or Evin prisons at an alarming pace, SAVAK seemed to have deemed Rouhani not important enough to arrest. Reproduced in Rouhani's memoirs, one SAVAK document reads: 'Most theology students are of the belief that his sermons are dull and uninteresting, but he manages to attract crowds because he uses the title "Dr" before his name.'

The death of Mostafa Khomeini, the eldest son of the Grand Ayatollah in exile, changed perceptions of the young cleric. Mostafa had died in a car crash in Najaf, Iraq, and Khomeini's supporters, including Rouhani, were quick to blame SAVAK for his death, although no evidence exists to suggest this is at all true.

At the request of Ayatollah Morteza Motahari, Rouhani delivered the funeral sermon. He relays that the mosque was 'shaken' as he compared the elder Khomeini to Abraham and, to the shock of many, referred to him as an Imam. Not to be confused with the use of the word 'imam' to describe a prayer leader in a mosque, for Twelver Shia Muslims in this context, the title Imam connotes something much more divine—the belief that sole leadership of the Muslim community is passed through the holy line of descendants of the Prophet Mohammad: the Twelve Imams. Rouhani had elevated Khomeini to that status, and it is believed it was the first time anyone had done so in public.

If Rouhani was an unexceptional agitator at that point, unworthy of a cell next to revolutionary giants, the sermon certainly increased his credentials. A year later, on the advice of his mentor Ayatollah Mohammad Beheshti, Rouhani left Iran, first travelling to London, then to Paris, to join Khomeini in exile.

As the imam of Sorkheh put it decades later, 'Rouhani held many positions, working his way up from rung to rung' after the revolution.[15] Among them, he worked with Ali Khamenei, who was at that time a midranking cleric and trusted member of the revolutionary core, to purge the armed forces of Shah loyalists. He also became a parliamentarian representing Semnan.

It was after the onset of the Iran–Iraq War, in September 1980, that Rouhani came to form an alliance with one of Iran's most powerful men—Ali Akbar Hashemi Rafsanjani. From this point, their fates somehow intertwined, for better or for worse. And after Beheshti was killed in the mass Haft-e Tir bombing on 28 June 1981, along with seventy-two other officials of the Islamic Republic, Rafsanjani became Rouhani's most important mentor.

Rafsanjani, still chairman of the parliament, had also become the Iranian military's de facto commander-in-chief, and as such had grown increasingly uneasy at the burgeoning strength and independence of the newly formed Islamic Revolutionary Guard Corps. He had even sent Rouhani to the front to keep tabs on the Revolutionary Guards, and, according to Rafsanjani's own memoirs, Rouhani's reports were usually scathing. It seems even in its infancy, Rafsanjani, the pragmatist, could see how unchecked power would turn a group of brave revolutionary warriors into a political and economic force which would challenge the power of even the revolutionary class of clerics.

With Rouhani as a member of parliament and Rafsanjani as its chairman, the pair tried to curtail the IRGC's power by keeping it under parliamentary and executive oversight. They of course lost, and in 1982, the 'State of the Guards' became law, giving the IRGC vast powers and independence free from the checks and balances of elected officials—a problem which persisted into Rouhani's own administration.

* * *

It was no small coincidence, then, given his long history with Rafsanjani, that the Iranian kingmaker sat at Rouhani's left side during the swearing-in ceremony in parliament. The black-turbaned Hassan Khomeini, grandson of the late Supreme Leader, sat in the front row. The juxtaposition was highly telling. Ahmadinejad had shunned both men during the later years of his presidency, to the extreme point that his supporters had even booed the younger Khomeini at a ceremony marking the anniversary of his grandfather's death.

Rouhani's first moments in office indicated the direction his administration would take and offered a stark contrast to the previous eight years. Two people were missing, however—former president Mohammad Khatami, who was still banned from public events, and Ahmadinejad himself, despite custom mandating the latter's attendance.

Addressing the packed chamber, Rouhani stated: 'My government will make the most of its efforts ... reduce threats and increase opportunities. ... People want better lives, dignity, respect and stability. Iran should find its right place in the family of nations.' Many members of that family watched on, as dignitaries representing more than forty countries attended, as did Javier Solana, the EU's former foreign policy chief. Earlier, Rouhani had greeted each of them as they filed into the chamber, shifting between English, Persian and Arabic. Mohammad Javad Zarif, whom Rouhani had nominated as foreign minister, did the same. It was clear—this was a revival of the moderates.

But beyond a good photo op, the new president faced enormous challenges—internationally and at home. Rouhani had made sanctions removal the key priority of his campaign, and thus it was his first priority as president. But that could only be achieved through international negotiation.

Although it was not yet known to the public, secret direct talks between Iran and the US had already begun, facilitated by Oman. More than a year earlier, on 7 July 2012, US National Security Council Staffer Puneet Talwar and Hillary Clinton's deputy chief of staff, Jake Sullivan, had travelled to Muscat for the first direct meeting between Iran and the US, outside the often charged atmosphere of nuclear talks with the P5+1 (the five permanent members of the UN Security Council, plus Germany).[16] There inside Sultan Qaboos' palace waited a four-man Iranian team, which included Deputy Foreign Minister Ali Asghar Khaji and Reza Najafi, a disarmament and non-proliferations expert who would later become ambassador to the International Atomic Energy Agency.[17] It was an exploratory meeting and, for the Americans, a chance to see whether the Iranians were serious about further talks and negotiations. The Iranians wanted something different—to get the US to accept Iran's right to enrich uranium, which had for years been a sticking point in negotiations with the EU3 and its successor the P5+1. Of course, the US delegation could not deliver on that, which frustrated the Iranian team, who left empty-handed. But the little meeting did offer a base on which to build; both Obama and Khamenei approved of the back channel, and that in and of itself was pivotal.

Critically, inside the White House, Obama had recalculated his approach to the Iranian issue. Much like Trump, Obama had applied a strategy of maximum pressure, which included a punishing sanctions regime. While Trump's approach was unilateral, Obama's was multilateral and included consensus at the UN and among permanent members of the UN Security Council, including Russia and China. But after several years, Obama concluded there was very little to show for this strategy. Iran had not capitulated on its nuclear rights, including its right to enrich uranium, nor had sanctions or the threat of war stopped Iran's nuclear advances. In fact, by the time Rouhani was sworn in as president, Iran's nuclear activities had vastly increased. Wendy Sherman, who would become one of the States' lead negotiators in talks with Iran, observed: 'Every year that went by, they had more centrifuges, more capacity, and more capability.'[18] In addition, there were signs Iran's economy was not only adjusting to the outside pressure, but that America's ability to keep its sanctions coalition intact had begun to waiver, with some countries already skirting the US- and EU-led Iranian oil embargo.

Iran knew the US had very few options left short of war, and with the advent of Obama's second term in office, it seems the White House also came to realise this. John Kerry had also replaced the more hawkish Hillary Clinton as secretary of state, and this proved an important element during debates in the White House.

It was almost a year after the first Oman meeting that a follow-up took place. In March 2013, the US upped the ante, sending then US Deputy Secretary of State William Burns, along with Sullivan, who was considered a rising star in Washington, to meet Iranian officials.[19]

In part through Omani lobbying, the Obama White House had been reassessing at least some of its positions on Iran, including its refusal to acknowledge Iran's right to enrich uranium. Obama had given Burns the go-ahead to present this to the Iranians—in very limited and concise language, as a potential point of exploration rather than a solid acceptance or agreement. Kerry followed this up with a letter to Sultan Qaboos, who was acting as the interlocutor. The sultan then passed on his own thoughts to Ahmadinejad, saying that he believed the Americans were very serious about talks, and also compromise.

Despite the Supreme Leader's green light for the Oman backchannel and direct talks with the US, there were still huge obstacles in Tehran, most notably within the Ahmadinejad administration and among its key appointees, including Saeed Jalili, then chief nuclear negotiator. Reformists, moderates and even some of the more pragmatic conservatives, such as Velayati, knew that talks would go nowhere, regardless of what was happening in the White House. Velayati made that officially known during the 2013 presidential debates by criticising Jalili's stubborn and brusque stance as an obstacle to diplomatic progress. This criticism was also a public sign that there was more pragmatism towards the US within Khamenei's inner circle than ideological adherents assumed, and possibly wanted. Thus, many of the political elite knew the chance to strike a deal with Obama, who was looking for a legacy issue and unencumbered by the prospect of another election, was ripe.

Clearly, Iranians at large made no secret of the fact they wanted change and to see this issue resolved. What was more, the revolt against Ahmadinejad and anyone associated with him was widespread—not only within the high echelons of power in Tehran, but amongst the general populace. The overwhelming election of Rouhani, dubbed the 'diplomatic sheikh' in Iran, and the rejection of Jalili, who only garnered 11 per cent of the vote, proved as much.

Unsurprisingly, despite the shift in calculations at the White House towards a more realistic view of Iran's position, foreign policy advisors still made the same assumptions as their predecessors. Just as the Carter administration failed to predict the revolution, Obama and his advisors failed to predict the election of Rouhani.[20] It caught them completely off guard and proved once again that negative US assumptions were as much a hindrance to diplomacy as hardline ideologues in Tehran.

But at least a change in administration in Tehran made up some of the distance between the two sides. Parliament had confirmed Mohammad Javad Zarif's nomination as Rouhani's foreign minister, which was just one new appointment in a wide-ranging overhaul of key positions at the foreign ministry. Zarif had served as Iran's UN ambassador from 2002 to 2007 and before that had been a lead negotiator during some of the Republic's most important foreign policy decisions, including the UN-brokered ceasefire to end the Iran–Iraq War in 1988, and later secret talks to help the US in its war against the Taliban after 9/11.[21]

Zarif had spent many years in the US, first moving there in the 1970s as a teenager to go to prep school. He later attended San Francisco State University, where he gained a BA and MA, and also the University of Denver, where he obtained another MA and a PhD. As a lifelong diplomat and scholar, fluent in English and with high-level contacts in Washington and New York, Zarif was an exciting choice. His reputation as an intelligent, shrewd and pragmatic diplomat, who favoured the normalisation of ties with the US, was known further afield, including to Kerry, who had been chairman of the Senate Foreign Relations Committee since 2009. This would be important just a month after Zarif assumed office, when in September 2013 he travelled to New York a few days before the UN General Assembly. Although the secret channel between the US and Iran was not yet known publicly, there were signs something was happening.

Breaking with precedent, Khamenei had decided to hand responsibility of the nuclear dossier, and therefore talks, to the foreign minister, instead of to the incoming secretary of the Supreme National Security Council. In doing so, the Supreme Leader had ensured he and the SNSC 'would be one step removed from the talks if they failed.'[22] It was a hugely important decision, not just politically in terms of saving face, but also strategically. Although the SNSC continued to play a key role in terms of building consensus among the many branches of the Iranian political sphere, Khamenei's decision gave Zarif and Rouhani an important element of autonomy, free from domestic meddling.

Just days before the UN General Assembly, on 17 September Khamenei had also given a speech to IRGC commanders, in which he publicly signalled willingness to compromise through what he termed 'heroic flexibility'—a reference to Imam Hassan ibn Ali, the grandson of the Prophet Mohammad and second

Imam to Twelver Shias, who in 661 CE decided to seek peace with his rival Muawiyah I, instead of conflict. The Supreme Leader stated, 'Flexibility is necessary in many areas. It is good and there is nothing wrong with it,' but warned, 'the wrestler who is wrestling against his opponent and who shows flexibility for technical reasons should not forget who his opponent is. ... Our politicians too should know what they are doing, who they are faced with.'[23]

In New York, the mood surrounding the new Iranian delegation was in stark contrast to that of the Ahmadinejad days. In previous years, most Iranians had resigned themselves to the fact that there would be walkouts, protests and a belligerent speech that might or might not involve denying the Holocaust. As part of Rouhani's charm offensive, he brought Jewish MP Siamak More Sedgh with him to New York, to prove that Iran, which is home to one of the oldest Jewish populations in the world, is not antisemitic, or Holocaust-denying, but rather, as More Sedgh put it, 'anti-Zionist. I am Jewish and I myself am against Zionism.'[24]

When he is not in parliament, More Sedgh, a trained surgeon, is the head of the Jewish charity Dr Sapir Hospital in the old Jewish quarter of Tehran. From behind his desk, he leant his large frame back in his chair, dragging slowly from a cigarette. The ash tray on his desk was already full. From under the haze of smoke, More Sedgh explained another striking feature of Rouhani's trip, slightly amused: 'The president even made us stay in an average hotel, knowing Iranians back home were facing economic difficulties. Not like before where things were more lavish.'

The expectation that something better would now come of the UN General Assembly even helped to strengthen the Iranian currency to 29,500 rial against the US dollar, compared to about 39,000 rial against the dollar just a few months prior. The upswing was driven by hope alone, as Rouhani, at that point, had not even handed down a budget.

There was also an expectation, based on a sudden swirl of rumours, that Rouhani and Obama would meet and shake hands. In the Iranian capital, 10,000 kilometres away from New York, one of Iran's most respected former diplomats and political scientists watched on with interest. Davoud Hermidas-Bavand sat in his living room, surrounded by a curious mix of possessions gathered during a lifetime as a diplomat, from deer antler–framed chairs and ivory inlaid statues, to little paintings that had been gifted by former ambassadors. Dressed in a suit and silk tie, with the sophisticated bearing of a man of another era, Hermidas-Bavand summarised that Rouhani had at least three points in his favour at the General Assembly. First 'and primarily, it was the will and wish of the Iranian people that the existing problems' be solved and that Iran get out of its deadlock situation. Secondly, the international situation, 'particularly the regional crises', dictated that 'a new approach' be taken. Thirdly, the Supreme Leader's statements on the need for flexibility meant that Rouhani had 'enough authority, and to an extent, free authority, to handle the problems'.[25]

Elsewhere in the capital, political analyst Sadegh Zibakalam also heard the chatter of a breakthrough at the UN. 'It's an exciting time for Iranians,' he said. 'They're fed up with hostility, "death to America" ... they're all watching with anxiety and lots of hope for a breakthrough ... not a major breakthrough, even— as long as Rouhani and Obama shake hands, it's enough.'[26]

As it turned out, there was no handshake. And though both Rouhani and Obama had agreed to a private encounter, away from the cameras, in the end the Iranian delegation determined it was too much of a domestic political grenade and backed out.

Regardless, the General Assembly was a turning point. Obama recognised Iran's right to peaceful nuclear energy and bluntly stated the US was not seeking regime change. He invoked the Supreme Leader's religious decree against building nuclear weapons and acknowledged that as Rouhani had already received the mandate of the Iranian people, signs that the two sides could find a resolution were apparent. 'I don't believe history can be overcome overnight,' he said. 'But if we can resolve the nuclear issue, it's a major step down a long road to a different relationship.'[27]

Hours later, Rouhani took the podium to deliver his first address at the UN. He had paid attention to what Obama had said and addressed it in his speech, sometimes sending a backhand to the American president, who had stood firm on the US deploying all means necessary, including military ones, to protect its own interests in the Middle East. On this point, Rouhani replied, 'Securing peace and democracy and ensuring the legitimate rights of all countries in the world, including in the Middle East, cannot—and will not—be realised through militarism.'[28]

And though Rouhani noted that Iran was willing to remove all doubts about its nuclear intentions, it could not be without 'acceptance of and respect for the implementation of the right to enrichment inside Iran and enjoyment of other related nuclear rights.' Little did the public know, Obama had already indicated this acceptance.

On the sidelines of the UN General Assembly, a flurry of diplomatic activity was also going on, as Zarif and British Foreign Secretary William Hague agreed to start repairing the diplomatic freeze between Iran and the UK, which was sparked in 2011 when a group of radicals stormed the British embassy in Tehran. Zarif also sat down with US Secretary of State John Kerry, in what was the highest-level direct meeting between the US and Iran since the revolution. And with the rest of the P5+1, the group finally agreed to resume high-level nuclear talks.

As Rouhani headed for the airport, the trip had been deemed a success. And then the phone rang. It was Obama.

Through translators, Obama congratulated Rouhani on his election win and reiterated his view that diplomacy could work. It was a phone call that lasted fifteen minutes, after which

Rouhani bid Obama farewell, telling him in heavily accented English, 'Have a nice day.' In reply, Obama in equally awkward Persian responded, *'Khoda hafez'*—may God protect you.

When Obama told the White House Press Corps a few moments later, 'Just now, I spoke with President Rouhani of the Islamic Republic of Iran,' shock rippled through the room. Meanwhile in Tehran, word spread with speed, as mobile phones chimed and lit up with the news. For the most part, the Iranian press reflected the positive tone, with reform-leaning papers like *E'temad* calling the UNGA P5+1 meeting a 'historic proposal', juxtaposed with an image of a telephone under the headline, 'Obama called'.[29]

That same day, Tehran's provisional Friday prayer leader, the aging Ayatollah Mohammad Emami Kashani, used the pulpit to deliver his thoughts on Rouhani's efforts in the US. Speaking to the sea of hardliners, which notably included quite a large swathe of IRGC officials, Kashani stated: 'Iran has always been oppressed by the US and arrogant powers, so this is a movement to defend the nation. In different times, it requires different approaches. The strong and logical speech of the president was based on this, and I hope God helps Rouhani and his government.'[30] It was not simply Kashani's message, but also that of Khamenei. Back the president, but don't trust the enemy.

However, even with the positive developments in New York and clear support from the Supreme Leader, some were unmoved. A young, bestubbled worshipper outside Friday prayers, Mohsen Sarmadi, explained later that he didn't 'think relations with the US were a good idea. It goes back to the revolution. Whenever a problem or war has occurred it has been because of the US or Israel, and I don't think Iran benefits from it.'[31] Another older worshipper, wearing a business shirt and bright green scarf, was slightly more circumspect. 'If the US has no hostile plans and is humanitarian in nature, and our authorities agree to have friendly relations with the US, I think it's quite good. We will both benefit.' But he added, seriously, 'In the past few years, the US has not shown any kindness, neither to Iran nor any other country.' Hassan Hanizadeh, a conservative Tehran-based analyst, later surmised that the 'relationship between the US and Iran is complicated,' and indicated that US support for Israel and its meddling in the Middle East would remain the biggest obstacles to reconciliation.[32]

Rouhani's momentum on the international stage continued at a rapid pace—and so too did hardline attacks on the new president and his foreign minister. Radicals, bogged down in their own ideology and perhaps sensing their growing irrelevance, vociferously raged against Zarif for his audacity to talk to the Americans. They accused him of treason and questioned his loyalty to the Republic, citing his many years in the US as proof he was *gharbzardegi* or 'drowning in the West'. This angered the privately pious diplomat, who had spent his adult life in the service of the Republic, so immensely that he developed physiological issues. With crippling back spasms, which at times bound him to bed or a wheelchair, Zarif still managed to get to Geneva at the end of November for the third round of talks since the General Assembly. The day before, he released a video on YouTube in English, clearly aimed at a global audience, and asked, 'What is dignity? What is respect? Are they negotiable? Is there a price tag?' He reiterated the Rouhani administration's platform, saying, 'The choice is not submission or confrontation. This past summer our people chose constructive engagement through the ballot box. And through this they gave the world a historic opportunity to change course.'[33]

Four days later, by the sparkling waters of Lake Geneva, the P5+1 and Iran reached the Joint Plan of Action, or the Geneva interim agreement, which set out the parameters on which the parties would proceed to build a permanent resolution.[34] For six months, Iran agreed to numerous limitations, including no new enrichment of uranium over 5 per cent; suspending work at the Natanz Fuel Enrichment Plant, Fordow, and at the Arak reactor; and daily inspections by the International Atomic Energy Agency (IAEA). In return, through the P5+1, the EU and US agreed to suspend sanctions on Iranian petrochemical exports, gold and precious metals, while the US agreed to licence the supply and installation of spare parts for Iranian civilian airliners and to suspend sanctions on Iran's automotive industry. Parties also agreed to release around US$4.2 billion of Iran's foreign currency holdings, which had been seized by banks around the world due to US sanctions.

Back in Tehran, the news was greeted with a collective sigh of relief. Unbelievably, in less than four months, the Rouhani and Obama administrations had done what others could not or would not achieve in almost a decade. The agreement meant that the prospect of war and catastrophe had suddenly decreased, and there was a glimmer of hope that life would return to normal—whatever that looked like.

Emad Abshenas, the managing director of the Tehran-based think tank Iran Diplomatic, felt the change immediately. And though he would become critical of the process and of unkept promises on all sides, he agreed the psychological changes were positive, noting that 'some people expected more talks between Iran and the US' outside the frame of the nuclear issue.[35]

Much like the warm reception that met Rouhani in Tehran when he came back from the General Assembly—with hundreds of supporters flocking to his car at Mehrabad Airport—Zarif also returned from Geneva to a rock star's welcome.[36] Hundreds of supporters went to the airport in the middle of the night, bearing posters of Rouhani and signs for Zarif, reading 'Greetings to the ambassador of Peace'.[37]

The interim agreement came into force two months later in January 2014. And although it was welcomed, there was considerable apprehension in Iran that the P5+1 would not uphold their end of the bargain. But as Amir Mousavi, a researcher and advisor to the Iranian defence ministry, explained, the deal was based on reciprocity. 'If the agreement is not implemented simultaneously by both sides, [it] will be suspended. If they [the US] do not fulfil their commitments and release Iran's frozen money abroad, Iran is ready to resume enriching uranium to 20 per cent,' he said. Mousavi, who would later serve as a controversial cultural attaché to Algeria, also pointed out that inspectors from the IAEA were already in Iran, and that if the P5+1 reneged on its commitments, 'then in just one hour, Iran can restart everything again.'[38]

Aside from trepidation about trust, there were obvious issues that the deal did not address, as powerful Iranian businessman Masoud Daneshmand pointed out. Daneshmand was the managing director of a shipping line, a member of the Iran–United Arab Emirates Chamber of Commerce, and on the board of directors of Tehran's Chamber of Commerce. With little economic strategy from the previous government, it was up to private businessmen like him to find solutions to the country's litany of economic problems. 'Sanctions have mostly been imposed on our banking system, transport, insurance and on oil,' said Daneshmand.[39] 'It means they have blocked Iran's access to SWIFT and international banking. We have no way to transfer money; transport companies have been banned from coming to Iran's ports, and insurance for goods and transportation also suffers. What is supposed to happen from 20 January [when the interim agreement would be implemented] has no effective impact on sanctions, but its psychological aspect should be considered.' What Daneshmand alluded to was that the deal did not remove sanctions on Iran's Central Bank, nor give it access to SWIFT.

Many ordinary Iranians agreed it was troubling. On the streets of Tehran, resident Agha Karimi explained, 'There is a Persian proverb that says: "Show one death and one will be content with fever." That's where we are now. The world has put us under such enormous pressure that by such a little thing we've become hopeful and see a good future. So, for a beginning, it's good—but generally, not good enough.'[40]

Iran had been relying heavily on third-party brokers such as the United Arab Emirates to transfer money and to pay for goods and services, which was technically illegal under the embargo. 'The UAE—specifically Dubai—is one of our commercial partners,' Daneshmand explained. 'Why? Because it is a second business base for us. ... We export almost 97–98 per cent of our goods to Dubai before they reach their final destination. It works the same for imports. But, during the past year, our financial interaction with Dubai dropped $10 billion.'

It was clear that any relief, no matter if it had been written in an international agreement, would be slow. But as Daneshmand and Karimi observed, the psychological effect of a breakthrough was, in itself, also important.

However, as had been made startlingly clear in the years prior, international issues were only half the problem in Rouhani's Iran. The new administration was facing domestic challenges almost as great as the nuclear crisis. Aside from economic malaise, Rouhani had promised to fix the fortunes of the 'battered' youth, as Rouhani campaign manager Mohammed Reza Nematzadeh had put it. Students, reformists and activists had left the political scene, save for those brief few days in June, in a mass exodus of apathy and despair. And it was not simply that they had given up either; many had been forced out—targeted, ostracised and in the case of hundreds, if not thousands, of students, punished with bans on attending university.

Those students ended up on a blacklist. They were known as 'starred students' because the Ministry of Science, Research and Technology—which runs universities—had put an asterisk beside their names to identify them as members of the so-called 'seditious' movement. Journalist Foad Shams was one of them. At first glance, he was perhaps the most unassuming trouble-maker a person could meet. He wore thick glasses with clear plastic frames that cut through his long, dark-brown sideburns. And from behind a thick but neat moustache and goatee, he spoke quite softly. In his cream-coloured sweater and matching khaki pants, he looked like he would be right at home in the 1970s. As a socialist, Shams would also, in the coming years, become an avid supporter of US Senator Bernie Sanders.

But according to hardliners, Shams was a criminal. From the small office of the news magazine *Hashiyeh*, opposite Tehran's Bostan-e Honarmand, or Artists Park, Shams explained how, as a journalist, he was arrested during the wave of protests that gripped the country in 2009 and was subsequently sentenced to six months in prison for 'propaganda against the state'. According to Freedom House, that year, Iran was the world's leading jailer of journalists. Shams served his penance and went back to work, only to discover three years later, after undertaking an entrance exam for a master's degree in geography at Tehran University, that he was on a blacklist.

Apparently, 2009 was not as far in the past as he thought. 'I was waiting for my results, and when they didn't give them to me, I went to find out why. That's when they told me I was a starred student. I chased it up and was not given a clear response—just verbally was told I wasn't allowed to study.'[41]

Shams stayed in Iran. Others who had the means left. One young Shirazi named Mehdi recounted how he was picked up a month after the protests as he walked down the street because Iranian authorities had been tracking his phone.[42] As he was thrown into the back of a police van, a guard punched him in the face. With his nose bleeding and glasses cracked, he did something curious. He asked the guard to take his picture. 'I was lying on the floor and he looked down at me like I was crazy,' the soft-spoken former student recounted. When the guard asked why, Mehdi replied, 'I want to give it to my mother. She is a regime supporter. I want to show her what shit you really are.'[43] The young architect doesn't remember what happened next. He said he was beaten so badly he passed out. He now lives in Europe.

The new administration had promised to rectify at least some of the wrongs of 2009. Although it was much too early for Mehdi to try to return home, Shams noticed that his fortunes had started to shift only a few months after the election. He had been allowed back to the University of Tehran, as had other students who had been vilified for dissent. It was perhaps just one small victory on an exceptionally long list of woes—the death and fever paradox—but nonetheless, it was a start.

Aside from hope and promises of reform and change, another theme had begun to emerge under the Rouhani administration—unbalance. Within the Republic, the balance between elected vs unelected and reformist vs hardline officials is delicate, and there are long-understood traditional spheres of influence.[44] Since the revolution, hardliners have dominated unelected offices and state institutions, such as the judiciary, the Expediency Discernment Council, security and intelligence circles and the all-important Guardian Council. The political direction of parliament and of institutions such as the foreign ministry, however, is variable and subject to election outcomes and new presidents— provided both that the Guardian Council allows a variety of different factional representatives to run and that enough of the populace participates at the polls. Under reformist or moderate administrations, like-minded politicians are naturally appointed to key positions in malleable institutions, but changes cause friction between, and within, institutions dominated by entrenched personnel appointed by the state rather than the executive. Hardliners, in particular those from the more radical factions, saw the election of Rouhani as a threat to their positions, both in their institutions and in wider society. The nuclear deal and direct Iran–US talks did not just cause spoilers like Benyamin Netanyahu to hyperventilate with rage; there were many people within Iran who followed suit.

Indeed, even before the deal, radicals had shown opposition to the Rouhani agenda. Although he was greeted with cheers when he returned from New York after the historic phone call with Obama, a number of radicals had also headed to the airport, but not to cheer. They had thrown eggs at the president's car and sworn at him.[45] And even as the Rouhani doctrine gathered pace, they were not going away.

On the thirty-fifth anniversary of the revolution, the crowds covered the entire central roundabout at Tehran's Azadi Square and stretched down the highway.[46] Members of the armed forces, in their dress uniforms and polished shoes, had lined up in formation, straight as arrows in front of the large stage. Around them, a carnival atmosphere erupted, as paratroopers sailed down from the sky in synchronised displays, and airdrops of colourful balloons and confetti covered the crowd. Some held up photos of Khomeini and Khamenei, as well as Hezbollah flags. Others held aloft signs and balloons, or had painted their faces red, white and green.

It was Rouhani's most important address to the nation—the first major national event since his election—and it took place at Azadi Tower, a symbol of freedom, after which it took its name. The cheers that greeted the president as he walked on stage were deafening. Rouhani paid tribute to Khomeini and those who fought to establish the Republic, in a speech that Sadegh Zibakalam dubbed 'conciliatory' and devoid of the 'ferocious remarks of the past eight years.'[47]

But Rouhani also turned his attention to more modern issues, like the challenge with the US. In no uncertain terms, he stated: 'To those who hold the illusion that threats are on the table against the Iranian nation, I explicitly announce they need glasses. On no table in the world are there military threats against our nation.'[48]

The president did not reserve his criticisms for outsiders; he took aim at those much closer to home too, telling the crowd that 'the revolution belongs to the whole nation' and not to one faction or another. It was a revealing statement. To Zibakalam, this meant that hardliners should not monopolise the revolution and its legacy, and that 'all Iranians, namely reformists and others, should take part in decision making of the country.'

But as the crowd cheered and chanted, there was one group that remained at odds with the new president's pragmatic commentary. They had arrived early, to stake out positions in Rouhani's line of sight, and held aloft white banners of Khamenei—quite literally acting as flag bearers of the state. One of the men stated categorically that he did not like the president. Another looked quite repulsed by the thought of him. Why they would awaken at the crack of dawn to see a president they despised was clear— they wanted to warn Rouhani. For these men, who identified themselves as followers of Khamenei, just like for other hardliners during the election, Rouhani was not faithful to the leader of the Republic. They drew upon worn and often vague reasons for this belief—including the 'treasonous' phone call with Obama.

Analyst Zibakalam noted that many 'hardliners were focusing their attention and looking cautiously and nervously to the Supreme Leader' to see the direction he would take. And although Khamenei, in his own speech, had depicted US officials as 'controlling and meddlesome' liars, he had also warned: 'No more than a few months have passed since the [Rouhani] government took office. ... Authorities should be given the opportunity to push forward strongly. Critics should show tolerance towards the government.' Observers concluded that the Supreme Leader was not only trying to appease his hardline base, but in doing so to buy the president some time. The strategy would only work as long as Iran saw benefits from US engagement.

Aside from flags of the Supreme Leader, the group had come prepared with a variety of creative signs conveying a host of grievances. One read 'If they [the US and Israel] misbehave in anyway, Tel Aviv and Haifa will be torn to pieces', while another depicted John Kerry and US Under Secretary of State for Political Affairs Wendy Sherman in a rubbish bin, under the words 'Out of Service'. Two other men held up a large sign of a boot superimposed on Obama's face. But perhaps most disturbingly, one man, remarkably stone-faced, brandished a picture of Green Movement leader Mir Hossein Mousavi under a mock hangman's noose.

The latter image, which was unsurprising in its message but startling in its audacity, made clear that for some, opposition to the president rested on more than long-held grievances against America or nuclear talks. Rouhani was not just fighting a battle against Western powers; he was also fighting one much closer to home. This was something he seemed to acknowledge himself; after a student at Sharif University asked him what he would do, if elected, about the ongoing detention of Karroubi and Mousavi (and the latter's wife Zahra Rahnavard), Rouhani replied:

> I hope the next government is able to bring about a non-securitised environment. I don't think it will be difficult to bring about a condition in the next year where not only those under house arrest, but those who have been detained after the 2009 elections, will be released.[49]

The statement was met with wild applause and chants of 'Rouhani, we love you.'

And yet, as the months and years of Rouhani's presidency passed, the leaders of the Green Movement remained under house arrest. It was perhaps the most visceral reminder that reality remained the greatest impediment to reform.

6

DELIVERANCE

In Iran's largest car manufacturing plant, in the industrial city of Karaj, sparks were, quite literally, flying. Employees of Iran Khodro (IKCO) were once again assembling cars on the production line with a sense of optimism that had long been absent.[1] It was not simply pride in their work, although that was arguably obvious in some of the employees, but also a hope for the burgeoning trade deals, of which IKCO was part.

One of the engineers on the shop floor, dressed in blue overalls, said it had been quite stressful coming to work every day during the sanctions crisis not knowing from one day to the next whether he would keep his job, when an estimated 100,000 others had not.

Automotives accounted for 5 per cent of Iranian manufacturing jobs before 2011. And that year, at its peak, Iran produced 1.7 million vehicles annually—of which 850,000 rolled off the Iran Khodro production line. A vast number were Peugeot 206s and 405s, which had become as much an essential part of the Iranian traffic landscape as the Paykan had been generations before.

The Peugeots were assembled in Iran from imported kits, originally under a licencing deal with the French automotive giant PSA Peugeot Citroën. But sanctions caused a litany of problems, not least of which was the abrupt departure of foreign companies like PSA. Suddenly, automotive production dropped 40 per cent, and thousands of workers lost their jobs. Automakers were forced to slow production and to source and even engineer parts themselves. It was a stinging blow, particularly around Karaj, which is home to some of the country's largest manufacturing plants in addition to IKCO. Labour strikes increased, unemployment rose and businesses struggling with rising costs and export bans ran into the red, unable to pay salaries, sometimes for months on end.

Well-known labour union leader Shapour Ehsanirad, recognisable in his golfer's cap, was exasperated by the troubles, which he said had hit blue-collar workers day after day in an unending wave of misfortune.[2] Ehsanirad had been organising workers to demand their rights—and pay from private companies—as well as to lobby the government.

Despite the financial crisis and the fact that sanctions relief had not yet materialised, Ehsanirad had little time for excuses, pointing out that the government had not fulfilled one of its key promises to raise wages in line with inflation. 'Now 40,000 workers have signed a petition asking him [Rouhani] to do it. If he wants to make changes, we workers need to be able to see this on our tables,' he stated.

Given the problems facing the industry, it had not been an ideal year for young mechanic Shahab Ashori to find a job at one of the car factories. But building cars was a dream the young man had held since he was in his early teens, and he was not giving up. He had been searching for work all over the capital without luck, and so he sat in the waiting room of a labour agency diligently filling out his forms, hoping by some chance they could place him. 'I always wanted to work in a car factory, but now they're mostly firing their employees, rather than employing people. For sure, it [the economy] has impacted the job market,' he lamented. But Ashori was nonetheless optimistic that Rouhani's election and Iran's bettering relations with the US and its allies would soon turn things around.

The fortunes of so many blue-collar workers seemed to rest on the nuclear deal and the promised benefits. Certainly, there were already hundreds of companies around the world—not least in France—that were eagerly awaiting the chance to do business in Iran. At an investment conference in the capital in February 2014, it was a who's who of French business. A hundred and fifty representatives from as many companies, including oil giant Total, PSA Peugeot Citroën and Renault, had flown in for the three-day meeting commandeered by Mohammad Nahavandian—Rouhani's chief of staff and economic advisor (later to be appointed vice president of economic affairs).[3]

Like PSA, other French companies that had once worked in Iran were hoping to resume operations, including the Marseille-based CIS Group, which worked across industries including oil and gas, and the SFPI Group, which had identified the Iranian market as a possible component in its strategy to diversify profits outside its home market of France. Oliver Blake of SFPI was buoyant, saying he saw 'big potential' in Iran, but added that contracts would be contingent on a permanent and lasting solution to international issues—in other words, economic embargoes. Despite optimism and clear excitement for such a money-making opportunity, this remained a very real concern.

Boutique investment firm Turquoise Partners handled 90 per cent of foreign investment in the Tehran Stock Exchange, which despite the doom and gloom in the economy had continued to be one of the best-performing markets in the world. Its manager, Ramin Rabii, said international trepidation about investing in Iran was still a huge problem, despite the nuclear deal and election of Rouhani. Rabii also pointed to perceptions as another hurdle. 'Iran is a relatively modern country, with proper institutions in place, with a very active and dynamic young population, very well educated—and that's not usually the image they [foreigners] have of the country,' he said.[4]

But the country that French and European businesses had abandoned during the nuclear and sanctions crisis was not the same as the one to which they were hoping to return. As Mohammad Reza Najafi-Manesh, head of the Iranian Association of Auto Parts Manufacturers, explained from his Tehran office, 'Of course the industry didn't remain silent or seated to see what will happen—of course they went to other sources.'[5] At the Iran Khodro plant, Hossein Najari, vice president of the company, said that had meant a need for self-reliance. His company and others had focused on engineering their own parts to make up for the gap left by France and other suppliers. Najari identified overreliance on imports as the main 'weakness point' of Iran's automotive industry, and hoped manufacturers—indeed the whole country—had learned that lesson.

However, despite the propagation of the 'resistance economy', the proof was very much in the product. Sanctions blocked access to many raw materials and foreign technical expertise and thus, as Najafi conceded, some domestically engineered parts, especially patented or highly specialised technology, or parts sourced elsewhere in places like China, were not as good as the originals. And the price of the cars made that clear; a second-hand Peugeot or Citroën made with original parts still cost more than a brand-new Iranian-engineered model.

The wait for change, for sanctions relief, for deliverance from misery would mark the months—and indeed, for many, the years—that followed Rouhani's election and the interim nuclear deal.

At Tehran's Muscular Dystrophy Association, Neda Anisi was hoping for something more concrete from diplomats so she could restart her treatment. As the twenty-something-year-old explained, she was only taking her medication when she could save enough money to afford it, even though that was not effective.

The association's chief, Ramak Heydari, found it concerning that anyone had been forced to make such a serious decision, given how time-sensitive muscular dystrophy was. 'If the patients don't take the medication, the deterioration rate in six months is the equivalent of what would usually occur over the course of two years, with treatment.'[6]

Anisi was already in a wheelchair. Eventually her lung function would deteriorate and force her onto a ventilator to breathe. That in itself was an astronomical expense for the average patient if they were to be ventilated at home, which was a possibility; a ventilator cost about 20 million toman, or US$5,000–7,000 depending on the exchange rate. And Anisi was just one of an estimated 30,000 to 35,000 Iranians who suffered from the disease.

Heydari, herself diagnosed with limb-girdle muscular dystrophy, for which there was no known cure, sat behind her desk in a no-frills office, as patients came in for blood tests and results. The clinic's main function was to provide a diagnosis and treatment plans. The latter mostly involved physical therapy and medication, which, according to Heydari, 'does not cure muscular dystrophy patients completely. It's really drug assistance to slow down the speed of the disease's growth and to slow down the speed of heart and lung failure.'

The key for a cure was in science, but under international embargoes, even medical advancements were scuttled. Iran's leading stem cell research centre, the Royan Institute, had begun work on one specific study into facioscapulohumeral muscular dystrophy (FSHD), a type of dystrophy which primarily attacks muscles in the face, shoulders and upper arms. But a lack of funding and raw materials, which it could no longer import, forced the institute to cancel what looked like a promising programme.

A cure, as Anisi pointed out, would benefit not only Iran, but sufferers the world over. As she put it: 'If sanctions are lifted, naturally I think it will have a positive impact on my life. Actually, all dystrophy patients are hopeful that research can be done. If there are no sanctions, research in Iran for a total cure could continue as it does all over the world. And if a drug or treatment is produced, it could be supplied easier.'[7]

The international stalemate over sanctions was only the latest chapter in a four-decade-long saga, in which the US and its allies had attempted, and largely succeeded, in making Iran the world's pariah. For all Iran's domestic political machinations, many economists held more than a modicum of understanding for a developing nation that was quite literally prevented from developing by the world's most powerful country. Naturally, they argued, a state dealing with perpetual external crisis must choose its spending priorities carefully. And in the absence of significant foreign investment in domestic projects and sectors, much is left to neglect.

High in the Alborz Mountains, powdery snow fields stretch out in a seemingly never-ending moonscape of brilliant blinding white. Above the clouds, where the peaks have disappeared to pierce the clean blue sky, skiers and snowboarders line up to jump on lifts. Some casually sip on flasks full of spirits to stay warm; others look on, attempting to hide their disapproval. Stretching more than 3,600 metres above sea level, Dizin is not just Iran's but arguably the Middle East's best ski field, lauded for the quality of its powder. Less than an hour and a half's drive due north of the capital, it is an easy reach for Tehranis, as well as for the many European tourists who have discovered its slopes. Like Shemshak down the road, known for its steep slopes, loud parties and DJ sets, Dizin was fast gathering a reputation amongst adventurous travellers. The atmosphere had even prompted *Vogue* to ask in a 2015 piece, 'Could Tehran (Yes, Tehran) Be the Next Aspen?'[8]

But as far as reality went, the short answer was no. Dizin, for all its wonders, was falling apart. As Olympic skier Baqer Kalhor explained, as he waited for a chairlift, 'The equipment is old— nothing has been updated in thirty-seven, thirty-eight years, and just three new facilities have been added.'[9]

Kalhor, also a member of the Iranian Ski Federation, would know. He was born and bred in Dizin and had skied there since he was old enough to walk. He had even trained on its slopes to compete in the Men's Slalom at the 2002 Winter Olympics in Salt Lake City. While other members of the Iranian national ski team waited nearby, Kalhor lamented that a lack of investment meant Dizin's facilities did not match its ski fields. 'Dizin has so much potential,' he said. 'The whole mountain can be used. I hope investors in the company that supervises this resort invest more and make it bigger and bigger so we can introduce it to the world, secure its future and make money.'

As he awkwardly tottered off in his ski boots, the chairlifts came to a grinding halt. Those on the ground looked up to see skiers and snowboarders suspended in mid-air, their snow boots dangling over the edge, with literally nowhere to go. It would take an hour for engineers to get the old machines working again and to pull the stranded adventurers to safety. With loud sighs of frustration, Kalhor and his colleagues shuffled back down the mountain. There would be no more training today.

It was not simply a matter of fun or adventure; foreign tourists meant money. Iran was hoping the change in international atmosphere would restart its tourism industry, which was largely reliant on neighbouring visitors or Chinese tourists. In 2013, around four million foreign visitors travelled to Iran, for a mix of reasons, including medical tourism, but the Rouhani administration wanted to increase that number to 10 million. It had begun to reshuffle the tourism industry to facilitate its goals.

The 500-year-old Golestan Palace, opposite Tehran's Grand Bazaar, was just one of Iran's twenty-four UNESCO-listed World Heritage sites—the highest number of any country in West Asia and the wider Middle East.[10] In its glittering halls, museum manager Shafi Khani lamented that although there were many Iranian tourists, 'for now, there are few foreigners'.[11] However, then Deputy of the Iranian Tourism Organisation Morteza Rahmani Movahed, whom Zarif would later appoint as ambassador to Japan, took a different view, saying that within only a few months of the new presidency, the tourism board had started to see more visitors than usual. 'I think there are two reasons,' Movahed said. 'First is related to the election of Hassan Rouhani; the other is the safety and stability that Iran enjoys, compared to other regional countries. But the most important issue is there is a new attitude for cultural visitors to come to Iran. For example, this Christmas more than 200 European groups have planned to spend Christmas in Iran. This is a change if you want to compare it to the past.'[12]

* * *

The diminishing psychological burden of impending war had allowed life to dramatically improve. And on a tangible level, companies like Iran Khodro were once again hiring and boosting productivity, while small businesses were popping up all over the country. Many of the new businesses were cafés, opened by young Iranians who had caught on to the global trend of hipster coffee houses, and who believed the country was turning a corner. In the heart of downtown Tehran, on the quaint cobbled 30 Tir Street, the new lively mood was most apparent. The City of Tehran had granted permission for vendors to set up a new mobile food hub in an area of the capital which had traditionally reflected the many different faiths that have called Iran home for millennia. Surrounded by museums and religious centres, including the Haim Synagogue, Zoroastrian fire temple and Greek and Armenian Orthodox churches, young Iranians milled about, meandering between the neon lights and brightly painted food trucks, selling everything from the northern specialty Mirza Qasemi or Ahvazi Arab falafel to US-style hotdogs, complete with string cheese and cheap yellow mustard. Iranians, who readily offer the self-characterisation of *shekamoo* (a playful version of gluttonous), knew that even in bad economic times, there was always a market for food.

As the sun dipped, the old area suddenly came alive with cheerful voices that wafted into the night sky with the mingled scents of a dozen different foods. Although there was still a mountain of problems that had not been solved by the new administration, the lively atmosphere reflected the mood of many Iranians. Nothing was perfect, but at the very least, life had regained its colour.

But there was one glaring area of concern that desperately needed attention. It was not reform promises, nor imports, nor even the unemployment rate. It was the environment.

By Rouhani's first term in office, Iran had already been gripped by fifteen years of drought that had swallowed villages, rivers and livelihoods. It had ravaged a nation, on which Iranians had built one of the world's oldest civilisations and sustained life for thousands of years, even with limited water and semi-arid conditions.

A 2016 report co-authored by Kaveh Madani, Iran's former deputy at the Department of Environment, stated: 'Drying lakes and rivers, declining groundwater levels, land subsidence, deteriorating water quality, desertification, soil erosion and dust storms are the modern problems of a nation which was once one of the world's pioneers in sustainable water management.'[13]

Nowhere was that more apparent than in the storied city of Esfahan, lauded for its otherworldly mosques, mosaics and historic bridges. It was almost unimaginable that the Zayande Rud, literally the 'birth-giving river', which had lapped at the edges of the mighty Si-o-se Pol, swimming under the bridge's vaulted arches since the sixteenth century, had run dry. But for the first time in living memory, the riverbeds had become dustbowls.

In years past, the plastic swan-shaped boats, popular with tourists and lovers, had cut gentle wakes in the river's surface under the glow of moonlight and nearby lamps. *Ghelyoon* smoke had wafted lazily into the night sky from a tiny old teahouse nestled under the bridge, which had brimmed with men's business, as advertised by a tattered, hand-scrawled 'no women allowed' sign. But in the great dry expanse where the river had run, the boats sat forlornly at its edges, row upon row, tethered to better times. The teahouse, with its antiques and trinkets still hanging from the ceiling, had fallen silent to voices, save for the few who came to surround themselves in nostalgia. For Esfahanis, so proud of the city's culture, its landmarks and attractions, the missing river was the epitome of heartbreak.[14]

But they were not alone in their sorrow. In the Northwest of the country, Lake Urumiyeh disappeared into ruin. It was once the largest lake in the Middle East and a little piece of heaven between the majestic mountains of East and West Azerbaijan Province. But it had been a long time since anyone would describe it that way. The lake held just 5 per cent water. It had dried up, leaving behind salt-cracked earth, rusting boats and an environmental calamity.

This is not just a story about a lake. It is a story of what has happened to the whole area—the whole country's environment, in fact. The largest lake in the Middle East does not just go dry without peripheral effects. And that's because villages around Urumiyeh relied on two things for income: tourism and agriculture.

DELIVERANCE

The lake brought tourists—a lot of them. And with tourists came money. Now the remnants of that time lay scattered about, as if some kind of cataclysmic event had come one day and turned resorts into relics. With their weeping hulls, ships rusted along the shore, marooned and forgotten. The washrooms and bungalows had been abandoned to the growing weeds, time sweeping away windows, ceilings and doors. Water toys—paddle boats and kayaks—were stubbornly bound to the dirt in which they lay, rotting and bleached by the sun.

One road away from the lake, Haidar Ali Taqizadeh sat on a peeling chair outside his small, run-down corner shop, leaning forward heavily on his cane. His eyes were milky with age, his face expressionless. He was watching time pass by, rather slowly. Taqizadeh used to own property on the lake shore, prime real estate for tourism, but that was many years ago. With an air of regret and of someone who lives in the past, he related: 'We had inherited the land from our fathers. ... At that time our income was really low, but for a little bit of money people came to rent rooms. We had built some washrooms, but even with that little money we had a good life, and we were happy with that. After the lake dried up, we earned nothing. The government subsidies are not enough. Look,' he pointed past a gate next to the shop, 'this is my house and its back wall is falling down.[15]

'When there was water here,' he continued, 'there were many tourists, and everything was flourishing. There was enough income. There wasn't a water shortage for agriculture either. But if this avenue does not exist, would you come here? Of course not. The lake dried up, people stopped coming and we lost everything.'

Beside the gate to his house was a little dip in the wet dirt. There the clucks of chickens could be heard coming from their little pen. Beside them, two plastic swans stuck out, half covered in a tarp, half buried in chicken feed and hay. They were the same type of paddle boats that sat unmoving at Si-o-se Pol in

147

Esfahan. One was white, the other red, their painted black beaks chipped and fading.

A local boy, no more than ten years old, played in one of the plastic swans. He was too young to remember a time when water brimmed in the lake. Unlike the elders of the village, who worried about money, the young boy's greatest wish was to know what it felt like to play in the salty waters of Urumiyeh. 'This is mine,' he said, tapping the plastic swan. 'When the water comes back, I'm going to take it out all day,' he smiled.

Back at the lake, the pier jutted out, its beams and salt-encrusted pillars exposed for all to see. Underneath, a small motorboat was marooned, its Yamaha engine sitting lifeless on the lakebed. Omid Bonabi stared at it as he had done countless times before. A manager with the West Azerbaijan branch of the Department of Environment, it was his job to come up with policies to protect the waterways of the province, including Urumiyeh. 'As an Iranian and as a person who lives in Azerbaijan, when we see this situation, it makes us sad,' he said. 'Once there were good opportunities for tourism here, but unfortunately no tourist comes to Urumiyeh just for the lake anymore.'[16]

A man-made bridge cut through the lake's middle, trapping low water levels in unnatural spots. It was a Shah-era project, finished by Ahmadinejad in a flurry of monument building. A small gap, about 100 metres long at the lake's deepest point, was the only place water could move freely. In a time of drought, it was a white elephant in the salty sludge.

Bonabi was frustrated. 'There is not only one reason that led to this situation. Many different factors combined and led to the drying of the lake,' he said. 'The main reason is climate change; average rainfall in the area was about 330–340mm annually, but over the past ten years it reduced significantly.'

'The situation in Urumiyeh didn't happen in one day,' said Mohsen Roozbani at the Department of Environment in Tehran, 'and it's not something that can be reversed in a day or even a year. Even if we start now, it's very optimistic to think we will see an improvement in the next three to five years.'[17]

But men are as much to blame as God for this predicament, if not more so, he contended. Dams, like the Shahr Chai in West Azerbaijan Province, were supposed to be a solution. Shahr Chai rises resplendently out of a little valley, ringed by mountains, snow-capped and imposing. The light reflects off them in an almost mythical way. The seal of the Islamic Republic is embossed proudly across the dam's face. It is one of an estimated 600 dams built since 1979, as part of a strategy to irrigate farms and provide power in a semi-arid country.[18]

Although it is beautiful, its effects on the regional economy, as well as on the environment, are a point of contention. One environment official claimed that dams had helped to save water, and that only around 5–6 per cent of the dry conditions could be blamed on like-minded projects. Other environmental scientists say that unmitigated dam building—a construction spree rivalling even that of Iran's petrochemical industry—has caused severe environmental degradation and desertification. Farmers also complain that the dams are blocking the rivers upstream, so the flows no longer reach them as they once did.

But, Bonabi explains, farmers are as much to blame as anyone else. 'Expansion of farmland and irrigation mismanagement are problems, because the amount of water that farmers use here is more than the global average,' he said, surveying the white shimmering salty lakebed. 'More than 80 per cent of [the region's] water is used in agriculture. If we can just manage land irrigation better, we can save more water.' Across the country, agriculture uses up to 92 per cent of Iran's water resources, and inefficient water use means up to 70 per cent of that is wasted.[19]

And Ahmadinejad's government helped them do it. The seventh and eight parliaments (2004–12) introduced two laws that resulted in 'a colossal loss and damage to underground water tables'.[20] They did it by allocating free water for agriculture and cutting supervision of wells and drawing underground water. It was a free for all, which resulted in farmers and businesses depleting underground water resources at twice the global average. According to Masoud Assadi, chairman of the National Assembly of Agricultural Associations, 'the water crisis of today is not necessarily a result of drought and climate change, but also a product of inefficient policies and mismanagement in several organisations.' He lamented that these policies 'consumed all the national resources which were meant for future generations.'

Scientists warned that without drastic intervention, Iran was heading towards total environmental destruction—from Urumiyeh in the West and the drying marshes of the Karoun River further south, to the central plateaus of Esfahan, and east across to the mountains and valleys in Sistan-Baluchestan.

The government brought in a team of Japanese experts to provide solutions for Urumiyeh and took up nineteen plans to save the lake.[21] Rouhani appointed former vice president Masoumeh Ebtekar as the head of the Department of the Environment and began a process of water-saving measures, including restrictions on irrigation, well digging and consumption itself. It also halted dam building and imposed water restrictions on cities like Tehran, which at times consumed four times the daily global average.[22]

With Lake Urumiyeh virtually dead, Roozbani suggested that although it might take years to fix the lake—if it was even possible at all—'one of the most important keys to saving the lake are the people who live in the vicinity.' Although some within the Department conceded the environment was damaged beyond repair, they were at the very least, finally paying attention.[23]

* * *

By the end of his first year in office, Rouhani had attempted to address environmental policy, put an end to Ahmadinejad's free-wheeling spending, balanced the budget despite falling oil prices, halved inflation and stabilised the Iranian rial.[24] Meanwhile, the US treasury had finally granted Boeing a licence to export spare commercial airline parts to Iran, while General Electric had also received permission to overhaul eighteen engines sold to Iran in the late 1970s.[25] At the same time, while the French scrambled to re-stake their claim on Iran's economy, other European states were doing the same, including Germany, which posted a 33 per cent increase in exports to the Islamic Republic.[26]

It was a positive sign. Yet although most Iranians were pleased to see things improving, many were still incensed that this was even a topic of discussion. 'Imagine how ridiculous one has to be to celebrate such a thing,' remarked one career diplomat outside the foreign ministry in Tehran. 'They [the West] deny us our basic rights, and we are supposed to say thanks. They can go to hell.'[27] Still, this anger notwithstanding, for the first time in a long time, Iranians could celebrate Norooz in March 2015 with a sense of stability.

However, there was no certainty that the nuclear talks would end in a final agreement. As Iranians prepared to welcome spring and shed the darkness of winter, Israeli Prime Minister Benyamin 'Bibi' Netanyahu was in Washington, DC. He was livid that the US and the P5+1 had reached an interim deal with Iran, and thus he threw his efforts into sabotaging a permanent agreement. And he had been invited by then House Speaker John Boehner and Senate Majority Leader Mitch McConnell to do so on the floor of Congress no less.

In his address on 3 March 2015, his third to Congress, Bibi claimed a deal 'would all but guarantee that Iran gets [nuclear] weapons, lots of them.' He decried Iran as another ISIL, lambasted the country for not acting 'normal' and finished by telling

Congress, 'This is a bad deal—a very bad deal. We're better off without it.'[28] While almost sixty of the 232 Democrats boycotted the address, twenty-six Republicans gave Bibi's thirty-nine-minute speech a standing ovation.[29]

A few days after Netanyahu's speech, forty-six senators, led by right-wing Republican Tom Cotton, signed an open letter to Iran's parliament, which warned that any deal reached without legislative approval could be overturned by the next president 'with the stroke of a pen'.[30] In effect, swathes of lawmakers were not only at war with Obama—they were also, of course, at war with Iran.

The atmosphere pointed to something quite troubling, said Trita Parsi, founder and former president of the National Iranian American Council. 'I think there is evidence that the depth of enmity towards Iran in the United States, arguably, is deeper than the depth of enmity towards the United States in Iran, even though it's always assumed to be the opposite,' he contended.[31]

Back in Tehran, the Netanyahu roadshow and Cotton's letter were met with the usual eyerolls. Parliament Speaker Ali Larijani called the move 'amateurish', noting, 'Even their political experts denounced them because they undermined their own integrity.'[32]

Supreme Leader Khamenei called the letter 'the ultimate degree of the collapse of political ethics and the U.S. system's internal disintegration'.[33] Meanwhile, Foreign Minister Mohammad Javad Zarif, who was preparing to depart for nuclear talks in Lausanne, declared that the letter was:

> mostly a propaganda ploy. It is very interesting that while negotiations are still in progress and while no agreement has been reached, some political pressure groups are so afraid even of the prospect of an agreement that they resort to unconventional methods, unprecedented in diplomatic history. This indicates that like Netanyahu, who considers peace as an existential threat, some are opposed to any agreement, regardless of its content.[34]

Although the reaction was expected, there was great uneasiness in Iran. The letter, like the Netanyahu speech, was a reminder of Iran's perilous position vis-à-vis the US. It laid bare that no matter the progress made since mid-2013, or even good intentions, everything could just as quickly revert to the bad old days. And that kind of uncertainty, like a house built on water, left a sinking feeling in the pit of one's stomach, as Parsi recalled:

> I already drew the conclusion towards the end of the Obama administration that the nuclear deal and a relationship could not survive unless there was a broader shift in the United States' approach to the region. It could not continue with an approach in which it set aside its own interests to defend Saudi Arabia, the UAE and Israel.

By the end of June, the P5+1 was in Vienna.[35] Much like Zarif, who had been bedridden and riddled with back issues numerous times during talks, Kerry was himself worse for wear, having broken his leg in a cycling accident in France in May. On crutches, the towering secretary of state spoke with the huge throng of journalists outside the Palais Coburg Hotel, with both optimism and an absolute sense of realism. 'This negotiation could go either way,' Kerry said. 'If hard choices get made in the next couple of days, and made quickly, we could get an agreement this week. But if they are not made, we will not.'[36] Rouhani, for his part, had already commented, 'Some think that we should either fight or we should surrender ... but we believe none of that. There is a third path. We can cooperate with the world.'[37]

Although the agreed deadline to conclude talks by 30 June came and went, talks pressed on for another two weeks. Across the street from the Palais Coburg, journalists milled about the Marriott Hotel. Most had followed talks for months across Europe and were running out of clean clothes, red-eyed and exhausted, and seemingly solely fuelled by filter coffee and Wiener Schnitzel.

Back in the Iranian capital, as the crowds of morning commuters huddled by newsstands to peruse the day's offerings after the weekend, word of a possible deal had trickled back. Pictures of the Vienna diplomats were splashed across the front pages, under mostly optimistic headlines. Perhaps the most telling of all was the cartoon on the front of the reformist daily *E'temad*, in which a sullen Netanyahu sat alone with his show-and-tell of guns and bombs, under the headline, *'tanhaye bi sharike Netanyahu'*—the loneliness of Netanyahu.

Twelve years after the nuclear crisis began, on 14 July 2015, the foreign ministers of all seven nations posed for photos and announced the Joint Comprehensive Plan of Action (JCPOA).

The Iranian foreign minister, with his trademark broad smile, called it a 'historic moment', adding that the agreement was 'not perfect for anybody but is what we could accomplish. Today could have been the end of hope ... but now we are starting a new chapter of hope.'[38] Federica Mogherini, who had replaced Catherine Ashton as the EU's top foreign policy tsar, said the JCPOA could 'open the way to a new chapter in international relations and show that diplomacy, coordination, cooperation can overcome decades of tensions and confrontations. ... I think this is a sign of hope for the entire world.'[39]

The JCPOA, which comprised 159 pages, including five annexes, laid out the specifics of how the P5+1 and Iran planned to solve the nuclear dilemma.[40]

The key points of the accord established that Iran would:

- submit to further International Atomic Energy Agency (IAEA) monitoring and inspections;
- clear up IAEA questions regarding pre-2003 activity;
- redesign the Arak heavy water reactor for research and development, remove its core and fill it with concrete;
- not build a heavy water reactor for fifteen years;

- restrict uranium enrichment to a low purity of 3.67 per cent for fifteen years;
- cut its gas centrifuge capacity by more than two thirds;
- cut the stockpile of Low Enriched Uranium (LEU) from 7,500kg to 300kg, by either diluting or shipping excess abroad;
- and restrict research and development for ten years.

In return the P5+1 agreed to:

- lift all nuclear-related UN Security Council sanctions, as well as multilateral and national sanctions—which included the EU oil embargo, the ban on SWIFT and US sanctions prohibiting the sale of new civilian aircraft and spare parts;
- endorse the JCPOA through a new UNSC resolution (2231), which terminated prior declarations;[41]
- and refrain from any action inconsistent with the 'letter, spirit and intent' of the JCPOA, including the imposition of 'discriminatory' measures in lieu of sanctions.

Importantly the JCPOA, through Resolution 2231, also provided for the continuation of UN arms embargoes on Iran, which banned the sale and receipt of conventional weapons, technology or knowhow for five years—until October 2020. It also banned the transfer of non-conventional weapons, including ballistic missile–related technology, for a further eight years.[42]

The deal also provided a 'snapback' mechanism, in which the UNSC could reinstate old sanctions quickly in the case of Iranian non-compliance. But as would become painfully clear, no one had considered the prospect that one party might go beyond non-compliance to actually sabotage the entire enterprise.

'I think there was this assumption perhaps that these are all serious countries and they will stick to the deal,' said Parsi. 'So even when the Americans are thinking about these types of things, they were talking about a scenario in which the Iranians were caught cheating—they were not talking about a scenario in which the Iranians were caught sabotaging.'

Both Iran and the US had to subject the JCPOA to domestic approval—through Congress in the US and the Iranian parliament—and it was not an easy task. In Washington, Republicans delayed implementation of the JCPOA through the Iran Nuclear Agreement Review Act and for months tried not only to block the accord in Congress but to prevent an Obama veto.[43]

In Tehran, parliamentarians debated the JCPOA in two rounds, although no one expected the legislature to reject the accord. In the first session, Zarif, his deputies Abbas Araghchi and Majid Takht-e Ravanchi, and the head of the Atomic Energy Organization of Iran, Ali Akbar Salehi, who played a critical role in negotiating the JCPOA's technicalities, attended to defend the deal. But the group was subjected to a verbal melee of threats and accusations that they had sold out the country's rights. At times Zarif slouched low in his seat, head in hands, clearly tired and frustrated. But it was Salehi who revealed something much more troubling. 'A dear brother from the parliament came to me and swore that he would kill me,' he told the chamber. 'Is this the way to talk to a servant of the system, and tell him that they would kill him by pouring cement on him and burying him under the Arak nuclear reactor?'[44]

Parliament Speaker Larijani, not wishing for a repeat, fast-tracked the final session two days later, refusing to allow opposition MPs to present further amendments. In another fiery, though short, session, hardliners accused the speaker of circumventing process. Later, one of the lawmakers, Mehdi Kouchakzadeh, said the bill's wording had been vetted outside parliament—by Larijani, Supreme National Security Council secretary Ali Shamkhani and Asghar Hejazi—a senior representative in the Supreme Leader's office.[45] Hardliner Ali-Asghar Zarei openly wept as he shouted, 'at least appearances [of an independent parliament] should have been kept.'

In the end, 20 per cent of MPs didn't bother showing up for the final vote. And of the 233 that did, fifty-nine lawmakers voted 'no'.[46] A day later, the Guardian Council, which vets all parliamentary bills, ratified the legislation.[47]

While the JPCOA process itself, including efforts by Saudi Arabia, the UAE and Israel to sabotage the accord, emphasised what many Iranians considered unjust international political realities, the debates in Washington and Tehran highlighted how the realities at home could be just as bad. And it was difficult to avoid this hostility and pushback, whether domestic or foreign.

The attacks on Zarif, who had become the face of the JCPOA and détente with the US, worsened when news leaked that he had run into Obama on the sidelines of that year's UN General Assembly.[48] The pair shook hands and exchanged a few polite words about the nuclear talks. Hardliners called him a traitor, and some even demanded his impeachment.[49] According to journalist Saeed Laylaz, the attacks against Zarif inside and out of parliament indicated 'the heightening of tensions ... as well as the further isolation of hardliners.'[50] Another journalist, Foad Shams, knew first-hand how much Rouhani's election had changed the landscape and agreed that the immediate atmosphere, conducive to progress, weakened the position of hardliners. The government's success in nuclear talks contributed.

Emad Abshenas from think tank Iran Diplomatic surmised, 'We have a lot of influential people who benefit from the enmity between Iran and the US, and some who even benefit from sanctions. They will all be negatively affected if relations between Iran and the US get better and if the economic situation of Iran moves towards normal trade with [the] international community.'[51]

The more these actors lashed out in the face of clear benefits, which had materialised first and foremost in the fact war no longer felt like a breath away, the more isolated they became, and the more the general public grew visibly frustrated by their constant negative attacks and impediments. Hardliners were mocked in cartoons, while on Telegram and other social media platforms, supporters started the hashtags 'I support Zarif' and 'Zarif is not alone'.

If, as Laylaz suggested, the uproar proved how isolated hardliners were, then it also proved how out of touch they were with the public—their constituents. Indeed, opinion polls, both official and otherwise, consistently showed Zarif to be the most popular man in Iran—a clear clapback to those who opposed the nuclear deal and Zarif's conduct, including the Obama handshake.

Rohollah Faghihi was following the political struggles closely. The young journalist, who was born in the seminary city of Qom only two years after the end of the Iran–Iraq War, could not remember a day in his young life free from outside political tension. He recalled how Zarif became a national hero, because people believed he would change that. 'People looked at Zarif as their saviour,' he explained, acknowledging it was perhaps an unrealistic expectation. But, 'we were all under such extreme pressure ... people were relieved to see the shadow of war, the shadow of more devastating economic conditions had gone ... at least for a brief period of time.'[52]

With the deal done, the Rouhani administration was hoping to attract US$200 billion of foreign investment, or $40 billion per year, over the next five years. At an oil conference in the capital, attended by a who's who of the petroleum world, the oil ministry revealed long-awaited contract reforms to make foreign investment in Iran's most important asset much more enticing.[53] It was the first-time investors had an understanding of what business in Iran post-JCPOA might look like.

By the official implementation day of the JCPOA on 16 January 2016, petroleum investors were not alone. Once the IAEA certified that Tehran had met all its obligations under the nuclear deal, which triggered sanctions removal, pen was already being put to paper. PSA Peugeot Citroën announced the much-anticipated deal that was supposed to revive Iran's auto industry.[54] The $435 million joint venture, which then Iran Khodro CEO Hashem Yekke Zare termed 'compensation', included upgrades to the fifty-year-old Karaj factory to produce three new models. Under the venture, IKCO and its French investors aimed to produce 100,000 new cars by the end of 2017, with the intent of doubling output soon after.[55] After five years of battles, job losses and anxieties, Hossein Najari, Iran Khodro's vice president, finally had some good news for his employees. It also meant that he could hire back some of the workers he'd been forced to let go.

* * *

Only a month after the nuclear deal came into effect, Iranians were back at the polls. All 290 seats in parliament were up for election, as well as all seats in the Assembly of Experts.

It was a much more relaxed atmosphere than that which surrounded the vote in 2013, primarily because there was no threat of war looming overhead and the nuclear problem had, seemingly, been resolved. Without the need to resist and push back in a constant state of crisis, many people were of the belief that a new parliament could set about righting some other wrongs—particularly if that parliament supported the Rouhani administration.

The main blocs had organised themselves into lists. The first, 'Voice of the Nation', was headed by one of Iran's most well-known politicians, Ali Motahari. Known as a maverick, and at times unpredictable, Motahari swings across the political divide between reformists and hardliners, depending on the issue. He is known as a social hardliner—an advocate of compulsory hijab and the ban on women at football games, for example—but also as a critic of the authoritarian atmosphere that pervaded during the Ahmadinejad years. Motahari also advocated the release of Karroubi and Mousavi and supported the nuclear deal. His election list comprised moderates and more pragmatic conservatives.

The second list, dubbed the 'List of Hope', was headed by Mohammad Reza Aref. It was made up of reformists and moderates, including members of Karroubi's National Trust and Rouhani's Moderation and Development Party. Meanwhile, Larijani—a principlist who had mellowed into a pragmatic conservative—opted to run as an independent.

The third list, the 'Grand Coalition of Principlists', was led by Gholam Ali Haddad-Adel, who unsuccessfully ran for president in 2013. The four-time MP, who was parliamentary speaker between 2005 and 2008, was also a known Khamenei confidant; his daughter is married to Khamenei's son, Mojtaba.[56]

At the same time as the parliamentary elections, elections for the eighty-eight-seat Assembly of Experts were also on the cards. And it was perhaps the most crucial vote in a generation, given that elected members would sit until 2024, and may therefore be in the position to choose the next Supreme Leader. In the Assembly, Rafsanjani led the charge to unseat conservatives, along with Rouhani, who was also running for a seat. The pair issued their own sixteen-member list for Tehran, dubbed the 'People's Experts', comprising moderate and reformist-leaning clerics. Hassan Khomeini, grandson of the Republic's founder, was close to both men and would have been on that list, had the Guardian Council not controversially disqualified his candidacy.[57]

Former president Khatami, who was still banned from state TV, threw his support behind the reformist and moderate campaigns, and in a video released on YouTube and Telegram told voters: 'Those who are concerned about the country's interests, progress and removal of threats and limitations should vote for all individuals on both lists'—referring to both the List of Hope and the People's Experts. He added that the vote was 'a step to secure the country's dignity, strengthen its security and stability and improve the reform of its affairs.'[58]

Some of Iran's most prominent artists and actors, including Reza Kianian and Taraneh Alidoosti, also came out to publicly support the two lists and encourage people to vote.[59] Kianian, quoted by the 'We Vote Iran' Telegram page, said, 'Our achievement today is the result of yesterday's choice. ... Despite all the social ups and downs, we know, our vote is influential.'[60]

In the Assembly, the Rafsanjani–Rouhani List won fifty-two of eighty-eight seats, including fifteen belonging to Tehran.[61] Rafsanjani polled the highest, with 2.3 million votes, followed by Tehran Friday prayer leader Emami-Kashani and Rouhani. In what was also the icing on the cake for progressives, Assembly Chairman Ayatollah Mohammad Yazdi and radical Mohammad-Taqi Mesbah-Yazdi lost their seats. The latter had become a spiritual advisor to Ahmadinejad and had also advocated violent crackdowns on reformists, before and after 2009.

In Parliament, Aref's List of Hope also performed well, despite the Guardian Council's disqualification of such a large number of prominent reformists that they had been forced to run untested candidates in their place. Reformists and moderates won all thirty Tehran seats and 121 all told.[62] They had also ousted the Grand Coalition of Principlists' leader, Haddad-Adel, in the process.

The 2016 parliamentary sweep was an important referendum on the obvious domestic changes in Rouhani's Iran. As Faghihi put it, 'People were hoping Rouhani could have the same success domestically as he did with the JCPOA.'

But as a leading Iran analyst and author, Mehrzad Boroujerdi, explained not long after Rouhani's election, the success of domestic reform would 'depend on what Rouhani accomplishes on the foreign policy front. If he is successful, then he will have the necessary political capital to take on the conservatives on a range of domestic issues including press freedom.'[63]

The change of administration and early steps to success had already given Rouhani a small amount of leverage. He had used it to order the much-loathed morality police, known as Gasht-e Ershad, to stop harassing and arresting women in the streets. The force, recognisable in its white-and-green vans, was certainly one of the most malign sights in Tehran and had sent liberal women, who wore hijab loosely slipping off the back of their heads, sprinting to escape.

In another positive development, several famous prisoners, such as celebrated human rights lawyer Nasrin Sotoudeh, were released from prison almost immediately after Rouhani took office. Sotoudeh had been sentenced to six years in prison on appeal in 2011, for 'spreading propaganda and conspiring against state security'. Much like her colleague Nobel Peace Prize laureate Shirin Ebadi, Sotoudeh had been involved in high-profile cases, representing journalists, activists and ordinary citizens, including minors, who had run afoul of either the intelligence ministry or the judiciary.

Another group that had faced an onslaught of attacks was the hard-working, clever, and competitive Iranian press corps. The eight years prior to Rouhani's presidency saw a record number of press closures, including of the popular feminist magazine *Zanan*, as well as arrests and an intimidation campaign that had forced many prominent Iranian journalists who had managed to avoid jail to either flee abroad or quit the profession.

But the Rouhani administration changed the landscape. As Foad Shams explained, 'In the early years of Rouhani's government, the situation improved. Not only that, there was more hope that the environment in which journalists worked would become freer. Especially after the JCPOA, the government paid more attention to the media. Freedom was somewhat greater.'[64]

Changes in key ministries, such as the Ministry of Culture and Islamic Guidance, known as Ershad, which controls media permissions, facilitated the more relaxed atmosphere. There was also less encouragement of the judiciary and intelligence ministry to crack down on newspapers or journalists that radicals disliked.

Rouhani himself had reached out beyond Iran's borders to their foreign counterparts, by granting interviews with notable international journalists, writing op-eds in English-language papers, including *The Washington Post*, and through social media. His office ran Twitter and Instagram accounts in both Persian and English, the latter of which was a clear sign of not only outreach but also an understanding of the influence and power of social media in international politics.

However, Rouhani's initiatives had their limits. At his first press conference after his election win, attended by throngs of Iranian and foreign journalists, the president was asked about the widely respected and popular Association of Iranian Journalists— an organisation of some 4,000 professionals that had come under attack during the Ahmadinejad years and closed down. Rouhani told the packed room: 'I believe that not only the Association [of Iranian Journalists] but all associations should be revived legally because these organisations are the best tools to manage the issues of society. ... I will put my efforts into this.'[65]

But three years later, despite countless efforts by journalists to re-register the organisation, the Association was still closed. Of course, others had sprung up, but the largest organisation had not been revived—seemingly, according to Shams, because the administration had not followed up.

Worse, human rights activists were still being arrested. Sotoudeh's colleague at the Defenders of Human Rights Centre, Narges Mohammadi, had been in and out of prison, detention and court for years as a campaigner against the death penalty. But shortly after the 2016 parliamentary election, she was sentenced to sixteen years in prison for running the campaign through what the judiciary termed an 'illegal' organisation.[66]

Further, although Rouhani had curbed the powers of the morality police, the organisation had re-organised to deploy thousands of undercover members—7,000 in Tehran alone—to inform on supposed infractions. Although Rouhani was critical of Gasht-e Ershad and contended it was not the government's job to police personal freedoms, the continued presence of the force proved the president's power had its limits.[67]

It was not simply Rouhani's inability to make wider changes; conservative factions were also pushing hard. Not long after Rouhani's election, Qalibaf, still the mayor of Tehran, was still pursuing a strategy to recalibrate his image, from a moderate public servant into a hardliner. He had ordered a series of unexpected changes in the capital, including an order to segregate all municipality workers. Under the decree, he also demanded male managers only hire other men as administrative assistants, saying, 'Women should not spend most of their time every day next to men other than their husbands because it harms the foundations of the family.'[68]

City officials in Tehran, the most liberal city in Iran, said work hours were too long and the move was in women's best interest, reported the Iranian Labour News Agency. The order had widespread effects—according to the Tehran Municipality, 15 per cent of its workforce were women, some of whom were fired and replaced with men.

When the news filtered down, Tehrani women were incensed, and so too was the Rouhani administration, which scoffed at the order and refused to acknowledge it. Shahindokht Molaverdi, the vice president for women and family affairs, stated that the plan was being implemented in defiance of the government.[69] Mohammad Taqi Hosseini, then deputy minister of labour (and later ambassador to Mexico), criticised the policy in an official letter as 'discrimination' and a breach of international conventions in which Iran is a participant.[70]

At the same time as Qalibaf was overhauling the municipality and challenging the new government, the city's police chief was also applying the pressure. Colonel Khalil Halali, chief of police for public places, announced that women would no longer be allowed to work in visible areas of the city's booming café and restaurant scene. It was an unbelievable order, affecting thousands of establishments, many of which were owned and run by women.

In the inner west suburb of Gisha, a new two-tiered café had sprung up near the busy bridge, which separated the suburb from its neighbour, Shahrarah.[71] Stuck between a hole-in-the-wall meat shop and a small language school, the coffee shop had just been starting to attract customers when the new bans were announced. Although the coffee was nothing special, the young owners, Amir and Shila, had thrown everything they had into the business. They took turns cheerfully taking orders, serving customers, and working in the tiny kitchen behind the counter. They offered a small selection of breakfast dishes, cakes and toasted sandwiches, the latter always accompanied by a side of potato chips. But under the new directives, even if the couple held a joint permit, Shila would be banned from working everywhere but the kitchen. And that was despite the fact her name was on all the paperwork and the permit mounted on the wall behind the counter.

Unlike many other Persian Gulf countries, Iran did not practice segregation in restaurants, or even offer the feature of 'family rooms', so common in petro-kingdoms like Qatar, Saudi Arabia and the UAE. In fact, one of the main achievements of the revolution was that women had become as visible as men, if not more so. They drove taxis, ran their own businesses, led student unions and held cabinet positions and seats in parliament. They outperformed their male counterparts at university, dominated the press corps and were the loudest and most persistent voices for reform across the country. Especially in the urbanised capital, public segregation had really only existed in some schools, buses and trains.

In the new Iran of hope and prudence, pushback politics was not limited to simply the capital. The National Organization for

Civil Registration, which operates under the Ministry of Interior, had issued a decree that caused much more fury than anything Qalibaf had done. The body, which issues identification documents, had decided that a woman could remove the name of her husband from her most important identification paper—the *she-nasname*—only if they had separated and if she could prove she was still a virgin.[72] The same rule of course did not apply to men.

At a late-night gathering of young artists in Tehran, the consensus was that the new decree signalled a 'revoltingly offensive' double standard.[73] But, with a hint of the dark humour that would get Iranians through some of their darkest days, one crassly remarked it was a useless exercise; there were no virgins left in Tehran anyway.

7

SABOTAGE

As the Iranian parliament tipped towards moderates and some Iranian analysts predicted a period of stability, progress and economic resurrection, the shadow of international politics started to darken once more. Donald John Trump had become the presumptive Republican nominee for the pending US presidential election.[1] Hillary Clinton would lead the Democrats, and despite her hawkish leanings on Iran policy, this prospect didn't trouble many in Iran, as she supported the JCPOA.

In 2016 Tehran, a Trump victory seemed as far-fetched as it was in Washington, yet Trump's pronouncements that his 'number-one priority is to dismantle the disastrous deal with Iran' was rattling nerves.[2] Trump, who claimed at a rally for the American Israel Public Affairs Committee (AIPAC) that the deal was 'catastrophic for America, for Israel and for the whole of the Middle East', offered no alternative other than promises to renegotiate a 'better' deal on his own terms. It astounded analysts and politicians alike that the New York businessman would seek to revamp a crisis that took twelve years to sort out.

The atmosphere, coupled with the continued economic slump and miniscule benefits from the JCPOA, prompted economist and journalist Saeed Laylaz, in an in-depth interview with reformist website Aftab News, to claim Iran had not faced such an attack since the Mongol invasion. Laylaz stated, 'I do not know of a nation or country named Iran that has endured such pressure since 618 AH (1221 CE) when Genghis invaded Iran. In the last eight centuries, such pressure on the Iranian nation has been unprecedented.'[3]

In Tehran, Iranians, including those in the Rouhani administration and at the foreign ministry, consoled themselves with the belief that there was no way Trump could ever win the presidency. Many even chuckled at the idea.

Elsewhere, at one of Iran's most important missions in the Middle East, one deputy ambassador dismissed fears Trump would keep his campaign promises even if he did win. Indeed, politicians were certainly not known for truthfulness. 'It's just talk,' said the diplomat, seated on an ornate chair in the embassy's sitting room. 'Trump will have advisors and other people telling him what to do. I don't believe they will allow him to do that [abandon the JCPOA].' But that was presuming his advisors, who were at that point still unselected, understood the lengths it took to reach the deal. 'Yes,' said the diplomat, 'they would know. We [the Iranian foreign ministry] are not too concerned.'[4]

In the early hours of 9 November 2016, a stunned world watched as Trump became president-elect of the United States.[5] He had pulled off the unthinkable. From the Midtown Hilton in New York, the real-estate mogul thanked his supporters and pledged to Make America Great Again. Trump said, although he would 'always put America's interests first, we will deal fairly with everyone. ... We will seek common ground, not hostility; partnership, not conflict ... we will get along with all other nations willing to get along with us.'[6]

On his Twitter account, Rouhani's deputy chief of staff for political affairs, Hamid Aboutalebi—a lifelong diplomat—noted with a sense of optimism: 'The image that Trump displayed of himself in his victory speech as the president-elect was different from his image in the election campaign. This is a considerable point.'[7] Still, the Iranian president was palpably nervous, even as he claimed the outcome of the US election would have 'no effect' on Iran, as it was on an 'irreversible path' with regards to international relations. Rouhani indicated that diplomats had had enough foresight not to enter an agreement solely with the US or any single nation; instead they had made sure that the deal was based on a 'UN Security Council resolution that cannot be changed by a government decision.'[8]

Meanwhile, in the Romanian capital, Bucharest, Foreign Minister Mohammad Javad Zarif was on the first leg of a three-nation European tour. Since coming into office, Zarif had been crisscrossing the globe for trade and diplomatic talks, with everyone from the Turkish foreign minister to Vladimir Putin.[9]

Although Trump had repeatedly lambasted the Iran deal and threatened a so-called 'Muslim ban' that would affect Iranian travellers, Zarif stated, 'We do not interfere in the internal affairs of other countries. ... This is the American people's election. ... But, the US must carry out what it has undertaken as an international multilateral commitment in the JCPOA.'[10]

Threats to abandon the nuclear deal equated to the end of so-called sanctions relief, which itself was moderate at best. Still, it was something. The difference between death and a fever. When less than a month after the election, in the last weeks of the Obama presidency, both Boeing and Airbus signed firm deals with Iran, many Iranian businessmen saw that as proof that things might be fine after all.[11] It was a critical and urgent step, especially given that Abbas Akhoundi, the minister of roads and urban development, had estimated that Iran would need 551 airplanes in the next decade to overhaul its aviation sector.[12] The minister relayed that Iranian airlines operated a total of 266 planes, of which 100 were inoperable. And according to Hooshang Shahbazi, the pilot who had pulled off an exceptional emergency landing at Mehrabad Airport in 2011, those still flying were well past their use by date.

'From an economic point of view, anyone who uses old planes loses out,' Shahbazi said. 'When the age of a plane increases, so too do expenses and safety issues. For that reason, most countries sell or retire their planes after ten years. For example, the average age of Emirates aircraft is six years. After six years they sell them. But the average age of our entire fleet is twenty-four to twenty-five years.'[13]

Boeing was to play a major part in the rehaul, agreeing to sell Iran Air eighty aircraft, including fifty 737 MAX 8s, fifteen 777–300ERs and fifteen 777–9s. The US$16.6 billion agreement was the largest trade deal between the US and Iran in four decades and had only been reached after lengthy negotiations, which crucially included a US treasury export licence.[14]

Meanwhile, Airbus went even further, signing a 100-plane deal with Iran Air, which included forty-six aircraft from the A320 line, thirty-eight A330s and sixteen A350s. The deal, worth US$10–20 billion, depending on list price, would allow Iran Air to expand its international reach and overhaul its battered reputation.[15]

The deals added to the €1 billion deal already signed in February of the same year between Iran Air and the Franco-Italian aviation company ATR, which Airbus partly owned.[16] ATR, which first began operating in Iran in 1992 but had faced serious difficulties and trepidation doing so under sanctions, had identified the country as a 'freshly open market' with whom it was eager to work.

And whilst the Airbus and Boeing deals were crucial for foreign flights, the deal of forty new generation ATR 72–600s was the key to making local air travel, particularly in regional areas, safe again.

Although it had taken an agonising amount of time for the JCPOA to reach any confirmed deals, there was elation on 11 January 2017 in Toulouse, when Iran took delivery of its first new Airbus in forty years. The next day, it glided into Iranian airspace, over Tehran, and touched down smoothly on the tarmac at Mehrabad Airport. It was a moment of pride for anyone standing on the ground who happened to catch sight of the A321, painted with the navy-blue motifs of Iran Air and the recognisable *Homa* on the tail.

The plane's arrival was such a big deal that a pack of media had assembled at the hangar to film the occasion, whilst Reuters broadcasted the delivery live on its newsfeed. Seda va Sima called it 'a historic moment for Iran, signalling the end of the sanctions era for the country'.[17]

Shahbazi himself watched on with a smile. 'We were so happy at the sight,' he said. 'We thought we had been freed from sanctions and we had left those troubles behind. That ... good, safe new-generation planes would come to Iran and we could relax again.'

As the Airbus taxied towards its new home in the Iran Air hangar, two firefighting rigs shot streams of water into the sky, creating a double arc in the airliner's path. The water salute, a long-held aviation tradition to celebrate milestones such as maiden flights, was just one element of the ceremony, which was almost befitting a head of state.

The small crowd waiting in the hangar included Ali Akbar Salehi, the head of the Atomic Energy Organization of Iran. If it were not for Salehi and the other small group of Iranian negotiators, the arrival in Iran of any new aircraft would never have happened.

Claps and cheers erupted as the Airbus came to a stop, with the pilots billowing the Iranian and Iran Air flags out of the cockpit windows. The pilots and officials, including Iranian

Transport Minister Abbas Akhoundi and Airbus CEO Fabrice Bregier, beamed as they disembarked, while an Iran Air stewardess handed them red roses.

Akhoundi described the delivery as 'a symbol of the beginning of a new era in Iran's aviation industry,' but added with caution that Iran would live up to its contractual commitments, and he hoped that 'despite the changes in the US government, Airbus will also continue to do so.'[18] His deputy, Asghar Fakhrieh Kashani, went even further, saying, 'given that the contracts for the purchase of these aircraft were concluded after the signing of the JCPOA, they will not be revoked if sanctions return.'

The Iranian position in the post–nuclear deal world was that parties to the JCPOA had to keep their commitments, despite political ruptures in Washington. Iranian diplomats were sticklers for protocol and procedure and expected the other signatories to abide by the accord to the letter. However, despite the fact that the JCPOA was an international accord and not some backroom gentlemen's agreement, more than anything, it was still an exercise in good faith.

* * *

While some people busied themselves with making the best out of challenging times, others saw these efforts as a smokescreen: superficial changes, colour, big announcements with little tangible effect on the lives of average, working-class Iranians, even eighteen months after the JCPOA was reached.

As Saeed Laylaz and Foad Shams had suggested, radicals saw the JCPOA as a chance for reformists and moderates to marginalise them—possibly for a lot longer than one or two terms. This was why, according to journalist Rohollah Faghihi, hardliners 'started provocations as soon as the deal was implemented, and unfortunately Obama helped them, by continuing to obstruct some banking and financial actions. It gave hardliners more pretext for provocation.'[19]

Political analyst Emad Abshenas agreed. 'Of course hardliners didn't want the agreement, because they believed Americans wanted to fool Iran and wouldn't sign a deal in Iran's favour,' he said. 'At the time, the overall social situation was not in their [the hardliners'] favour so they had to retreat. But Obama hesitating to implement US commitments ... gave hardliners the opportunity to strengthen again.'[20]

Iranian MPs attacked the Rouhani administration every chance they could, while likeminded papers ran editorials casting doubt on the nuclear deal, or fanned the flames of baseless rumours that foreign companies, including Airbus, had ripped off Iran by selling the country second-hand planes rather than new ones. They viewed the Airbus deal as a waste of limited resources that should have been spent elsewhere and especially should not have gone to foreign companies based in countries like France, which had actively pursued sanctions and a tough line against Iran for years. As Faghihi suggested, the tepid pace of progress, aided by business stalling in the US and Europe, played a role in giving hardliners more fuel.

Perhaps even worse, the nuclear deal, known by the acronym BARJAM in Iran, hadn't resolved issues around some humanitarian imports, and Iranians themselves were still having to rely on smugglers, friends and family. 'BARJAM did not really change much about medicine,' recalled Neda Anisi, who suffered from muscular dystrophy. She had been trying out the glucocorticoid Deflazacort and had noticed it was having positive effects on her condition. But, she lamented, 'It could barely be found and was still having to be smuggled in.'[21]

Given the demoralising realities, it was no surprise that the administration made a big deal of foreign trade deals, or indeed the arrival of a new jetliner. Every deal was important—not just in an economic sense, but also politically. And as the nuclear deal was predicated on continued Iranian adherence and placed limitations on even peaceful nuclear development, there was still a need for the government to justify continued restrictions even after the accord was signed. The Rouhani administration had to prove to both the public and politicians on a daily basis that their strategy was working.

As analyst Mehrzad Boroujerdi had predicted, the success of domestic reform was tied to foreign policy. He also warned that Rouhani's 'failure on the foreign policy front will embolden the conservatives to torpedo his domestic initiatives as a way of discrediting him.'[22] These domestic initiatives included an attempt at ending the securitisation of society. But because of the nature of the Republic's political system, the presidential administration had little to no control over certain security and intelligence agencies, some of which, including the IRGC, very clearly had their own agendas.

While the Rouhani administration was attempting to rehabilitate Iran's image abroad as a diplomatically engaged, moderate government, the IRGC stepped up its campaign of arresting dual nationals. Among them were Iranian-American *Washington Post* journalist Jason Rezaian and his Iranian wife, Yeganeh Salehi; Iranian-American businessman Siamak Namazi and his father, Baquer; and British-Iranian charity worker Nazanin Zaghari-Ratcliffe.[23]

The arrests were of great embarrassment to the Rouhani administration, particularly the foreign minister, who had to field question after question both at home and abroad as to why so many dual nationals were in prison. Despite Zarif's attempts to distance the administration from the judicial process and the IRGC, over which the government has no control, his remarks rang hollow.[24] The basis of arrests, according to those with knowledge of the cases, was to command political leverage, or, as in the case of Namazi, to sabotage Rouhani's initiatives to draw in foreign business, including with Iranians abroad. According to

National Iranian American Council founder Trita Parsi, the IRGC 'were targeting people who were trying to build bridges, because if people like that [Namazi] were not safe then there would be no bridges.' He went on to say that the IRGC 'could accept the JCPOA, but they could not accept that it would lead to an onslaught of other people coming to Iran and diluting their control and their power in the country.'[25]

Although Salehi was released after two months, her husband, Rezaian, remained in Evin Prison for 544 days. His detention included four trials and a guilty verdict, which Martin Baron, executive editor of *The Washington Post*, described as 'a sick brew of farce and tragedy.'[26] Rezaian was finally released in a prisoner swap on 16 January 2016, which also coincided with the date that the JCPOA came into effect.[27] As of February 2021, Siamak Namazi is still in prison, while his father, Baquer, is barred from leaving Iran. Ratcliffe-Zaghari is still in Iran under house arrest, with her sentence due to end in March 2021.

To Rezaian, this constitutes state-sponsored hostage taking. But behind all the politics is the fact that all these individuals were only in Iran because they loved the country, or, in Salehi's case, were born and raised there. The Rouhani administration had encouraged young Iranians living abroad, including dual nationals, to come back to help rebuild a new Iran. Many, including those who had never lived in Iran at any time in their lives, answered the call. But like the lesson handed to older generations, the revolution continued to devour its children.

* * *

If the Rouhani administration was already navigating a fragile environment, both domestically and abroad, one event pitched its moderate and reformist backers into a sea of anxiety. During an evening broadcast on 8 January 2017, Seda va Sima interrupted its usual programming with an update from a female news presenter. She began, voice quivering slightly as she read from a prepared script, 'After a life full of restless efforts in the path of Islam and revolution ... [Hashemi Rafsanjani] departed for lofty heaven.' The political kingmaker Rafsanjani was dead.

Rafsanjani had suffered a massive heart attack that afternoon, and although doctors tried to resuscitate him for an hour, the eighty-two-year-old could not be saved. Despite his advanced years, the death of the former president sent shockwaves through the country. To many, Rafsanjani was the revolution. He defied political factionalism as he shifted across platforms and messages, adapting to changing challenges decade by decade, until at last he had reinvented himself as a reformist. To old Khomeinists, Rafsanjani was in many ways more of an extension of Khomeini's ideals than the latter's own successor, Supreme Leader Khamenei. Rafsanjani's death also ended up proving correct the Guardian Council's decision, whatever their motivation, to disqualify him from running for president in 2013—if he had won, he would not have served out the full term.

Officially, Iran declared three days of mourning, while newspapers the next morning had plastered their front pages, many of which were bordered in black, with images of the white-turbaned Ayatollah. *Arman-e Emruz* called Rafsanjani a 'contemporary Amir Kabir', in reference to the nineteenth-century advisor and prime minister, considered Iran's first great reformer and moderniser, while *Iran Daily* described Rafsanjani's death as an 'irretrievable loss'.[28] Even the hardline *Vatan-e Emrooz* described the late Ayatollah as 'one of the pillars' of the revolution.

The Supreme Leader issued a lengthy statement, saying, 'The loss of a comrade and ally, with whom I share a friendship that dates back fifty-nine years, is difficult and heart-rending.'[29] Indeed, it was Rafsanjani who had helped Khamenei to become Supreme Leader upon Khomeini's death in 1989. In a subtle reference to the disputes that had caused the pair to fall on con-

1. From left to right: Ahmad Khomeini, Ali Khamenei and Ayatollah Ruhollah Khomeini, c. 1979. Source: Khamenei.ir.

2. Four presidents of the Islamic Republic: Hashemi Rafsanjani (far left), Ali Khamenei, Mohammad Khatami and Mahmoud Ahmadinejad (far right). Above them hangs a portrait of Ayatollah Khomeini, 3 Aug. 2005. Source: Khamenei.ir.

3. Grand Ayatollah Montazeri with Mohsen Kadivar, 30 Jan. 2003.
Courtesy of Mohsen Kadivar.

4. Mugshots of Ali Khamenei and Hashemi Rafsanjani on the wall of
Towhid Prison, Tehran, 2014. Photograph by Soraya Lennie.

5. The disappearing Lake Urumiyeh, 2014. Photograph by Soraya Lennie.

6. Coffins carrying the newly returned remains of Iranian soldiers killed in the Iran–Iraq War are lifted through a crowd at Imam Hossein Square, Tehran, 2014. Photograph by Soraya Lennie.

7. US Secretary of State John Kerry shakes hands with Iranian Foreign Minister Mohammad Javad Zarif at the end of negotiations on Iran's nuclear programme, marking the agreement of the Joint Comprehensive Plan of Action, Vienna, 14 July 2015. Public domain.

8. Hashemi Rafsanjani registers his candidacy for the Assembly of Experts election, 21 Dec. 2015. Photograph by Ahmad Halabisaz.

9. President Hassan Rouhani and Defence Minister Hossein Dehghan at a mourning ceremony for Hashemi Rafsanjani, 9 Jan. 2017. Photograph by Ahmad Halabisaz.

10. Supporters of Hassan Rouhani at a campaign rally in Tehran, 4 May 2017. Photograph by Ahmad Halabisaz.

11. Security agents rescue a boy during an attack by ISIL on the Iranian parliament, 7 June 2017. Source: Omid Vahabzadeh, Fars News Agency.

12. The funeral of Qasem Soleimani, Tehran, 6 Jan. 2020. Photograph by Ahmad Halabisaz.

13. Supreme Leader Ali Khamenei conducts funeral prayers for Qasem Soleimani, Tehran, 6 Jan. 2020. Source: Khamenei.ir.

14. A rescue worker holds pictures found in the wreckage of Ukraine International Airlines Flight 752, 8 Jan. 2020. Photograph by Ahmad Halabisaz.

15. A local man inspects part of the wreckage of Ukraine International Airlines Flight 752, 8 Jan. 2020. Photograph by Ahmad Halabisaz.

16. A funeral for a Covid-19 victim, 2020. Photograph by Ahmad Halabisaz.

trary sides of the political spectrum, Khamenei continued, saying, 'Differences in views and interpretations of Islamic law in various points of this long time could never break the friendship. ... After him, I cannot think of anyone with whom I share such long history and experience along the highs and lows of historical moments.'[30]

But as Rafsanjani's casket lay in state at Hosseinieh Jamaran, one man cut the sullenest figure. Rouhani sat beside the coffin, eyes red, reciting prayers from the Quran. In the days that followed, the president looked bereft, rudderless and pensive, as though the weight of the world had suddenly landed upon him. He claimed, 'The soul of a giant man of revolution, politics, a symbol of patience and strength, has ascended to the skies.'[31] And in doing so, Rafsanjani had left Rouhani without his most important ally in the fight against radicals.

Rouhani was not only faced with Trump's threats to abandon the JCPOA, a sluggish economy and increasingly vicious attacks from hardliners; parliament had also begun a mutiny. Many of those unknown first term MPs on the reformist and moderate lists had betrayed the movement to side with hardliners, fearing that if they remained reformists, the Guardian Council would bar their re-election bids in 2020. Barely a dozen MPs, including Ali Motahari, Parvaneh Salahshouri and Mahmoud Sadeghi, remained loyal.

Amid this confluence of calamity, Rafsanjani's death had a devastating impact. And it was at this moment, journalist Rohollah Faghihi suggested, that Rouhani, in effect, lost the fight for reform. 'When Rouhani lost his most important supporter, he didn't have anyone to back him. He started giving up on his promises and surrendering to hardline pressure. Hashemi's loss caused a lot of damage to the reformist and moderate camp,' he lamented.

Rafsanjani's death cast a long shadow of uncertainty across the country. Although his power had diminished since 2009, to the point that radicals openly attacked and mocked him, Rafsanjani had not wavered in his campaign against those he termed 'Islamic fascists'. And despite the widening gap between Rafsanjani and the Supreme Leader, the former's standing as a pillar of the revolution and comrade of Khamenei meant any punishment stopped short of those meted out to other revolutionaries, such as Karroubi or Mousavi.

As Faghihi explained, 'Hashemi Rafsanjani played an important role, bridging that gap between the establishment and reformists. Even though most of the establishment hated Hashemi—they accused him of being a liberal and trying to turn the theocratic state of Iran into a secular one—at least unofficially, they couldn't do much, because he had vast influence over many sectors. They hated him but could not ignore him.'

With Rafsanjani's death, pragmatists—including the president—were suddenly exposed. The balance between unelected hardliners and elected moderates had well and truly tipped.

The loss of the revolutionary icon had plunged not just the revolutionary elite into mourning, but Iranians far and wide, many of whom dressed in black, set up makeshift candlelight vigils, or taped the cleric's posters to shop and car windows. Especially for the war generation, many remarked that the presence of Rafsanjani had at times seemed more certain than even the survival of the Republic. And for anyone born after 1979, Iranian politics did not exist without his Cheshire-cat grin. The death of Rafsanjani was indeed the end of an era.

His funeral was, at that point, the largest Iran had seen since the death of Khomeini.[32] On 10 January 2017, government and military officials packed into the Tehran University prayer hall to bid farewell to the Ayatollah, whose recognisable white turban had been placed atop his coffin before the sea of mourners. A tearful Khamenei, who sobbed as he led the prayers himself, recited the *namaz-e janaza*, the Muslim prayer for the deceased.

The crowd was filled with notable figures, including Rouhani, who stood beside the Supreme Leader, Sadeq and Ali Larijani, and radical cleric Ayatollah Ahmad Jannati. A large swathe of military leaders, past and present, including IRGC commander Mohammad Ali Jafari, Quds Force commander Qasem Soleimani and former IRGC commander Mohsen Rezaee, had also shown up. The men had known Rafsanjani for four decades, having worked closely with him during the Iran–Iraq War years. By contrast, it was no surprise that former president Khatami—who was close to the late Rafsanjani—had been banned from attending.

Outside, the coffin made its way through some of Tehran's most famous streets, including the aptly named Enghelab, or revolution, in the midst of hundreds of thousands of black-cloaked mourners. Some estimates, including from Hossein Hashemi, the Tehran governor, put the number as high as 2.5 million people.[33]

Despite Rafsanjani falling from favour in his last decade of life, it was not difficult to believe that millions would flock to bid him farewell. There were very few sectors in Iran that Hashemi, as he is more commonly known, had not influenced. As commander of the armed forces, he helped lead the country through the war—the most traumatic years in Iran's modern history. As president, he led the reconstruction effort to repair ruined, decimated cities, as well as institutions that had suffered from neglect and malaise during those years of bloody conflict. Rafsanjani, who famously became known as the 'commander of construction', also founded a chain of affordable private universities throughout the country, including the massive Islamic Azad University. The model was so popular, for a time, that the IAU enrolled more students than the entire state university system combined.[34]

Rafsanjani had also used his time first as president and later as chairman of the Expediency Council and Assembly of Experts to foster cordial ties with Iran's regional rivals in the Persian Gulf, primarily Saudi Arabia.[35] And he had long advocated a resumption of ties with the United States, arguing it was an inevitability and vital to the survival of the Republic.

Unsurprisingly, then, his funeral procession itself reflected a polarised society and the struggle over the Republic's legacy and future. While thousands inside the gates of Tehran University mourned Rafsanjani as a pillar of the revolution and a symbol of the Republic and chanted support for Khamenei, thousands of others held aloft pictures of both Khatami and Rafsanjani as symbols of moderation and reform. Along the line of procession, which snaked through the heart of the capital, pockets of mourners chanted, 'Hashemi, your path continues', 'Greetings to Khatami', 'condolences to Mousavi, Karroubi', and the catchphrase of the Green Movement, 'ya Hossein, Mir Hossein'. The chanting was so loud—and repeated sporadically throughout the procession—that Seda va Sima was forced to dip the volume on its live feed and replace it with music of mourning.

But as millions lamented the passing of Rafsanjani, radicals revelled in the knowledge that their greatest opponent was no longer.

Those in the halls of power kept their criticisms largely to themselves, but on social media it was a different story, as statements of mourning were laced with backhanded jibes, and sometimes outright hostility. Perhaps the most vociferous commentary came from young, social media–savvy Iranians, who posted messages of criticism and slander against the departed Ayatollah and his family, rather than condolences. Many referred to the revolutionary stalwart as a traitor and a thief, who had used his position to sabotage and undermine the Supreme Leader with a so-called invisible hand. Others called for his family, namely his children, to join him in the grave. A few had posted laughter emojis over a picture of his daughter Fatemeh Hashemi crying on her brother Mehdi's shoulder.[36] Mehdi was serving a ten-year prison sentence for embezzlement but had been granted furlough to attend his father's funeral.

For hardliners, Rafsanjani's death was not a loss—it was an opportunity, of which they would make good use in the years to come.

* * *

Just ten days after Rafsanjani was buried next to Khomeini in his sprawling mausoleum south of Tehran, Trump was sworn into office. It was 20 January 2017. Rouhani himself was facing re-election in the coming summer.

Although life, particularly on a social level, had improved, as the fractures in Rafsanjani's funeral proved, there were outstanding issues that had not been addressed.

The leaders of the Green Movement were still under house arrest, despite Rouhani's own speculation that he could solve their situation within a year of coming to office. Meanwhile, political prisoners like Narges Mohammadi had been joined by dozens of other activists in jail, including anti-death penalty campaigner Atena Daemi, writer Golrokh Ebrahimi Iraee and labour activist Shapour Ehsanirad. The latter had been arrested for organising a strike of unpaid workers at the Safa Rolling and Pipe Mills Company in Saveh.[37] He had lamented earlier, when Rouhani took office, that he didn't think the new president would be able to keep many of his campaign promises to improve the rights of workers, because the state was seemingly so opposed to organised unions and activism. He had also, rather knowingly, predicted that his own judicial troubles would not end simply with a change of government.[38]

Labour strikes had become more and more common during the economic crisis, as businesses struggled with high costs that had cut into profitability, and thus the ability to pay workers on time. Some activists, like Ehsanirad, pointed out that corruption and a lack of transparency was also a driving factor, as money meant for employee salaries often ending up 'missing' or 'mismanaged' by company executives.

These issues followed Rouhani into his re-election campaign. The high drama of the nuclear issue and international politics had cast a long shadow over 2013, but almost four years later, those issues were of lesser importance at the ballot box. Unlike in the US elections, no Iranian candidate was threatening to tear up the nuclear deal.

The greatest challenge Rouhani faced was exactly what some voters had warned of four years earlier—disappointment. Lofty promises to fix the economy and create jobs had largely fallen flat, because the promised economic benefits of the nuclear deal did not eventuate.

It would take a lot longer, and a lot more investment, for middle-class and poorer Iranians to see a life-changing reward. But Rouhani's 2013 campaign had created so much excitement and expectation that there was no way he could have lived up to those hopes, especially in such a short amount of time.

As for domestic reform, the president faced three problems. First, he did not have the exclusive power to enact what he had promised without launching a battle against entrenched conservative unelected institutions, including the Guardian Council, the intelligence ministry and the judiciary. Second, Rafsanjani was no longer alive to mediate between the government and the establishment. And thirdly, the erosion of the JCPOA and its promised economic benefits destroyed Rouhani's domestic political leverage.

In the 2017 election, Rouhani faced a number of familiar opponents, including Mayor Mohammad Baqer Qalibaf, who was running for president for the third time. He had used the past four years to bolster his conservative credentials—including with the sex-segregation plan in Tehran—but had also started complaining about Rouhani's economic record. In the televised debates, he went a step further, accusing the president's administration of corruption. Qalibaf came up with his own version of Occupy Wall Street's '1 per cent', arguing that Iran's wealth was in the hands of an elite 4 per cent, which included the president and his men.

His attacks were met with scoffs of derision from spectators watching at home, given that the corruption scandals embroiling Qalibaf himself had only increased with time. Rouhani smiled and thanked the mayor for the opportunity to address the topic, although the debate was supposed to be focused on the environment. He launched into a stinging attack on his sharp-suited opponent, listing projects and public spaces in Tehran that the city had sold or destroyed in murky circumstances, including a deal with billionaire businessman Babak Zanjani, who had been sentenced to death on charges of corruption.[39] Rouhani asked, 'You who promote this 4 per cent, to whom did you give permission to build that big tower? You gave permission for a thirty-three-story building to a person who stole the people's assets.'[40]

But Qalibaf was not the only conservative in the race who was using a populist platform to damage Rouhani. The black-turbaned Ebrahim Raisi, a rising force in the hardline establishment, proved the biggest threat to the incumbent president.

Raisi had not been well known as a political man before election speculation had started in earnest a few months earlier. He had held a variety of judicial positions since the 1980s, as Tehran's prosecutor general, deputy chief justice and attorney general. He was also a member of the Assembly of Experts. And although his name was known to some Iranians, it was usually connected to two things: the 1988 massacre of political prisoners, which Montazeri had opposed and later revealed, and for managing Astan-e Quds Razavi, the country's richest *bonyad,* or foundation, based in the holy city of Mashhad.[41] Raisi was appointed head of the powerful charity, which manages the shrine of Imam Reza, in 2016, sparking speculation that the country's ruling elite had put him on a trajectory that would one day lead to the Republic's highest office—that of Supreme Leader.[42]

His candidacy also once again raised the profile of the Republic's *bonyad*s, which are 'quasi-governmental institution[s], military, paramilitary or religious, set up to perform charitable activities on behalf of the Iranian state.'[43] There are at least three such major organisations, including Astan-e Quds Razavi, which were established after the revolution to redistribute confiscated wealth, care for veterans and the poor and manage other charitable projects. However, although *bonyad*s are government-funded, they operate with no government oversight and have, according to researchers, become 'sprawling, for-profit conglomerates' that control thousands of businesses, including in petrochemicals and banking. And as a budget leak would later show, the *bonyad*s, which pay no tax, were a serious threat to the Iranian economy.[44]

Nonetheless, even as the head of a multi-billion-dollar charity conglomerate, Raisi had engineered his campaign on populist principles. It was in many ways a rehashing of the Ahmadinejad age, complete with promises of a 300 per cent increase in cash handouts to the disadvantaged to offset subsidy reduction. The economic promises were so wanton that Ali Larijani was forced to publicly denounce them in frustration, asking, 'Where do the candidates want to find resources to fulfil their promises?'[45] The parliamentary speaker pointed out that cash handouts and subsidy offsets were under the purview of parliament, not the presidential administration.

Economic management was a wildly punishing arena for dispute, and the question of subsidies was one element that had started to emerge with ferocity. Under the Subsidy Reform Plan, backed by the World Bank and IMF, the Ahmadinejad administration had reduced some subsidies, including on energy, and replaced them with a monthly cash handout of IR455,000 (US$12).

The Rouhani administration was opposed to continuing the handouts, given the fact that, at least initially, too many Iranians had access. So after taking office, the administration narrowed the eligibility, removing almost five million mostly rich and upper-middle-class Iranians from the list, and another 24 million people two years later.[46]

However, even if Raisi's promise to increase handouts did not gain much traction, his constant criticisms of corruption and economic management did. In an opinion poll conducted a month before the vote, it was clear why. Only 11 per cent of respondents said their economic situation had improved since Rouhani came to office, while 42 per cent said unemployment was the most important issue the next president should solve.[47] And rather tellingly, 72 per cent of respondents said the economic situation of ordinary Iranians had not improved with the nuclear deal.

Given the disappointment over the slow pace of economic recovery, and the sluggish enthusiasm which greeted the prospect of another election, the Rouhani campaign was forced to push itself off the ropes through some political daring. The moderate cleric had become, at least in promise, a reformist.

In the last debate, the most watched of the three, Rouhani, his daring first vice president—Eshaq Jahangiri—(also a candidate), Raisi and Qalibaf led a blistering exchange of allegations and smears. Qalibaf, using the Ahmadinejad tactic of show-and-tell, held up two deeds he claimed were evidence that Jahangiri and Rouhani had been buying land at cut-throat prices since the 1980s. In what seemed to be a coordinated effort, the IRGC-linked Tasnim News Agency released the alleged Jahangiri documents online.[48]

Rouhani also threw down the gauntlet, traversing the traditional bounds of criticism, which usually fell short of airing the dirty laundry of the IRGC and the judiciary. Rouhani told Qalibaf he was a hypocrite and should look at his own family's finances before slandering anyone else. He also lambasted the mayor for using the past four years to try to 'destroy' his administration and warned him about boasts he had made about beating student protesters when he was Tehran's police chief. Rouhani even told Qalibaf that he had been in possession of a file more than a decade earlier that could have ruined his career, saying, 'If I had not prevented disclosure [of the file], you would not be sitting here.'[49] For Iranians watching the debates from their homes, it was a remarkable encounter. Seldom could anyone remember a more scathing, biting election campaign, which traversed taboos and red lines.

The president also raised an issue that he and Rafsanjani had warned against during the war days, namely the cartel-like practices of the IRGC and its stranglehold on Iranian business—a not-so-subtle dig at Qalibaf who, between 1994 and 1997, served as the managing director of the IRGC's engineering conglomerate Khatam al-Anbiya.[50]

Like Qalibaf, Raisi also used the debates to increase accusations that Rouhani had allowed corruption and endemic tax evasion to run rampant during his administration. He raised the controversy surrounding Rouhani's brother and advisor Hossein Fereydoun, who had become the target of hardline MPs who accused him of corruption.

In return, the president accused the former attorney general of abusing religion as the head of Astan-e Quds Razavi and of knowing nothing but 'death and imprisonment', which many took as a reference to the mass executions of 1988.[51] Indeed, just days before the debate, Rouhani had stood before a crowd of thousands of supporters at Lake Urumiyeh and thundered:

> They talk about freedom of speech and criticism—those who cut out tongues and sewed mouths closed. What was issued to you over the years was the word prohibition; a prohibition of the pen, a prohibition of an image. Please, do not speak of freedom, for freedom itself would be embarrassed. Do not talk of criticism. You work in an institution that no one dares to criticise. Destruction is taking place in this society, but our men and women have consciously stood up to their blackmail.[52]

The re-energised Rouhani campaign had gathered speed once again and his rallies, including a star-studded event at Azadi complex, felt more like entertainment festivals than political conventions. Maestro Mohammad-Reza Shajarian's version of the Rabbana, a religious prayer, rang out across the stadium packed with 20,000 people, to raucous applause and salutation. The song had been a Ramadan fixture on state TV and radio for three decades, used to signal the beginning of the evening *iftar*. But it had been pulled almost a decade earlier, ostensibly because the beloved singer and composer had supported the Green Movement in 2009.[53]

Actors and singers took to the stage with messages of hope and unity. Singer Hussein Zaman recalled how he had been under 'artistic siege' for fifteen years, but that the Rouhani government had offered a new hope. Footballer Ali Mansoorian appealed for unity to continue the movement, eliciting the colours of Iran's two main football teams, Esteghlal and Persepolis, saying, 'Today, blue and red have come together to create purple!' Actress Sahar Dolatshahi reminded Rouhani of why many people had put faith in him in the first place, saying:

> I am here talking to you about freedom in this stadium that many girls wish they could attend just once. I salute freedom! Mr President

... I have not forgotten that you arrived in an atmosphere of promises of gender justice. You promised us equal job opportunities and promised to review civil laws. Mr President, the Charter of Civil Rights is before us. We believe in your promises. To distance the policy of denial and cover-ups of social harm is the top of your political platform. We have many demands, and we have come to accompany you on this difficult path. We will not go back.[54]

The crowd roared, 'Greetings to Mousavi! Greetings to Hashemi! Khatami must endure!'

In this environment, where supporters openly pushed for civil liberties and Rouhani himself broke taboos and riled against the more nefarious aspects of the Republic, it is not difficult to understand why many reformists were energised to vote. The bold strategy worked, and polls showed an upward surge not only in voter turnout but also in support for the incumbent.[55]

Rouhani's message even swayed Mohsen Kadivar, who was living in the United States, to cast a ballot, which he had not done for two decades. 'I thought maybe he [Rouhani] could achieve something, that he was telling the truth,' he recounted.

With forty-eight hours to go until the polls opened, there were only two main candidates left: Rouhani and Raisi. Qalibaf had dropped out so as to not split the conservative vote.[56] And while Rouhani's message convinced some reformists to vote, others came out for the same reason as they had in 2013—to prevent a hardline victory. They reasoned that even if Rouhani could not make things better, someone else could always make it worse.

Rouhani trounced his chief rival, taking 57.14 per cent of the vote compared to Raisi's 38.28 per cent.[57] However, unlike in 2013, Rouhani lost eight of Iran's thirty-one provinces, including his home district of Semnan. Of the eight provinces that Raisi won, he was victorious in four capitals—Mashhad, his hometown and the capital of Razavi Khorasan; Birjand in South Khorasan; Bojnourd in North Khorasan; and Qom.[58] And though it wasn't clear at the time, the concentration of votes for Raisi in conservative strongholds would foreshadow a gathering storm of opposition that was about to explode.

8

HARDENING HEARTS

By the time Rouhani was re-elected, the mountain of pressure, including from the Trump administration, had grown. Arguably, with the country at large facing such strangulation, Rouhani gave up on reform. Iranians no longer seemed to be moving forward; they were simply trying to survive an onslaught.

And more than that, some of the earlier progress Rouhani had achieved was slipping backwards. Journalists like Foad Shams commented that the more liberal atmosphere for the press diminished as securitisation increased. As the Rouhani administration was forced to focus on saving the JCPOA and the Iranian economy, it no longer had the bandwidth to push back against the security establishment or the judiciary. It was exactly as Mehrzad Boroujerdi had predicted.

External crisis had undermined Iran's internal development, and 80 million Iranians were paying the price. Suddenly the debate over compulsory hijab seemed less important, as the challenge of putting food on the table increased.

But outside pressures on Iran were also much closer to home than Washington. Regional catastrophes were seeping into the country's soil. In addition to struggles over the JCPOA and domestic reform, the Islamic Republic was also very literally at war.

Rouhani had only been in office for less than a year when, in June 2014, the Islamic State of Iraq and the Levant (ISIL) declared a caliphate that stretched from Aleppo in Syria's north to Diyala province in Iraq's east.[1] At the heart of the so-called state, led by former Al-Qaeda in Iraq operative Abu Bakr al-Baghdadi, was Iraq's second-largest city, Mosul. There, more than a few residents—even the imam of famed twelfth-century Great al-Nouri Mosque—had welcomed Baghdadi and his men with 'exhilaration and enthusiasm'.[2]

As the militants drove their Toyota pickup trucks across the Syrian border into Iraq, 1,000 kilometres to the east of Tehran, urgency shrouded a snap meeting of Iran's Supreme National Security Council. Members, including the SNSC secretary, Rear Admiral Ali Shamkhani, were not surprised that the militants had received such a warm welcome, but they were alarmed by reports that Iraqi commanders had deserted their posts, while the few who tried to fight were so poorly equipped that they ran out of ammunition.[3] Later investigations revealed that up to a third of rank-and-file troops, so-called 'ghost soldiers', had only ever existed on paper.[4]

As the Syria–Iraq border disappeared, Iran put its troops and air force on full alert, while the SNSC ordered thousands of reinforcements to its western border, which stretched more than 1,458 kilometres, from the Shatt al-Arab, or Arvand River, in the south to the Turkish border in the north. Within forty-eight hours, three IRGC battalions had crossed into Iraq, while ammunition and supplies had made it to the Kurds.[5] The Kurdish Peshmerga was the only real fighting force left in the north, and Kurds feared that if it was overrun, they would face a genocide.[6]

The terrain and the fear were familiar to Shamkhani, who was born and raised in Ahvaz, the unbearably hot and humid capital of Khuzestan Province, which shares a 320-kilometre border with Iraq. It was arguably the worst-hit province during the eight-year Iran–Iraq War, which the Shamkhani family felt first-hand. All four brothers joined the war effort, with Ali rising through the ranks as commander of the IRGC Navy. But two of his brothers, Hamid and Mohammad, were killed in action.[7] Three decades later, it was up to men like Shamkhani to help lead Iran's strategy in a new war against a medusa of ideological psychosis, two failed states and inept leadership.

Despite the catastrophe that now straddled two countries, it took the US two months to launch its first airstrike, prompted by the Yazidi genocide that was unfolding—beamed live to televisions around the world—near Mount Sinjar.[8] But while the US dithered, and ISIL was less than 90 kilometres from Baghdad and even closer to Iran's border with Iraq's Diyala Province, the Iranians were already in the fight.

Shamkhani's old IRGC comrades, Quds Force commander Qasem Soleimani and a small group of senior IRGC leaders, including a fellow Ahvazi, Brigadier General Hamid Taqavi, were organising both the IRGC and volunteer Iraqi fighters, known as al-Hashd al-Shaabi, who had followed Grand Ayatollah Sistani's fatwa to mobilise en masse.[9]

Soleimani looked an unlikely warrior; slight of build and short, he walked with a trademark stoop. His jet-black hair had turned silver with the years, and his soldier's physique, toned in youth by battle and exercise at the traditional *Zurkhaneh*, had morphed into that of a middle-aged man. Those who met Soleimani described him as 'softly spoken and reasonable, very polite', and both measured and 'professional in his dealings'.[10] In his formal civilian clothes, black suit and typical Iranian grandpa collared shirt, Hajj Qasem, as he was popularly known to Iranians, looked every bit the local bureaucrat. But appearances can be deceiving. Not long before the ISIL advance into Iraq, former CIA operative John Maguire described the commander as 'the single most powerful operative in the Middle East today ... and no one's ever heard of him.'[11] Of course, that was not entirely true. Soleimani was in many respects a household name in Iran by the time he took the lead in the fight against ISIL.

During that conflict, Soleimani's reputation took on an almost mythical status, but his origin story was not unlike that of other veterans of the Iran–Iraq War. The commander was born in 1957 and grew up in a humble family in the village of Rabor, some 200 kilometres from the historic city of Bam. He left school at the age of thirteen, and with a relative travelled to Kerman city to work in construction. According to his recollections, he needed the money to repay a debt of 9,000 rial, which his family owed to the government.[12] A decade later, Soleimani had become a supporter of revolution, and after 1979 he joined the fledgling Revolutionary Guards in Kerman. The IRGC doctrine is to protect the Supreme Leader, to whom it directly answers, and to defend the revolution and the nation's interests.[13]

Soleimani recalled, 'We were all young and wanted to serve the revolution in a way. This is how I joined the Guards.'[14] He stood out amongst his comrades and, even without prior military experience, was appointed an instructor. His first real combat experience arrived soon after, when he was sent to Mahabad in West Azerbaijan to suppress a Kurdish separatist uprising.[15] But it was not that experience that turned Soleimani into a household name or even a war hero—it was the Iran–Iraq War.

From Kerman, after war broke out in 1980, Soleimani trained and dispatched several contingents to the southern front and later led his own company to Sousangerd, west of Ahvaz. The company formed the basis of what would eventually become the vaunted 41st Sarollah Division, which he commanded until he was appointed to lead the Quds Force in 1997.[16] Soleimani is quoted as saying that he was only supposed to be at the front for fifteen days, but instead remained there for the next eight years. Like so many other veterans, in some ways he never left that battlefield.

With the Sarollah Division becoming one of the most reliable during the war, Soleimani took part in almost all the key battles, including the joint Army–IRGC operation Tarigh-e Quds to liberate the city of Bostan in late 1981; Operation Fath al-Mobin to free western parts of Dezful in 1982; and Operation Karbala I to retake Mehran in the summer of 1986. He was wounded in Operation Tarigh-e Quds, and his unit was also gassed with chemical agents as it advanced towards the Iraqi city of Sulaymaniyah in summer 1987.[17] By all accounts, Soleimani's reputation as a brave and brilliant soldier was well known amid the rank and file on the front.

Although Soleimani spent most of the war on the southern front, fighting to defend and liberate parts of Khuzestan, he also played an important role in leading irregular warfare operations inside Iraq from the Ramezan base in Marivan, Kurdistan Province. And it would be those operations, as well as the relationships that he formed inside Iraq, that proved crucial more than three decades later.

The men from the Ramezan base, including Brigadier General Hamid Taqavi, formed the early core of the Quds Force. They spent decades building a network of ties in Saddam Hussein's Iraq, from the Shia in the south to Kurdish Sunni leaders in the north, specifically Jalal Talabani's Patriotic Union of Kurdistan Party (PUK), and, to a lesser degree, Masoud Barzani's Kurdish Democratic Party of Iraq (KDPI). Another Ramezan base alumnus, Brigadier General Iraj Masjedi, would later be appointed Iran's ambassador to Iraq. According to Bilal Sulaiman, a Kurdish party official who previously served in Tehran, Masjedi had been an important mediator in the dispute between the KDPI and the PUK in the 1990s.[18]

Those ties gave the men the ability to reach out to the Kurds, when even Baghdad could not.

After the US invasion and removal of Iran's enemy, Saddam Hussein, the ties increased, said the scholar Fawas Gerges. 'They [Iran] have built critical capital, social capital inside the country. And really what the Iranians tried to do was translate these ties into resources, which they did after the Americans [left]. It's not surprising, all they did was deepen and thicken their ties inside Iraq, with the dominant social group. Iran's influence goes beyond … the Shia, this is important, its influence is bottom up.'[19]

As a Shia-majority country, Iran was already the enemy of Al-Qaeda in Iraq and ISIL, both of which had sworn to wipe out Shia Muslims wherever they found them. The growing list of atrocities in both Syria and Iraq, often filmed and used for propaganda and recruiting, proved as much. But the bloodletting, although disturbing, was not a great surprise to the myriad of diplomats and intelligence analysts from Tehran to Amman to Erbil that had been warning the Syrian Civil War would resurrect AQI and spill over its borders.

Both Baghdad and Kurdish Regional Government (KRG) officials derided the 'grotesque' amount of money flowing to rebels trying to overthrow the Assad regime, particularly the large sums emanating from Paris and Persian Gulf petro-kingdoms like Qatar.[20] But those opposed to Assad, who had been sending weapons and money to rebels, slammed Iran for supporting a ruthless dictator, who allowed his country's destruction, hundreds of thousands of deaths and a global refugee crisis, in an effort to hold onto power.

Zarif put it differently:

Following the fall of Saddam in Iraq, there is a disequilibrium in the region they [Saudi Arabia and Persian Gulf Arab states] want to redress … and everything that is happening is caused by that perception of disequilibrium. And they give it all the flavours of 'Bashar al-Assad is democratic, undemocratic, ruthless.' But are we talking about democracies in our region criticising Bashar al-Assad? ... Let's be serious. This is not about democracy, it's not about the rights of the Syrian people. This is all about a convoluted, perverted concept of regional equilibrium.[21]

As was clear, atrocities on all sides were bountiful. But over the border in Iraq, the KRG knew it would not be spared either. And it had already identified ISIL and AQI sleeper cells in Mosul, a city under the jurisdiction of the Iraqi central government. Yet, despite Baghdad's own fears about a militant resurrection (it was already fighting to wrest back parts of Anbar Province, including Fallujah and Ramadi, from Al-Qaeda, ISIL and other fighters), KRG Prime Minister Nechirvan Barzani revealed: 'We tried with [Iraqi] Prime Minister [Nouri al-] Maliki to do something [in Mosul] ... we offered them a joint operation six months ago. ... He just refused ... he said everything is fine, there is no problem.'[22]

Barzani had also implored the US to pressure Baghdad to act. The plea, according to Barzani, fell on deaf ears, despite the fact that the US Department of Defense had predicted, with almost clairvoyant accuracy, the very same thing, two years earlier. A redacted preliminary report read:

This [the Syrian war] creates the ideal atmosphere for AQI to return to its old pockets in Mosul and Ramadi, and will provide a renewed momentum under the presumption of unifying the jihad among Sunni Iraq and Syria, and the rest of the Sunnis in the Arab world against what it considers one enemy, the dissenters. ISI [Islamic State of Iraq] could also declare an Islamic State through its union with other terrorist organizations in Iraq and Syria, which will create grave danger in regards to unifying Iraq and the protection of its territory.[23]

The report also identified Iran as a target—not simply because it was Shia, but because of its regionally unpopular intervention in Syria, along with Hezbollah and, after 2015, Russia, at the request of the Assad regime.[24]

Indeed, in 2013, a year before ISIL announced its caliphate, two suicide bombers killed twenty-three people, including Iran's cultural attaché, Ebrahim Ansari, outside the Iranian embassy in Beirut.[25] The Al-Qaeda-linked Abdullah Azzam Brigades, led by Saudi Majid al-Majidi, claimed responsibility for the attack and threatened more bombings if Iran did not pull out of Syria.[26] It prompted Lebanese security analyst Kamel Wazne to warn: 'This attack raised the bar and made the Iranians a direct target. ... Once you destroy these barriers, you open the gate for a very complicated game in the Middle East.'[27]

Wazne was correct. And by summer 2014, that game was playing out right on Iran's doorstep. The crisis in Iraq didn't just present a catastrophic challenge to Iraqi life and sovereignty; it also posed the most serious threat to Iranian security since the days of the Iran–Iraq War.

The war against ISIL also made the US and Iran curious bedfellows. Much like in the war against the Taliban almost fifteen years earlier, the two enemies were once again on the same side, with their respective forces at times operating only kilometres away from each other. Even so, the US did not invite Iran— the first foreign power with boots on the ground—to join its Global Coalition to Counter ISIL, which convened in Paris.[28] This prompted Zarif to ruminate that the Paris conference was a 'coalition of repenters, because most participants in that meeting, in one form or another, provided support to ISIS [ISIL] in the course of its creation and upbringing and expansion—actually, at the end of the day, creating a Frankenstein that came to haunt its creators.'[29]

But three years later, in June 2017, Iraqi troops, supported by a small band of US and allied special forces on the ground and in the air, had wrested back control of most ISIL-occupied territory in Iraq, and cornered the most diehard fighters into the twisting little alleys around the now ruined Great al-Nouri Mosque in Mosul's old city. The war came at great cost to Iraqi civilians, Iraqi forces and those fighting to help them—including Brigadier General Hamid Taqavi, who was shot dead by an ISIL sniper in Samarra in December 2014.[30] At his memorial, SNSC secretary Ali Shamkhani responded to those who questioned Iran's role in Syria and Iraq, saying, 'The answer to this question is clear: if the pious do not shed blood in Samarra, we must shed blood in Sistan, Azerbaijan, Shiraz and Esfahan ... Tehran.'[31]

* * *

By 7 June 2017, as the so-called caliphate crumbled and Iraqi leaders predicted the liberation of Mosul was imminent, Tehran awoke to a brilliantly bright morning. The warm sun beamed so strongly through the grimy windows that even before 10 a.m., it was clear the summer heat would be unforgiving. Outside, in downtown Tehran, the brown, creeping pollution that usually stained the sky had somehow been batted away, revealing a rare hue of blue. Mercifully, it was also almost the end of the sweltering work week, which saw Celsius temperatures creep into the high thirties. Downtown can be a stifling place, especially in summer, when the heat radiates off every surface and renders the traffic jams and hustle and bustle of annoyed commuters even more unbearable. Millions of cars clogged the streets; millions more people jammed the avenues and pathways in between, trying to get to work on time. Others had packed like sardines, shoulder to shoulder, into the city's long, red BRT buses, sweating and praying that even a small breeze would reach down to them from the high windows. Amid all the chaos, Iran's oldest democratic institution—the parliament—had convened.

The parliament building itself, shaped like a giant white pyramid, is ringed by the traffic and tree-lined wide avenues of old

Tehran. It was the third building in which parliament had sat since first being established in 1906 during the Constitutional Revolution, or *Enghelab-e Mashrute*. The hallowed institution is the oldest elected legislative body in the Middle East.[32] Men fought and died, many brutally, for its establishment, and later its survival, during the reign of the despotic Qajar Dynasty. The *Enghelab-e Mashrute*, which heralded a constitutional monarchy, was Iran's first revolution of the twentieth century—but, of course, not its last.

The original parliament building, named *Baharestan*, after the neighbourhood in which it stands, is not far away. It is a spectacular display of Qajar-era architecture, of white tiles and mosaics, pillars and brick. It has withstood political upheaval, earthquakes and, most notably, the 1908 bombing, carried out by Iranian and Russian Cossacks with British support to kill Iran's fledgling democratic movement. The building, like the origins of the institution itself, continues to be a symbol of the Iranian struggle against foreign imperialism.

At about 10.15 on that hot morning, inside the newer, pyramid building, with its expansive green-carpeted chamber, the parliament session had entered its second hour. MPs had gathered on the floor to discuss some very routine issues: the annulment of old laws, judicial agreements with Indonesia and South Korea, and questions for Communications and Information Technology Minister Mahmoud Vaezi. Parliamentarians who had bothered to attend lounged in their high-backed green leather chairs. Some gazed ahead towards Ali Larijani in the speaker's chair, with the glassy-eyed look of the deathly bored. And as usual, some were already falling asleep.

But what began as a routine June day did not end as one. A sudden series of loud bursts echoed through the vaulted chamber and jolted the bored parliamentarians upright. Several more bangs pierced the air. The MPs looked around, clearly confused about what they were hearing. Presumably some builders were working in another part of the building, banging hammers or tools. In the upper tier overlooking the chamber floor, members of the small Iranian press corps stopped their quiet chattering. Photographers too stopped clicking their cameras and strained to listen. But when the sounds of muffled screams reached the chamber, it became clear—something was very wrong.[33]

A few moments earlier, Maryam Shahriari and her sister had arrived at parliament, determined to speak with her local MP about an issue she had been having with her insurance company. As the pair talked about what they would say, they paid little attention to the men who had followed them off the street and calmly through the main gates.

It was only when the pair stopped at the security checkpoint that Maryam became aware of someone else, dressed in a woman's chador, standing right behind her. But before anyone could register that something was wrong, the unknown figure had thrown off the chador to reveal, that he—not she—was carrying a Kalashnikov.

Security cameras would capture the moment that four men, with automatic weapons and a handgun, shot their way into the building.[34]

'From the moment they started firing, people fled. ... We were in front of them and we had no escape route,' Maryam recounted later. 'There was no wall or even a chair that we could take refuge behind. We just threw ourselves to the ground.'[35] The sisters were both shot as they lay on the concrete, but they somehow survived.

On the second floor of the administration building, Hamid Emdadi was at work as office manager for the MP for Urumiyeh, Hadi Bahadori. Bahadori, one of the youngest candidates on the reformist List of Hope, had only won the seat in West Azerbaijan Province less than a year earlier. Emdadi himself hailed from northern Iran, from a mountain village on the edges of the expansive Mishu Daq protected reserve. Born to a farming family of three brothers and three sisters, Emdadi developed a love for the outdoors, which he took with him when he moved to Tehran after university. On the weekends, the young man, known for being quiet and thoughtful, could often be found trekking up the hills around Darband or Tochal, stick in hand.

But on that Wednesday, Emdadi was at his desk when he heard gunshots on the floor below. Unlike for those sitting in parliament on the other side of the complex, the noise was not muffled by distance. The young man, who had completed compulsory military service, recognised the sound immediately. As parliamentary staff ran for the stairs, Emdadi followed, but suddenly turned back to rescue another colleague who was hiding under a desk. But it was too late. A gunman bounded up the stairs and shot the clerk at point-blank range.

Two floors up, Hesam Khoshbinfar, the office manager for veteran MP Alaeddin Boroujerdi, was attending to two constituents who needed the conservative politician's help. As he tapped out a letter on his computer, he heard a loud banging below. 'I thought to myself, maybe it's the sound of repairs, so I kept working,' he recounted later. 'I wrote the lady the letter she wanted and gave it to her, and she went down the elevator.'[36] Another man, who had come in looking for help with a job, soon followed her out, accompanied by his friend.

Khoshbinfar, stocky and with a stubbly beard, turned his attention to his phone. Unbeknownst to him, the woman had got off the elevator and had come face to face with a gunman. Somehow, she escaped the barrage of shots that followed her as she ran. Meanwhile, the two men who had also filed out of the office were taking the stairs. There, one was shot in the leg, while the other managed to throw himself out of a second-floor window to safety.

Khoshbinfar says it was then that thirty-nine-year-old Ali Tudeh Fallah, who worked for one of the MPs and had been on the third floor, burst through the door. 'He said there was a terrorist attack. Lock the door. Mute your cell phone and all the phones. ... He went and shouted to everyone else in the corridor ... to do the same,' recounted Khoshbinfar. Fallah's older brother, who also worked in parliament, said Ali had implored him 'to escape, go into your rooms, hide, lock the door.' Instead of joining them, Ali headed back down the stairs to try to stop the attack. He was shot in the neck on the second-floor landing.

News of the shootings spread fast. Within minutes, police and IRGC special forces, known as the Saberin unit, had raced to Baharestan, led by Brigadier General Mohammad Pakpour. Two of the IRGC's most senior leaders—its chief commander, Major General Mohammad Ali Jafari, and his deputy, Brigadier General Hossein Salami—joined him on the ground, as snipers appeared on rooftops, and military choppers circled overhead.

Inside, security guards were trying desperately to keep the attackers at bay, despite being outgunned. In addition to automatic weapons and handguns, at least two of the assailants carried explosive-laden backpacks. The Saberin unit joined the fray, moving quietly from floor to floor. In a firefight, one of the attackers' backpacks blew up, killing its owner instantly.

At the end of the fourth-floor corridor, another employee, Seyed Amir Abbas Hashemi, was hiding in his office with seven colleagues, one of whom was pregnant. They had used desks, a cupboard and even files to barricade the door. As the explosion roared through the building, the false ceiling collapsed and water pipes burst. All the while, 'the terrorists repeatedly kicked and bombarded the door to open it,' said Hashemi, 'because the room overlooked the area where the IRGC and security forces had set up. ... It was indescribable.'[37]

Hashemi had managed to communicate with commanders on the ground, by holding his phone number, scrawled on a book cover, to the window. Via text message, he told the security forces the remaining attackers were on the fourth floor, and that civilians, including his pregnant colleague, were trapped.

Word of the attack had just reached across the city. On the outskirts of Tehran, security guards at Khomeini's sprawling mausoleum heard there had been a shooting, but knew little else. They barely had time to speculate on what might be happening downtown when they were confronted by two men carrying automatic weapons and suicide vests.

CCTV captured the moment when one of the men blew himself up as the security guards tried to stop him. The second attacker was shot dead in the courtyard.

There had been two attacks in Tehran in the space of half an hour. Fear spread quickly, permeating every conversation, text message or phone call. Those taking the bus or train, or working near landmarks like Azadi Square or the Bazaar, wondered if they were next.

Although every country that surrounded Iran was engulfed by war, terrorism, sectarianism or political chaos, the same was uncommon within Iran's borders. At the very least, Iranians were thankful to be living in a pocket of stability in a neighbourhood that had been ripped apart by turmoil, generation after generation. It was certainly true that Iran had suffered its own horrors over eight years of war with Iraq, but since the ceasefire in 1988, terrorism in major cities was almost unheard of. Security forces were most concerned about areas along the country's Pakistani border, where Sunni militants from groups like Jundullah and Jaish al-Adl routinely killed or attacked soldiers and police before running back to their bases in Pakistan.[38] Although such incidents occurred with an uncomfortable regularity in some rural parts of the country, terrorism, at least until that Wednesday morning, did not happen in Tehran.

Back in parliament, at the other end of the fourth-floor corridor, Khoshbinfar was hiding under his desk. He prayed and texted friends and colleagues, including Boroujerdi, to keep himself calm. The gunmen were skulking around in the corridor outside, and he could hear them trying to break into Hashemi's office. 'I was locked in my room,' he said. 'One of them was behind [the door] for three hours, and I could hear them talking and even cursing in Persian. The miracle of God was that this terrorist did not break into my room. He just checked if the door was locked and that was it.'

After a four-hour ordeal, a young IRGC soldier pulled Khoshbinfar to safety, using himself as a human shield while the stocky clerk escaped down the stairs. There he saw Ali Tudeh Fallah, who had risked his own life to warn his colleagues, lying in a pool of blood.

During the long siege, the phone in Fallah's pocket rang over and over. His wife, having heard news of the attack, was desperately trying to reach him. The phone rang out. She knew he was dead.[39]

While parliament's administration building was under attack, something odd was happening across the annex in the chamber. Although MPs were well aware of what was going on, and security guards had barricaded the door, parliament was still in session.

From the speaker's chair, Ali Larijani, appeared nonplussed. Surrounded by a group of lawmakers, Larijani thanked the MPs who 'continued their work calmly'. He continued, 'As you know, some cowardly terrorists infiltrated a building, but they were seriously confronted. ... This is a minor issue but reveals that the terrorists are pursuing trouble-making, especially here in Iran, which is an active and effective bastion against terrorism.'[40]

Around him, MPs broke out into a tepid chant of 'death to America', while others, such as the wheelchair-bound war veteran Gholam Ali Jafarzadeh, reformist politician Gholam Reza Tajgardoon and Gholam Mohammad Zaraee, took smiling selfies for Instagram. The trio were heavily criticised for looking so chipper when so many people were being killed not far away.

It took five hours for the security forces to kill the four gunmen. All the while, journalists in the press gallery waited and wondered how on earth the attackers had managed to carry so much ammunition. Security forces had brought in ladders, which they used to climb down from the press gallery into the main chamber, where Jafari and Larijani personally led them to safety. Meanwhile, other survivors, including a toddler, had been rescued from windows by firemen and security agents.

Upstairs, the IRGC gave Hashemi and his colleagues the okay to leave. They pulled the barricades aside and stepped out into the bullet-riddled hallway 'in disbelief'.[41] Bullet holes had ripped apart the walls, furniture had been tipped over, water was gushing from pipes and bodies were strewn in between.[42]

From the moment of the first shot, questions were being asked. Who and why? But before the attacks were even over, while dozens of employees were still cowering in their offices, there came an answer.

In a video posted on its propaganda channel, *Amaq*, the Islamic State of Iraq and the Levant (ISIL) claimed responsibility. The video, filmed by one of the attackers inside the building, shocked Iran. As alarms ring out, the unmoving body of a clerk lies behind his desk. In Arabic, a gunman exclaims, 'Oh God, thank you...' He shoots the man twice and yells, 'Do you think we will leave? No! We will remain, God-willing'.[43]

The attackers had killed at least fifteen clerks, civilians and security guards in parliament, and a gardener at the mausoleum. Almost fifty others had been wounded.

'If it were not for Fallah,' said Khoshbinfar later, 'a much larger number of employees and officials on the fourth floor would have been martyred.'

Fallah's grief-stricken mother, her face battered by mourning, recalled the last time she saw her son. The night before his death, they had brokem the Ramadan fast together. 'Every time he left [the house], I would look out the window. But as it happens, that day I didn't look,' she said, her voice cracking, 'Now, I will never see him again.'

At Behesht-e Zahra Cemetery, opposite Khomeini's mausoleum, where the courtyard tiles were still scorched from the bombing, many of the attack victims were laid to rest. On a shiny black tombstone, Hamid Emdadi's young face is etched, frozen in time. Underneath, the word 'martyr' is emblazoned in red.

It was the first 'successful' ISIL attack inside Iran. But only sixteen months later, more Iranians would end up like Emdadi, lying in martyrs' graves.

In Ahvaz, on 22 September 2018, gunmen opened fire on a military parade commemorating the thirty-eight-year anniversary of the Sacred Defence, a commemoration of the Iran–Iraq War. At least four men, disguised as soldiers, shot at the parading troops and the crowd of civilians, made up of local families, disabled war veterans and even children. At least twenty-five people were killed, including a four-year-old boy. Though twelve of the dead were Revolutionary Guardsmen who were marching in the parade, they were far from military targets. Most of the soldiers were young, unarmed recruits, and those that carried guns had unloaded them before the ceremony.

On its Al-Furqan Telegram channel, ISIL claimed responsibility, saying, 'The Ahvaz attack will not be the last, God-willing.'[44]

Though members of another insurgent group—the Arab Struggle Movement for the Liberation of Ahvaz (ASMLA)—also claimed responsibility for what they called a 'heroic' attack, its leaders, based primarily in Denmark and the Netherlands, denied involvement. Two years after the Ahvaz attacks, Danish intelligence arrested three members of ASMLA on suspicion of spying for Saudi Arabia.[45]

The Ahvaz shooting was the worst terror attack in Iran since the 2010 bombing of the Imam Hussein Mosque in Chabahar,

Sistan-Baluchestan Province. That attack, carried out by a Jundullah suicide bomber, killed thirty-nine worshipers who had gathered during the most important period of mourning for Shia Muslims, on Tasu'a, the eve of Ashura, which marks the seventh-century martyrdom of Imam Hussein, grandson of the Prophet.

The Tehran and Ahvaz attacks were seen as a reaction to Iran's involvement in the war against ISIL, and certainly, as the group came under bombardment in both Iraq and Syria, it struck out with headline-grabbing bombings across the world. But the war on ISIL was not the sole reason for the escalation of violence and tension in the region.

Since the election of Trump, a crisis had been brewing in the Persian Gulf. Although the Obama administration had made record levels of weapons sales to Saudi Arabia, even as it bombed neighbouring Yemen—the poorest country in the Arab world— into oblivion, it did not encourage Saudi adventurism much further than that. Crucially, it had resisted Saudi calls to bomb Iran. As Obama's secretary of defence, Robert Gates, had put it in 2010, the Saudis wanted to 'fight the Iranians to the last American'.[46]

'Obama himself said to King Abdullah, which really ticked off the Saudis, that "we're resolving our tensions with Iran, I suggest you do the same". He was just really not interested in playing that game,' recalled Trita Parsi, former president of the National Iranian American Council.[47]

But with Trump, the Saudis found a sympathetic ear. So too did the Emirates and Benyamin Netanyahu in Tel Aviv. 'The belief is it's motivated by a common threat from Iran. And while I think those countries do have all of their own rivalries with Iran, the degree of threat is dramatically exaggerated for other purposes,' argued Parsi, who had spent a lifetime navigating the US relationship with the Middle East. He continued:

> The main threat these countries are faced with is an America that's sick and tired of the Middle East and wants to come home. If the

United States leaves the region militarily, ceases to have nineteen-plus bases and 200,000 troops there, which essentially provides them [Saudi Arabia, the UAE and Israel] with that military umbrella, and tips the balance of power scale in their favour, that balance will shift away from them ... and they cannot engage in the kind of reckless behaviour they do now because there's no United States to bail them out.

Trump's first foreign trip as president was to Saudi Arabia, offering further evidence that the administration had pushed itself further towards Riyadh. Comparatively, Obama had travelled to Canada for his first trip; George W. Bush had visited Mexico, while Bill Clinton also travelled to Canada, for a historic meeting with Russian President Boris Yeltsin.[48]

Trump's visit to Riyadh took place just three weeks before the Tehran attacks. There, the new US president and Saudi King Salman finalised a 110-billion-dollar arms deal, which included 'cybersecurity technology, tanks, artillery, ships, helicopters and radar missile-defense systems.'[49] American companies also signed deals with Saudi leaders worth up to $380 billion.[50] In the words of Trump's then secretary of state, Rex Tillerson, it was a 'historic moment in US–Saudi relations'.[51]

Billboards featuring Trump and King Salman's official portraits lined highways and roads, inscribed with the slogan, 'Together We Prevail'. While ties between the Obama White House and Riyadh had strained, as the US president ignored Saudi attempts to block the JCPOA, to diplomats and political watchers around the world, Trump's visit signalled a realignment with Riyadh vis-à-vis Iran, and a green light for Saudi Arabia, the UAE and like-minded states in the Gulf Cooperation Council (GCC) to pursue a much more aggressive foreign policy agenda.

According to Parsi:

Trump doesn't hide what the United States always has done, that's the only real difference. It's perhaps a little more exaggerated than it was before. ... The US has always been treating the Saudis this way, turned a blind eye to their support for terrorism, kept on selling them weapons to keep oil prices low. ... The big difference is they [Trump's predecessors] all hide the real reasons and claim that Saudi Arabia is a strategic partner and an ally against terrorism and all kinds of nonsense like that, whereas Trump is going out and saying, 'They buy my weapons and I want to create jobs in the United States'. And he's kind of nakedly revealing what it's always been.[52]

It took little time for that aggressive stance to show itself. On 24 May 2017, Qatar's state news agency, QNA, was hacked and posted controversial comments attributed to Qatar's emir, Tamim bin Hamad al-Thani, praising Iran.[53] Qatari and US intelligence sources agreed the hack had originated in the UAE.[54] Two weeks later, on 5 June, Saudi, Bahrain, the UAE and Egypt severed diplomatic ties with Qatar and launched a land, sea and air blockade. They demanded Doha address thirteen conditions, which included ending political ties with Tehran.[55]

Qatari Defence Minister Khalid bin Mohammad al-Attiyah called the move an attempted coup to 'undermine Qatar's national sovereignty' and an endeavour by Mohammed bin Salman, the ambitious Saudi prince and defence minister, who a few weeks later became the Kingdom's crown prince, along with the crown prince of Abu Dhabi, Mohammed bin Zayed al-Nahyan, to 'dictate Doha's foreign policy'.[56]

Hamid Aboutalebi, Rouhani's chief of staff, explained, 'What is happening [to Qatar] is the preliminary result of the sword dance,' alluding to events that had taken place when Trump was in Riyadh.[57] Iranian officials saw a distinct correlation between the Riyadh meeting and the rapidly escalating crisis in the Persian Gulf, including the Tehran attacks. It did not help that only hours before gunmen had opened fire on the parliament and mausoleum, Saudi Foreign Minister Adel Jubeir had said that Iran should be 'punished' for interfering in the region.[58]

Unsurprisingly, the IRGC pointed the finger squarely at Riyadh. 'This terrorist act took place a week after a joint meeting between the US president and head of a reactionary regional country [Saudi Arabia] which has been a constant supporter of terrorism,' read the Revolutionary Guards' statement. 'The fact ISIL claimed responsibility proves that they [Saudi Arabia] were involved in the brutal attack.'[59] Jubeir denied that the Kingdom had anything to do with the events in Tehran.

Less than a month earlier, Mohammed bin Salman had warned the Islamic Republic, which in his view was 'a regime built on an extremist ideology ... [to] spread their Twelver Jaafari [Shia] sect', that his country was not waiting 'until the fight is inside Saudi Arabia. ... We will work so that the battle is ... inside Iran.'[60]

After the attacks in the Iranian capital, Iranian Foreign Minister Mohammad Javad Zarif tweeted, in a seeming reply to Mohammed bin Salman: 'Terror-sponsoring despots threaten to bring the fight to our homeland. Proxies attack what their masters despise most: the seat of democracy.'[61] Zarif later claimed that Iran had gathered intelligence that Saudi Arabia was 'actively engaged in promoting terrorist groups' on Iran's eastern and western borders.[62]

It wasn't just Iranian leaders who saw a Saudi hand in supporting terrorism. It was a popular public sentiment. Conversations between Iranians about the attacks in the days that followed almost always included statements of shock and blame. Even a public poll found that, although the majority of respondents believed ISIL was behind the attack, nearly 87 per cent thought Saudi Arabia had likely provided guidance and support to the perpetrators.[63] In the words of Hamidreza Taraghi, a former principlist MP turned analyst, 'ISIS [ISIL] ideologically, financially and logistically is fully supported and sponsored by Saudi Arabia. They are one and the same.'[64]

In the heightened war of words, many Western observers accused the Iranian government of paranoia. But Iranian officials knew, in reality, their position was not so alien, even in Washington. 'Look at the Clinton emails,' said one US security advisor, seated in a chain café in Doha's City Centre Mall. 'We [the US] know exactly what the Saudis and Emiratis, heck the Qataris too,' he said, gesturing around, 'are up to. After 9/11, we saw Saudi citizens celebrate! On the other hand, not to say Iran is by any stretch innocent—they support Hezbollah and Hamas—but their citizens held candlelight vigils. I think that is very telling.'[65]

What the advisor, who had worked in Iraq after the US invasion, was referring to was the tranche of emails that Wikileaks had hacked and leaked to the public, from Hillary Clinton to former White House advisor John Podesta just a year earlier.

Clinton wrote that both Qatar—home to the largest US base in the Middle East—and Saudi Arabia were 'providing clandestine financial and logistic support to ISIL and other radical Sunni groups in the region.'[66] She had also revealed separately that the US effort to support 'moderate' rebels in Syria was 'complicated by the fact that the Saudis and others are shipping large amounts of weapons—and pretty indiscriminately—not at all targeted toward the people that we think would be the more moderate, least likely, to cause problems in the future.'[67] It backed up the contents of an earlier, also leaked, State Department cable that stated, 'donors in Saudi Arabia constitute the most significant source of funding to Sunni terrorist groups worldwide.'[68] Even then Vice President Joe Biden, in a moment of public candour, explained that US allies in Turkey, Saudi and the Emirates:

> were so determined to take down Assad, and essentially have a proxy Sunni–Shia war ... They poured hundreds of millions of dollars and tens of tons of weapons into anyone who would fight against Assad—except that the people who were being supplied, were

Al-Nusra, and Al-Qaeda, and the extremist elements of jihadis who were coming from other parts of the world.[69]

Only a few years later, the Trump White House responded to the Tehran shootings by saying that although it grieved and prayed for 'the innocent victims of the terrorist attacks in Iran … we underscore that states that sponsor terrorism risk falling victim to the evil they promote'. In Iran, shock gave way to anger, and many hearts, which had been open to optimism and a détente with the US, hardened with hatred.

* * *

Back in Ahvaz, the Karoun River flows quietly and unassumingly through the capital of Khuzestan Province.[70] It is possible, in the steamy night, when glasses fog, skin sweats and insects lethargically buzz, to imagine the sky is actually clear. Clean, not choked with the pollution of a thousand years, not swimming with billions of particles from sandstorms from neighbouring Arab lands, not spent with munitions from wars that have left this very rich region heaving with promise and destitution at the same time, not to mention trauma. Pol-e Sefid, the white bridge which soars across the river, is a symbol of a better time; the river below, pockmarked with ancient marshes and river reeds, a symbol of something that has continued for millennia. A shadow of the marshes between which, not far away, soldiers crouched just decades earlier, fighting, dying, praying.

In the Kaveh market, dirty and colourful, the smell is so pungent it causes noses to crinkle and visitors to recoil. Fresh fish are piled from stall to stall, languishing on ice as flies buzz. Their owners hawk and barter with customers in that local accent of clipped vowels, too savvy to accept what they've been told. A sheep's head, teeth exposed, is propped on a table. A young boy, eyes wide, stares in shock. His parents, unnerved, haggle nearby. The ground is wet, glistening with a concoction of melted ice, fish blood and runoff. The local feel is a contrast to the capital's shops and markets, where just about everything, even in the Grand Bazaar, is made in China. There is still an old-world quality to Ahvaz, a city that bakes under a blistering sun for most of the year and is not for the weak-willed.

Khuzestan is important both historically and in Iran's present. Its oil was first discovered around Abadan in 1908; it is a place that has produced wild riches and abject poverty, prestige and shame, national pride and foreign plunder. Modern Khuzestan is a myth-making region of struggle against Iraqi invasion, bombs that fell like rain, civilians forced to run for shelter and dive into basements. It is here that heroes were made. Fahmideh.[71] Chamran.[72] Soleimani. Mention the name Khorramshahr to any Iranian, particularly a Khuzestani, and you feel it rather than hear it. The recapture of the city during the war became as important to the national struggle as the 1953 coup—a symbol of *azadi* (freedom) and *esteghlal* (independence), the two main and everlasting tenets of the revolution.

But war creates trauma—the sort that twists and turns the mind, everlasting, unwavering. It is evident in the generation that lived its formulative years with the threat of overhead death and doom, of chemical gas attacks and air raid sirens. Yet today, Saddam is gone. Most Iranians have reconciled themselves with the idea that his Iraq is in the past, that it dissipated at the end of a hangman's noose. But nobody forgets.

They say those who fail to understand history, indeed, who fail to remember it, as the Spanish philosopher George Santayana first said, are doomed to repeat it.

Decades later, as the Trump administration escalated the crisis in the Persian Gulf, accused Iran of terrorism while the country's own soldiers and people were dying because of it, and abandoned the JCPOA and re-imposed sanctions, Iranians came to understand that the US was addicted to war. Needless, avoidable, bloody war. And according to some Iranian war veterans, that was because very few Americans understood its true costs.

Bombs have not fallen on US soil since World War Two. Save for a few men and women, seventy odd years is outside the stretches of even the most infallible memories. In Iran however, war is not historical; it does not exist simply in black-and-white photographs or in schoolbooks, in parades, moments of silence or anniversaries. Loud noises still jolt survivors with chills. And the desert winds still blow traces of mankind's worst inventions through the air.

Conflict is so raw that bodies are still returning home in flag-covered coffins, and atrocities are still being unearthed decades after they occurred. The discovery of the bodies of 175 Iranian military divers, who had gone missing during the Karbala-4 offensive in 1986, is but one painful example. Their hands had been bound, and it was clear that many of the young men had been buried alive.[73] Their corpses were retrieved in 2015 as part of the ongoing mission to find and return both Iraqi and Iranian war-dead. The discovery, but also the shocking way in which the divers died, dragged up painful memories for a collective population. The divers were not mourned as relics of the past. In a massive public funeral, the men were laid to rest, grieved as though death had only just befallen them. Their families were still alive to cry over their coffins, their mothers young enough to remember war's heartbreak with disturbing familiarity, and their comrades still endowed with vivid memories of fighting, able to imagine how those last moments must have felt suffocating in the Iraqi sand. Even the millions of young Iranians who were not even born when the soldiers perished joined in the outpouring of grief, with hashtags, social media posts and pictures.

The divers were interred beside the hundreds of thousands of other soldiers already buried in martyrs' graves around Iran. The largest war cemetery, at Behesht-e Zahra outside Tehran, is row upon row of some 200,000 tombstones. Each bears an image of the deceased, mostly young faces, with eyes that would never crease from years of laughter and hair that would never turn grey with time. Many of the photographs, faded with the years, are entombed in metal framed glass boxes. Inside the little memorial chambers, family members leave trinkets or possessions of importance. Beside one young martyr, a pair of thin-rimmed glasses had been placed on a little ledge with care. Next to another, a Quran, prayer beads and a plastic carnation in a tiny vase. Another box had been decorated with curtains, which had been carefully parted and tied back to reveal the black-and-white photograph of a young soldier, surrounded by dried flowers. His picture peered out as though through the window of an imagined home, as though his life had not ended wretchedly on some battlefield.

And these were the lucky ones. Lucky enough to have found death, however gruesome, in battle. The martyrs are revered, and so they live forever. Martyrs never die.

The memory of sacrifice—why Iranians understood the high cost of war—was compounded by the fact that death had not finished with those who managed to survive a sniper's bullet, a buried mine or a falling bomb. The living dead were still dying, slowly, agonisingly, one by one.

Ahmad Zangiabadi was one of those unfortunate souls. He was a chemical warfare veteran, one of the 65,000 soldiers gassed by Saddam's men. Tens of thousands more civilians share his fate. As he walked along a narrow path outside his home in North Tehran, he presented a living reminder of the horrors of war. Each small step he took was as difficult as the next—slow, halting, hard.[74] He carried a blue umbrella to protect himself from the winter rain, while his son, Hesam, wheeled an oxygen tank beside him. Even this walk, a short 50 metres to the corner store, was torturous. Though the oxygen tubes under his nose allowed him to take small, shallow breaths, that was the very best he could hope for, with his damaged, collapsing lungs. In the winter of 2013, Zangiabadi knew it would not be long before he joined his fallen comrades in a martyr's grave.

Zangiabadi grew up in Kerman in south-central Iran. He was fifteen when war broke out, and by any estimation, there on the other side of the country, the young man would have been safe from the battle raging on the western front. But instead, like thousands of other young men from the province, including Qasem Soleimani, he volunteered. So it was that he was a soldier by the age of sixteen and a war veteran by twenty-two.

Zangiabadi had been at war for three years when his unit, holding a position on Iraq's Majnoon Island, was bombed with sulphur mustard gas. It was 6 p.m., 12 April 1985. The bombing was so intense, he recalled, that it trapped his unit on the ground for four hours. The young soldier, only nineteen years old, tried to hold a cloth to his mouth, but as he related later, the chemicals had saturated everything, even the material. As the gas wafted through the air with such a tantalising scent, like sautéed garlic and vegetables, for a moment his mind drifted back to his mother's kitchen—home in Kerman, safe and far away. The smell was so delicious and inviting, the memory so comforting, that the young soldier had to force himself to resist the desire to take just one deep, satisfying breath. He pressed the useless cloth across his nose and mouth even harder.

Although there was evidence the Iraqis had already been using chemical weapons for eighteen months, Zangiabadi said he had not encountered them until that day. At Tehran's Peace Museum, where the war veteran volunteered as a guide, he remembered, 'When they [Iraq] bombed us, we didn't detect the problem right away. But about four hours later, my body started reacting to the chemicals.'

It was about ten at night by the time Zangiabadi could leave for help. Feeling sick and realising he was in trouble, he asked one of his comrades to replace him at the front, so he could go to the medical centre. 'My eyes started to burn, then I started vomiting so badly I thought I was dying. My skin started to blister around my eyelids, my mouth, neck and anywhere else that was wet.' And on a steamy, deathly hot evening in the marshes, there was barely a dry inch of skin under his faded soldier's fatigues.

Other men from Zangiabadi's unit had also fallen ill. 'We lost consciousness and were taken to a hospital in Ahvaz,' he said. 'From there we were sent to Tehran.'

The nineteen-year-old's lungs were so badly burnt and his body in such agony that he fell into a coma for forty days. 'I do not remember much about that time,' he related. 'I was in hospital for another seven months after I woke up from the coma. After that, I returned to Kerman and started working at the Kerman War Headquarters, collecting aid to send to the front.'

After the war, Zangiabadi tried to get his life back on track. Given his age and level of fitness from years of martial arts, he didn't notice the effects on his lungs until years later. He enrolled in an English literature degree at Imam Hussein University and got married. But soon, the effects of the attack caught up to him. The gas had burned his cornea and destroyed his eyesight. Although he tried, he could no longer read the literature he loved so much and had to quit his studies. By then, other effects started to take hold. Zangiabadi grew nauseous and tired, debilitated by pain. And as the years passed, his lungs began to fail, trapping the young soldier in the body of a dying man. When once he had hoped for a good future and career, now he merely hoped to take a deep breath.

According to Iraq's own declarations, it used more than 101,000 chemical bombs and munitions, including sulphur mustard gas and nerve agents, during the war. Shahriar Khateri, perhaps Iran's leading expert in chemical weapons, said that despite this, the international community 'barely blinked an eye'.[75]

As early as November 1983, Iran had written to the UN Security Council to ask for an investigation. It was the first of fifteen letters of complaint Iran would send to the UN about Iraq's use of chemical weapons. Two subsequent UN investigations confirmed that Iraqi chemical attacks had occurred in both 1984 and 1985 and that 'attacks are still continuing in spite of appeals by the United Nations ... in direct contravention of the 1925 Geneva Protocol.'[76] The UN condemned the attacks, but the US, which knew full well that Iraq was using chemical weapons 'almost daily', managed to stop the UN from explicitly naming Iraq as the culprit in its statement.[77] The US also knew that components for such chemical weapons had been supplied to Saddam Hussein by Western firms, including possibly 'a U.S. foreign subsidiary'.[78]

A third UN mission, dispatched in April 1987, found attacks had not only continued, but had also targeted civilians.[79] It made little difference that the UN knew what Iraq was doing. Only two months later, on 28 June, Iraqi aircraft dropped four 250-kilogram bombs filled with mustard gas on the city of Sardasht in West Azerbaijan Province, 15 kilometres from the Iraqi border.[80] At least 8,000 of the city's 12,000 residents were exposed to the gas. It was the first city attacked by chemical weapons since the US had dropped atomic bombs on Nagasaki and Hiroshima during World War Two, but it wouldn't be the last. Less than a year later, on 16 March 1988, the Iraqi Air Force bombed the Iraqi Kurdish city of Halabja, killing up to 7,000 mostly Kurdish civilians.[81]

It is bad enough that thousands of people are still dying today from chemical weapons exposure during the war, that bodies are still returning home, that cemeteries and hospital wards continue to be busy places even thirty-two years after the ceasefire—but the knowledge that French, British, American, Swiss, German and Dutch companies supplied Saddam with the components and intelligence to carry out his chemical weapons attacks is what fills Iranians, not simply survivors, with anger and frustration.[82] Three of those countries—the US, France and the UK—are permanent members of the UN Security Council.

'They [the West] were complicit with Saddam,' said Shahriar Khateri. 'So, when they accuse us [Iran] about non-conventional weapons, they are hypocrites.'

'We had nothing to defend ourselves with,' said Zangiabadi. 'We couldn't do anything to stop the chemicals,' he recalled. 'We [Iran] were alone. No one helped us, not then, not during the war. The world sided with Saddam.'

The war ended on 20 August 1988, when Iran accepted a UN-brokered ceasefire. Iraq had threatened to escalate its chemical attacks to target large Iranian cities. Meanwhile just a month earlier, on 3 July, the US had mistakenly shot down a civilian airliner over the Persian Gulf, Iran Air Flight 655, killing all 290 people on board. The Iranian economy, just like many of its border cities, was in ruins. And the death toll—some estimate up to one million people were killed on both sides—was unprecedented. Khomeini likened the ceasefire to drinking a 'chalice of poison'.

Much of the modern Iranian psyche can be traced back to those battlefields and days of war. A country surrounded, alone, shocked, left with no option but to save itself. It is one reason Zarif says that 'Iranians are allergic to pressure'—that whether the challenge be war, threats or sanctions, Iran does not capitulate.[83] It reacts.

Decades later, a similar, sometimes visceral feeling spread through the Republic. Under maximum pressure—as Europe failed to deliver on its JCPOA commitments, and France and the US increased arms sales to the UAE and Saudi Arabia while in the same breath condemning Iran's own defence productions—many Iranians saw a pattern. Nothing had changed in four decades. And as the US pulled out of the nuclear deal and Europeans dithered, Iranian public sentiment followed. Between August 2015 and January 2018, support for the JCPOA slipped from 75.5 per cent to 55.1 per cent.

At the same time, support for Qasem Soleimani skyrocketed. The Quds Force commander overtook Zarif as the most popular man in Iran, with more than 82 per cent of Iranians declaring approval for Soleimani in one poll, compared to 67 per cent for the foreign minister. Many Iranians came to view Soleimani as once again having to fight to protect the country—and indeed others—from a menace not of Iran's own creation. And to many, Soleimani became a symbol of the Republic itself.

He became so popular that in the lead-up to the 2017 election, speculation was rife that Soleimani might run for president. Even some reformist voters supported the idea.[84] However, the commander, wedded to the battlefield, threw cold water on the idea very quickly. His aversion to politics was perhaps one reason why a wide cross-section of Iranians, including those who protested against the government, chanted anti-establishment slogans and boycotted elections, came to respect and even love him.

Only once was Soleimani known to have taken a political position in public: the July 1999 uprising at the University of Tehran. Twenty-four IRGC war veterans, including Soleimani, Qalibaf and Esmail Gha'ani, signed a letter to President Khatami, warning him that if he did not get the riots under control, the Revolutionary Guards would be forced to intervene.[85] But if it was the first time Soleimani publicly took a side in domestic politics, it was also the last. Privately, in fact, Soleimani was no radical. His devotion to the Republic and the revolution did not equate to devotion to radical politics, despite the persistent and successful attempts by hardliners to co-opt his image.

'He was completely in favour of reformists and [Mir Hussein] Mousavi,' said journalist Rohollah Faghihi. 'He had even agreed to mediate between the establishment and Mousavi in 2019. And he had also mediated to get the approval of the security apparatus to free some political prisoners, especially after the events of 2009.'[86]

And, unlike many other leaders in the IRGC, Soleimani was in favour of nuclear talks.

At rallies around the country, from wartime commemorations to those tied to the revolution and birth of the Republic, supporters, even young women who let their scarves slip off their heads and loathed conservatives, proudly held his image aloft. Arguably, there had never been a more prominent figure of resistance since Khomeini himself.

Abroad, the war against ISIL had also caused Soleimani's public profile to rise. Where once his picture rarely appeared in foreign press, suddenly the familiar arched black eyebrows and half-smile were everywhere. Articles about Iran's role in the Middle East rarely left out references to Soleimani, described in a 2013 *New Yorker* piece by Dexter Filkins as 'The Shadow Commander'.[87] *Time* magazine even named him as one of its 100 most influential people in 2017.[88]

What the Trump administration, Western media and foreign regime change activists failed to understand was that the negative framing of Iran, Soleimani and his supposed regional meddling meant nothing to Iranians inside Iran. As expressed in a 2011 op-ed in the conservative *Asr-Iran*:

> Qasem Soleimani is not a mystery, he is the commander of the Quds Force of Iran. There are astonishing stories about him in [foreign] languages that, with a mixture of truth and falsehood, present him as a terrifying ghost. ... The more frightening and terrifying they describe him, here in Iran, those who know him speak of his modesty and calmness. ... A nightmare that, as much as it frightens Westerners, pours sacred pride into our souls ... this strong commander, with buckwheat hair, thin body, and calm, sunburned face ... is down to earth, and familiar among his compatriots.'[89]

HARDENING HEARTS

Outsiders did not understand how the war, the ingrained culture of self-sacrifice for a greater cause, had coloured the Iranian psyche—how resistance and pride, green, white and red, formed the core of the modern Iranian identity. And under maximum pressure, Soleimani became the nation's flagbearer.

So why do some heroes live forever, while others fade into irrelevance?

In Iran, at least, they die.

9

MA CHEGOONE MA SHODIM?
(WHAT HAS BECOME OF US?)

'Each time history repeats itself, the price goes up.'

Anonymous

On 8 May 1945, US President Harry Truman announced the Allied acceptance of Nazi German surrender and the end of World War Two in Europe.[1] Although it took Imperial Japan another three months to surrender in the Pacific, 8 May marked a turning point in history—the day that the bloodiest war in Europe's history came to an end and a ruined continent could begin to rebuild itself after five years of desolation and despair.

On that same day in 2018, seventy-three years later, another US president, Donald J. Trump, made his own announcement—not to end a war, but in effect to begin one. 'I am announcing today that the United States will withdraw from the Iran nuclear deal,' he said. 'I will sign a presidential memorandum to begin reinstating US nuclear sanctions on the Iranian regime. ... The United States no longer makes empty threats. When I make promises, I keep them.'[2]

While Truman announced the end of a conflict that was not of America's making, Trump, according to John Kerry, 'has taken a situation where there was no crisis, and created crisis'.[3] Indeed, the IAEA—the sole agency responsible for monitoring Iranian compliance—had consistently reported Iran was abiding by the deal. Thus, the main aim of the JCPOA—to ensure the Iranian nuclear programme remained peaceful—was actually working.

'Here is the first time you actually have a deal,' said Trita Parsi from Washington, 'the first time there is a proper negotiation, extensive agreement, goes through all of the right channels, and guess who betrays it? Not Iran. The United States.'

The Trump announcement coincided with a cabinet reshuffle, in which Trump fired Secretary of State Rex Tillerson—on Twitter, no less—and National Security Adviser H.R. McMaster, both of whom were against abandoning the nuclear deal. Trump replaced them with Iran hawks: the former director of the Central Intelligence Agency Mike Pompeo, and John Bolton, George W. Bush's UN ambassador and one of the most vocal proponents of the Iraq War.[4] Bolton was Trump's third national security advisor in as many years. In his new role, Bolton affirmed that Trump was effectively 'reinstituting all of the nuclear-related sanctions that were waived' as part of the JCPOA, and that any new economic deals with Iran would be 'forbidden'.[5]

According to numerous diplomats from Tehran to Europe, Trump's actions did not constitute a withdrawal from the international accord as much as it did a violation. As John Kerry put it, 'We [the United States] are in breach of the agreement.'[6] Other members of the US JCPOA team, including Obama's under secretary of state for political affairs Wendy Sherman, further warned that Trump's actions would damage America's reputation abroad, as well as its ability to maintain the trust of its transatlantic partners.

Across the Atlantic, European leaders expressed 'regret' at Trump's decision, while the European Union's foreign policy chief, Federica Mogherini, said the EU was 'determined to pre-serve' the deal.[7] But perhaps the most provocative statement came from former French president Francois Hollande, who claimed the principles of the deal did not sway Trump 'since cynicism, vulgarity and egocentricity are the springs of his per-sonality'. Hollande continued, saying despite Trump's pronounce-ments to improve the deal, his only intention was to 'tear it up'. And that left countries like France, which had invested twelve years of diplomacy, in a precarious situation.[8]

In an effort to protect European businesses from the wrath of the US treasury, Brussels expanded its 'blocking statute' to ban any EU citizen or entity from complying with US sanctions, unless authorised to do so by the European Commission.[9]

Despite this, more than 100 major international companies abandoned Iran, including PSA Peugeot Citroën.[10] Though it had sold almost 445,000 vehicles through Iran Khodro and Saipa the year before, the French auto manufacturer prioritised pro-posed business ventures in the US. Total, the French oil giant, followed suit, cancelling its two-billion-dollar investment and its 50.1 per cent stake in the Phase 11 development of the massive South Pars Gas field.[11] And despite all the fanfare and red-carpet reception only eighteen months earlier, Airbus, Boeing and ATR refused to fulfil remaining orders. At that point, Airbus had only delivered three of the 100 planes intended for Iran Air, while ATR had delivered thirteen of twenty.[12] As for Boeing, the American behemoth had never even put in the order.

According to former pilot Hooshang Shahbazi, even after the deal,

> everything took such a long time. It's true that after the JCPOA, we could technically buy better planes. But first we didn't have the money to buy 200 planes from Airbus and Boeing at once. So, when we ordered the aircraft, by the time they [Airbus and Boeing] started processing it, it was too late. They didn't stick with us very long.

The deal was crushed. Trump gave us no time ... we need 600 passenger planes, but we only got three.[13]

With the benefit of hindsight, it was easy for some to criticise the Iranians for entering into a deal with the US. And inside Iran, hardliners placed all the blame on Rouhani and his foreign minister, Mohammad Javad Zarif—even though in 2015, no one, not even DC pundits, had predicted the rise of Trump.

'If you were there in 2015 and you had raised the idea, "What if a batshit crazy clown becomes president of the United States and starts leaving every international agreement there is, including Paris," do you think anyone would take you seriously?' Parsi asked, with a frustrated air of disbelief in his voice. 'It's easy for us in retrospect to point out, "Oh, how did they miss this?" but if you were there, raising that idea would have come across as some conspiracy theory, I suspect.'[14]

With every month that passed, the Trump administration turned the screws, finding new things to sanction. Between August 2017 and September 2020, the US made at least fifteen separate announcements of sanctions on Iran, targeting the country's most vital industries—petrochemicals, shipping, metals and banks—as well as individuals, including Supreme Leader Ali Khamenei and Mohammad Javad Zarif.[15] Trump had also designated the IRGC—a constitutionally recognised branch of Iran's armed forces—as a terrorist organisation and sanctioned more than a dozen of its senior officials, including aerospace commander Amir Ali Hajizadeh, naval commander Mansour Ravankar, whose maritime command extends across the South Pars gas field, and SNSC secretary Rear Admiral Ali Shamkhani.[16] The US also reimposed sanctions on Ground Force commander Mohammad Pakpour, who led the fight to rescue those trapped in parliament during the ISIL attack.

Soon, Iranians joked that there was nothing left to ban but *pofak*—cheese puffs.

At the same time as the US increased its sanctions regime, Pompeo issued Iran with a list of twelve demands, which included everything from an order to stop enriching uranium and developing ballistic missiles, to a demand for the effective end of the Quds Force.[17] One of the foremost scholars on Iran, Ervand Abrahamian explained that Pompeo's 'commandments' in effect amounted to a call for 'unconditional surrender'.[18]

In all, Trump's strategy laid waste to economic deals worth almost $45 billion, killed thousands of jobs, including for the struggling auto workers in Karaj, and put on hold desperately needed investments to modernise dozens of Iranian sectors, from petrochemicals to tourism. Dizin ski field was not about to become Aspen any time soon.

But perhaps worse than the collapse of big-ticket deals, SWIFT ignored the EU's ban on compliance with US sanctions and once again disconnected Iranian banks from its service, concluding that the prospect of US prosecution was far worse than falling foul of the EU.[19] Indeed, even before the election of Trump, the US treasury had already fined a number of European banks for violating US sanctions, including the French bank BNP Paribas. It was forced to pay almost $9 billion in fines in 2014, even though its actions were not prohibited in France.[20]

Even the EU's own special purpose vehicle (SPV) to facilitate business with Iran, named the Instrument in Support of Trade Exchanges (INSTEX), fell well short of Europe's own pronouncements to buck US sanctions.[21] Billed as a business saviour, in the face of pressure from the Trump White House, it ended up simply as a vehicle to enable transfers of items not technically sanctioned anyway—food, medicine and medical devices.[22]

US withdrawal and the imposition of sanctions, in conjunction with the failure of the agreement's European signatories to live up to their own commitments, triggered a step-by-step process of Iranian non-compliance. Iran increased its enriched uranium stockpile beyond the JCPOA's limits, began enriching uranium to purity rates above 3.76 per cent, started up advanced centrifuges, and began injecting gas into centrifuges at the Fordow plant, under the supervision of the IAEA.[23]

According to Abshenas, 'The P5+1 talks were officially between Iran and the US and the other countries were there to guarantee the outcome. Iran signed the deal on two bases: ending sanctions, especially on banking and oil, and normalising trade. Neither happened and the EU did nothing about it.'[24]

And as was clear during the Obama era, the so-called humanitarian exemption to sanctions meant little, as once again foreign businesses trading in the most basic necessities, from cancer drugs to flu vaccines, presented Iranian importers with roadblock after roadblock.

But there was another layer of trouble that had injected further crisis into the country. And at least in its initial hours, it had little to do with Trump—but rather with poultry. Avian flu had forced Iranian officials to cull 16 million chickens, which, along with an 80 per cent rise in feed prices compared to the year before, had caused the price of eggs to double by late December 2017.[25]

On 28 December 2017, hundreds of people began protesting in the holy city of Mashhad, Iran's second-most populous city. But it was clear from the direction of the group's anger— President Rouhani, at whom chants of death were directed—that the protests were not sporadic, nor simply about eggs. As journalist Saeed Laylaz surmised, 'The hands of political groups could be seen in today's gathering.'[26] He was alluding to supporters of Qalibaf and Raisi, two Mashhadis, who naturally drew most of their support base from the city and from the wider province of Razavi Khorasan. It was no secret that the former had tried to undermine the Rouhani administration since his presidential loss in 2013, while the government accused Raisi of doing the same since his own election defeat in 2017. Raisi's father-in-law, the radical Mashhad Friday prayer leader and vociferous Rouhani detractor Ahmad Alamolhoda, was also accused by government sympathisers of involvement in organising the protests.

A Tehran-based political analyst concluded that the protests were 'triggered by radicals to bring down Rouhani', and that they had simply used the pretext of economic dissatisfaction to do it.[27] But the initial core group of protesters had made a grave miscalculation, said the analyst: 'They didn't predict that it would get out of their hands and would actually spread to other cities. They didn't see that coming.'

The ploy backfired and protests spread, including to small villages, gathering steam as poorer Iranians, struggling with rising inflation and living costs, which by some estimates had risen 60 per cent since 2016, joined in. The chants against Rouhani were drowned out by chants against unelected officials and institutions, including those who had allegedly fanned the flames of protests in the first place. Protesters accused them, including *bonyad*s like Astan-e Quds Razavi, headed by Raisi, of bleeding the country dry.

The protests tapered out after two weeks, and although they were mostly peaceful, some of the protesters had set fire to banks and buildings, and, according to some reports, twenty-one people had been killed.[28]

The seemingly sudden fury of protesters and the targets of their rage were no coincidence. While the egg protest had started in Mashhad, the proposed budget for the coming year (March 2018– March 2019) had been leaked to the public, allegedly by Rouhani's own office. It showed that while the government was pushing ahead with its unpopular but IMF-approved plan to further cut subsidies, including on fuel, it was being forced to raise taxes and cut investments and social services, to make way for a massive allocation of taxpayer money to religious institutions and other affiliated entities. One figure that infuriated Iranians the most was the 31.1 trillion rials (US$853 million) earmarked for a dozen institutions that promote Islam and ideology—effectively 30 per cent of the entire budget. It was an increase of 9 per cent over the previous year and more than that which had been proposed for the foreign and culture ministries.[29]

Further, the leaked documents also revealed an increase in the IRGC's usually secretive budget, even though it itself had enormous financial holdings, which many economists—and even the president—argued had undermined the economy and almost eliminated the private sector.

A month after the protests broke out, Iran's defence minister, Amir Hatami, revealed that the IRGC and other branches of the armed forces had been instructed by the Supreme Leader to sell off business holdings and commercial assets 'irrelevant' to their main function.[30] The Supreme Leader himself acknowledged that many of the protesters had legitimate grievances and contended authorities needed to work harder to solve them.[31]

The protests revealed that economic dissatisfaction was rife. And unlike the protests of 2009, which were driven by the middle class seeking reform, the Rouhani-era protests were driven by the poor and the working class—the *mostazafin*, or dispossessed, that the Islamic Republic was established to protect.

According to Laylaz, three million Iranians were out of work, while 'more than 35 per cent of Iranians are under the poverty line.'[32] Laylaz contended that sanctions did not impact Iran's economy as much as many people imagined, but that corruption and mismanagement had long been the greatest drivers of 'misery'.[33]

Regardless of the cause of dissatisfaction, the protests were a mere taste of what was to come two years later, when the Rouhani administration pushed forward with its subsidy reform plan.

Late on Friday, 15 November 2019, the government announced a snap increase in the price of fuel and a rationing plan for private vehicles. Although it had been proposed two years earlier, the sudden implementation caught many people by surprise.

The price hike increased the cost of a litre of fuel from 10,000 rial for the first 250 litres to 15,000 rial (about 12.7 US cents) for the first sixty. The price would increase to 30,000 Rial for every additional litre after that. The point was not only to help the environment, but also to siphon the extra money into additional subsidies for 18 million families, including some of the poorest.[34]

Despite the price hike, fuel in Iran was still subsidised and sold at one of the cheapest rates in the world. But in a tinderbox of pressure, 40 per cent inflation and high living costs, it pushed thousands of Iranians over the edge.

Within hours, protests spread to at least twenty-one cities, including Mashhad and Ahvaz. Although the demonstrations were largely peaceful, some erupted into violence and chaos, as rioters ripped apart their cities.

In an attempt to stop the call to protest from spreading on popular social media apps like Telegram, the internet was switched off. For six days, save for a few sporadic moments, Iran went black. Information and Communications Technology Minister Mohammad-Javad Azari Jahromi, a former intelligence officer tipped as a future presidential contender, acknowledged that 'service providers were instructed to cut it off by the [Supreme] National Security Council.'[35] According to the connectivity tracking group NetBlocks, it took Iranian authorities twenty-four hours to block the nation's inbound and outbound online traffic.[36]

And as Iran went black to the outside world, inside, witnesses were shocked by what they saw. Rioters set fire to hundreds of buildings across the country and clashed with security forces in running street battles, from Tehran to Khuzestan. According to

Interior Minister Abdolreza Rahmani Fazli, an estimated 731 banks, 140 government sites, fifty bases belonging to security forces and seventy gas stations were burned down or ransacked.[37]

Unlike the protests in December 2017, security forces intervened immediately. And although it would take months for the truth to finally emerge, the crackdown was the bloodiest in the Republic's history. Even many ardent defenders of the Republic, from conservatives to reformists, lost faith. Witnesses on the ground said security forces, some perched on rooftops, had shot haphazardly into crowds, killing unarmed protesters, including those who were running away. Although it is difficult to pinpoint an exact death toll, an Amnesty International investigation found at least 302 people were killed, including security officers.[38] It also concluded that 'more than 220 of the recorded deaths took place over just two days on 16 and 17 November.'

Just as the events of 2009 continued to haunt the country in the decade after, the chaos and killings in 2019 further fractured an already traumatised society.

Abroad, politicians from DC to Tel Aviv predicted that the Republic was on the verge of collapse. Some right-wing analysts, including exiled Iranians who vehemently supported sanctions on their own people, gleefully boasted that the protests were proof that Trump's strategy of maximum pressure was working. But in reality, that was far from the truth. The Republic was not collapsing—instead it was the livelihoods and dreams of a nation that were falling into the abyss.

As Forough Farrokhzad, one of Iran's most influential feminist poets, once wrote in *Bazgasht* (Return), 'My city was the graveyard of my desires.'[39]

* * *

The shock of the riots had not yet dissipated as the Gregorian New Year approached. And shock was not limited to events taking place in Iranian streets. Towards the end of 2019, the tension between the Islamic Republic, the United States and its allies escalated to within a hair's breadth of war.

The Persian Gulf became a theatre of sabotage, which included the seizure of Iranian oil tankers, an attack on a Japanese-flagged ship and the bombing of the Saudi Aramco oil-processing facilities at Abqaiq and Khurais, which Riyadh blamed on Iran.[40] In the same period, Iran shot down an American RQ-4A Global Hawk BAMS-D surveillance drone that had flown into its airspace at the Strait of Hormuz. The incident led to revelations that although Trump initiated a retaliatory attack on Iran, he called it off at the last minute.[41]

Some recalled the last days of the Iran–Iraq War, where in those same warm waters, the US fought its largest naval battle since World War Two—and mostly in secret.[42] Back then, US warships had been escorting Kuwaiti oil tankers through the narrow Strait of Hormuz to protect them from Iranian harassment. On one such morning, 3 June 1988, the captain of the billion-dollar guided missile cruiser USS *Vincennes* ignored orders and international law and sailed into Iranian waters to open fire on half a dozen lightly armed Iranian speedboats. In the midst of a resulting, albeit one-sided, skirmish, Iran Air Flight 655, on its twice-weekly flight from Tehran to Dubai via Bandar Abbas, had flown overhead. The ship's crew, commanded by William C. Rogers III, whom fellow sailors described as 'trigger happy', had mistaken the plane for an Iranian F-14.[43] Rogers gave the order, and the USS *Vincennes*, equipped with the most sophisticated technology of its time, shot the plane and its 290 passengers and crew out of the sky.

As pieces of the Airbus A300 fell into the sea, it was immediately obvious it was no fighter jet. But instead of admitting the entire truth, senior American military officials, including Rear Admiral William Fogarty, who led the internal investigation, lied to both Congress and the Senate Armed Services Committee about the ship's true location.[44] Military leaders also lied about why the USS *Vincennes* had engaged the Iranian boats in the first place.[45] Meanwhile at the UN, then Vice President George Bush also repeated the narrative that Rogers 'acted in self-defence'.[46]

It took an Iranian lawsuit and an investigation by *Nightline* and *Newsweek* for the truth to come out three years later. And despite the deaths of 290 civilians and an attempted cover-up, Rogers was awarded the Legion of Merit, while Lieutenant Commander Scott E. Lustig, the ship's weapons and combat systems officer, was awarded a Navy Commendation.[47]

The whole disaster was catastrophic and, to Iranians, unforgivable. As the drums of war once again beat loudly three decades later, it became glaringly apparent just how avoidable such tragedies were, and how little had been learned since that fateful morning.

* * *

As 2019 approached its end, the tinderbox in the Persian Gulf triggered a sudden recalculation on the part of the UAE and Saudi Arabia, both of which had been encouraging Trump to take a more aggressive stance against Iran. According to Trita Parsi, Trump's failure to attack Iran after it shot down the American drone 'made clear that Trump was not going to go to war with Iran on their [the UAE and Saudi Arabia's] behalf. So, when suddenly the United States is not there to bail you [the UAE and Saudi Arabia] out, guess what happens? You discover how useful diplomacy can be.'

On 27 December, a rocket attack on an army base near Kirkuk, Iraq, killed an Iraqi-American contractor, which the US blamed on the Iranian-backed Kata'ib Hezbollah militia.[48] In response the US killed twenty-five Kata'ib Hezbollah soldiers in bombing raids in both Iraq and Syria.[49] Iraqi Prime Minister

Adil Abdul-Mahdi called it 'an unacceptable vicious assault' and a violation of Iraqi sovereignty.[50] Enraged Iraqis stormed the US embassy in Baghdad in a show of anger.[51]

Even without the US bombing and the embassy flare-up, two key Iraqi cities were already tense—Baghdad, and Basra in the south. For months Iraqis had been protesting their own government, against corruption, nepotism and what they perceived to be Iranian and American interference in Iraqi affairs. In the face of such intense grievance, Abdul-Mahdi, who had taken over the office of prime minister from Haider al-Abadi in October 2018, announced his resignation.

But unbeknownst to many, Abdul-Mahdi had another important role to play until parliament picked his replacement; he was privately acting as a go-between for Tehran and Riyadh. And his contact on the Iranian side was none other than Soleimani.

'The Saudis, who for such a long time rejected diplomacy with Iran, started to engage through the Iraqis,' said Parsi. 'Would it have worked? Would it have been painless? I'm sure it would have been super difficult, but the fact that Soleimani was a critical element of it makes perfect sense.'

Back in the Iranian capital, the crisis in Iraq was splashed across newspapers and television screens. But of the barrage of questions facing the Iranian president, few concerned Iraq's Iranian-backed militia group. Rouhani was asked why, after six and a half years in office, he had not made good on his election promises. Inflation was once again high, the value of the rial to the dollar had worsened, sanctions, although eased for some time, were back in force and worse than ever, political prisoners were either still being arrested or still in jail, and the environment of fear and war, so familiar in the days that preceded his wave of hope and moderation, had once again returned with a crushing terror.

Rouhani's response was quite simple: 'I made those [election campaign] promises during peace time, but we later entered a state of war, one which we did not choose or start.'[52] It was 30 December 2019. And three days later, as Qasem Soleimani took a flight from Damascus to Baghdad, Trump would prove just how correct the Iranian president was.

On 3 January 2020, at 12.36 a.m, Cham Wings Flight 6Q501 touched down at Baghdad International Airport.[53] It was dark and wintry as Soleimani, dressed in a dark blue jacket and trousers, stepped off the plane with two bodyguards, straight onto the tarmac. An old friend, Abu Mahdi al-Muhandis, deputy head of Iraq's al-Hashd al-Shaabi, waited for him with two armoured SUVs.

As Soleimani's bodyguards piled into the second vehicle, the Quds Force commander and Muhandis stepped into the first, driven by Muhandis' chief of protocol and personal driver, Mohammed Rida al-Jaberi.[54] They were headed to Muhandis' house in the heavily fortified Green Zone to discuss some business, widely believed to relate to the growing anti-government and anti-militia protests in Iraq. But what many people did not know was that Soleimani was also carrying a message for the Iraqi prime minister. It was Tehran's reply to Riyadh's outreach. But as the cars sped away, an MQ-9 Reaper drone hovered high above in the dark sky.

Despite Western media depictions of Soleimani as a 'Shadow Commander' and as elusive as smoke, he was travelling out in the open on the palm-lined airport road when the drone fired two missiles into the SUV. A third missile struck the second car, travelling not far behind.

The explosions rattled the otherwise quiet night, sending a huge wave of orange light across the black sky. It was a grotesque pulsing lightshow, so powerful that the Iraqi earth shook beneath. Boom. Boom. Boom.

Without Soleimani's knowledge, his itinerary, closely guarded and shared with only a few people, had been leaked and his movements in the preceding thirty-six hours tracked, as he criss-crossed from Tehran to Damascus to Beirut, back again to Damascus and finally to Baghdad.

Hit by two consecutive missiles, Soleimani's car flipped, the metal buckling and twisting in an intense fireball. Muhandis was pulverised. Soleimani was blown apart, but his face and ruby-ringed left hand remained intact. It was 12.47 a.m.

Found among the bodies were a wad of Iranian tomans, a handgun still in its holder, some car keys and a book of religious poetry.[55] The remains of a US AGM-114 Hellfire missile lay not far away.

Only a few hours later, as dawn finally broke over the carnage, both Iraqis and Iranians awoke to unbelievable news. In Tehran, Mehdi Taremi, a young university graduate, recounted staring at the television in disbelief. 'I was stunned,' he recalled. 'It shocked all of us. I remember thinking, in that moment when I heard they [the US] killed him, we are really at war. That bombs are going to begin dropping. I literally could not move, I was so afraid.'[56]

Taremi was not alone in his fear. Soleimani's death reverberated around Iran, like the chilling shudders and aftershocks of an earthquake. But this time no one was running for their lives. All anyone could do was wait.

It took three days for Hajj Qasem's body to return home to Kerman. He was given a multi-city funeral, which began in the Iraqi capital, before moving through the holy city of Najaf and across the border into Iranian Ahvaz.

There, a sea of black stretched across the Karoun River to greet him. Though many of the mourners had taken refuge on its banks during wartime, many others—dressed in black and walking in procession across the Fifth Bridge, railing to railing—had not even been born when shots were being fired here. They were not even walking when Soleimani was running through these battlefields, cheating death with each step he took. But it didn't matter.

In his simple wooden coffin, wrapped tightly in the shiny green, white and red flag of a country he fought to protect, the commander crossed the river for the last time. Some soldiers never leave the battlefield, even if the war ends. Soleimani was one such man. Here in Ahvaz, hands of mourners reached up to his coffin resting on the back of a truck, wishing to accompany him across the former battlefield with a reverence unseen in recent memory.

Songs of mourning rose from the crowd as they walked slowly along the road. Some had sung these laments before, not far from where they stood, as they saw off other fallen comrades lost to the carnage of conflict. Among the masses, national flags rose in the air; some carried the red flags of the Shia, while others bore Soleimani's image. Men slapped their chests in a well-practiced rhythm of mourning, as the eulogist cried, *'Hajj Qasem, be Khoda, pey basti!* Hajj Qasem, I swear to God, you have become [a martyr]! *Be hame shohada, pey basti!* You have joined all the martyrs!'

As the funeral float crawled through the crowds, men threw scarves, hoping a brief touch upon the coffin would bless them with the martyr's blood. And then from the speaker, the familiar call echoed: *Marg bar Amrika.* Death to America. The crowd chanted back. Though the mourners were shocked and saddened, an unmistakable current of defiance, anger and violation coursed through the procession. *'Ya Hussein! Ya Hussein! Ya Hussein!'* they cried. 'The enemy must hear this city!'

The chants echoed across the river. *'Ya Hussein be labe sardar naoftade hanuz!* "Oh Hussein" has not yet left the lips of the Commander! *Alam az daste alamdar naoftade hanuz!* The flag has not yet dropped from the flagbearer's hand!'

From the battlefields, the general was flown to the holy city of Mashhad, where the gilded tomb of the eighth Shia Imam takes pride of place. More than a million people, dressed head to toe in black, braved the cold to welcome Hajj Qasem. The outpouring was so large, it ran well into the night.

And here, in the dark human sea, a familiar song rose up, echoing through the holy city. A hypnotic rhythm, which decades earlier had accompanied young soldiers as they boarded buses to the battlefields. A song that affected them with an almost trance-like calm as they marched off to the front, and in many cases into minefields, seeking certain death.

'Oh, the army of the Master of Time [Imam Mahdi],
Be ready! Be ready!
The day of judgement is here.
The time of courage is here.'

From the holy city, Soleimani travelled to the capital, where millions more awaited. What was left of his body was not flown around the country in the back of an airplane, out of sight or hidden. His coffin, as well as those of Abu Mahdi and the two other Iranian dead, was lain across the seats in the economy class of normal flights. Although it was a curiosity to other passengers on the plane, apparently even in death, the commander was amongst his people.

On the ground in central Tehran, mourners lifted Soleimani's flag-covered coffin into the sky; in a crush, the devout scrambled to touch it, even briefly. Men openly wept. So too did the Supreme Leader, who himself conducted final prayers over Soleimani's coffin. Ebrahim Raisi stood at his left shoulder, and the president at his right. The last time Khamenei himself had conducted the *namaz-e janaza* had been for Hashemi Rafsanjani. And if Rafsanjani's funeral was the largest since the death of Khomeini, Soleimani's send-off was unlike anything the Republic had ever seen.

On 7 January 2020, Soleimani's body arrived at the Golzar Shohada cemetery in Kerman. The poor boy who had left home five decades earlier had finally returned, a martyr. He was buried in a sea of Kermani warriors, in a simple grave, not unlike those of the departed soldiers that surrounded him. One of those graves belonged to the chemical attack veteran Ahmad Zangiabadi, whose lungs had finally given up six years before—on 18 November 2014, a few months before his fiftieth birthday.

* * *

Not long before Soleimani was laid to rest, a barrage of surface-to-surface missiles began erupting into the sky above western Iran, heading for the Iraqi Ain al-Asad airbase, the main operating base for US troops still stationed in the country. IRGC aerospace commander Amir Ali Hajizadeh led 'Operation Martyr Soleimani' on the ground himself.[57]

According to the Iraqi military, the missiles were fired between 1.45 a.m. and 2.15 a.m. The IRGC confirmed thirteen missiles struck Ain al-Asad, while another launched toward the Erbil airbase also hit its target. By all accounts, it was the first direct engagement between Iranian and American troops since the naval battles in the Persian Gulf three decades before.

By 4 a.m. it was over.[58] It was by no means an attempt at slaughter; in fact Iran's leaders had told the Iraqi prime minister about the impending strikes to give him time to clear Iraqi and US troops from the area. According to Hajizadeh, the intention was to damage infrastructure and send a message. This claim was backed up by soldiers on the ground, including an American lieutenant colonel, who said his superiors had given him 'a couple hours of advance warning' to evacuate from their sleeping quarters and take shelter in fortified bunkers.[59]

Although Trump dismissed Iranian reports of any US casualties or injuries, in the weeks that followed, a clearer picture emerged. The Pentagon eventually confirmed at least 110 US service members had suffered traumatic brain injuries, and thirty-five had to be flown to Germany for treatment.[60]

MA CHEGOONE MA SHODIM?

Between the death of Soleimani and the missile strikes, a paralysing mix of sadness, anger and fear had infected Iran. And for three excruciating days, the sickening tension cut through everyday life. There was nowhere to hide from talk of the assassination. Everyday happenings were suddenly punctuated with confusion about what had transpired, how and why? And after the barrage of missiles hit the Iraqi bases, the uncertainty of what was to come had erupted into an angry serpent, twisting and lurching in the pits of stomachs, an agony of grim anticipation, sweaty skin, chills and nervous fever. As Taremi had said, 'we are really at war'.

At the same time as US and Iraqi troops were starting to come out of their bunkers, Sheida Shadkhoo was passing through passport control at Imam Khomeini Airport. It was dark and cold by the time she boarded Ukraine International Airlines Flight PS752 with 176 other passengers and crew, of whom 147 were Iranian. Like Shadkhoo, most of the plane's passengers would continue on to Toronto after a brief connection in Kiev. It was at the airport that most of the passengers learned about the missile strikes on Iraq.

As the chemist took her seat on the busy Boeing 737, she felt a wave of sadness at leaving people behind. Her trip to Tehran had been short, only three weeks to see her mother and her sisters, who still lived in the Iranian capital, while Shadkhoo had for the past several years lived in Toronto with her husband. From her plane seat, she was overcome with a sense of doom, which she decided to share on Instagram. In her last post, the forty-one-year-old wrote over a solemn selfie, 'I'm leaving but ... what's behind me worries me. Behind me, behind me. I'm scared for the people behind me.'[61]

Mitra Jonoobi, a friend of Shadkhoo back in Toronto, said they had been texting before the plane took off. Shadkhoo had sent a message to say that she and other passengers were nervous because of the missile attacks earlier that day. 'She told us every-body is frightened, and some of the people are crying because of the situation in the area,' Jonoobi told a local Canadian paper. 'I told her, "Please leave the airplane, tonight is very dangerous. The sky is full of missiles."'[62]

Before take-off, Shadkhoo had also spoken to her husband, Hassan, in Toronto. 'She wanted me to assure her that there wasn't going to be a war,' Hassan said.[63] 'I told her not to worry. Nothing is going to happen,' he recalled with devastation. 'She said, "OK. They're telling me to turn off my phone... goodbye." That was it.'

As the flight took off into the chilly Tehran night, not far away an IRGC base was on high alert. It was 6.10 a.m. Since the kill-ing of Soleimani and that morning's missile strikes, they had noticed more air traffic than usual, in particular US jets circling around the Persian Gulf and Iraq. One report came from defence command, alerting operators at the base that American war-planes had taken off from the United Arab Emirates and that cruise missiles were headed toward Iran.[64] The report was a false alarm, but soldiers were bracing themselves for US strikes.

They took the prospect so seriously that the military issued a new clearance protocol for civilian flights, so that only aircrafts that had been identified and cleared by defence would be given permission for take-off. Until then, the civil sector had had that responsibility. The change would ensure 'the correct identifica-tion of civil flights by the defense network and avoiding targeting them by mistake.'[65]

At the IRGC base, just a few kilometres away from the air-port, one of the anti-aircraft defence units had been relocated. But its operators had not correctly calibrated its alignment, and unbeknownst to the officers in charge, the target reading on its radar system was 107 degrees off its true location.

Three minutes after Flight 752 ascended into the sky, it flick-ered onto the defence radar system. The IRGC officer noted that the plane was off course and heading towards the base. In reality, the plane was actually headed straight and on its usual course to Kiev. The officer called in the aircraft's specifications to the air defence coordination centre to check its identity. A preliminary investigation shows the message was not received, and so the officer, assessing the information in front of him, determined the aircraft was a threat rather than a passenger plane. Four minutes after PS752 took off, and still without a response from the coordination centre, the officer fired an anti-aircraft missile, even though according to procedure, if the 'defence system operator cannot establish communication with the Coordination Center and does not receive the fire command, they are not authorized to fire.'[66]

The first missile ruptured the airplane's communications system, leaving the pilots unable to radio for help. The black box recorders reveal they had tried to control the damaged plane and that passengers, although it is unknown how many, were still alive. From the ground the soldier watched the plane continue to fly. He fired a second missile. Barely twenty-five seconds had passed. Some locals who were heading to work in those early hours saw the explosion in the sky. Although the plane had been hit with two missiles and was on fire, the pilots had managed to turn it back towards Imam Khomeini Airport. It flew for another fifty seconds before it finally exploded in mid-air.[67]

Against the dark sky, the fireball hurtled towards the earth like a comet. Around it, pieces of bodies began falling, like little grotesque raindrops, mingling in a moment of horrific fate that brought so many souls together. Unlike the scattering of ashes, what was left of somebody's beloved fell back to the earth without ceremony or reverence. It was 6.18 a.m.

Those who arrived first at the scene—locals, rescue workers and journalists—walked through the still smouldering debris field, dazed. The plane had first crashed into a playground in

Khalajabad near Shahedshahr and exploded on impact. Its speed caused what was left of the wreckage to bounce and career for hundreds of metres. The metal angrily tore at the earth and propelled pieces of the plane and its passengers across the playground, football field and an adjoining farm.

As the wintry grey dawn broke across the vast grim expanse, photojournalist Ahmad Halabisaz gingerly surveyed the scene. When his phone had beeped with news earlier that morning, he read the words across the screen unbelievingly. 'The Iraq attacks, then I hear a plane has crashed. I thought for sure we were at war,' he said. He drove from the capital out to the scene under such intense stress that he 'couldn't even concentrate on the road.'[68]

At the crash site, a passport, burnt at the edge, fluttered in the breeze. Elsewhere, a wallet lay open, revealng that its owner had carefully tucked inside a photo of a child. Halabisaz inspected what was left of a silver laptop. Nearby, the scattered contents of a makeup bag lay strewn on the brown dirt, in a broken array of colours. Blue, pink, red. Its owner in life clearly held a fondness for riotous hues.

Halabisaz had covered many catastrophes in his fifteen-year career, both natural disasters and those that were manmade, like wars in Iraq and Afghanistan. He'd also been to the sites of at least four major plane crashes in Iran. But the wreckage in front of him was unlike anything he'd ever seen. 'It stunned even me,' he said, 'there was nothing left. Just pieces. Little pieces everywhere.' As he traversed a drainage ditch to walk further into the field of wreckage, he trod on a small piece of the plane's twisted metal. It tore into his foot.

With his foot wrapped in a makeshift bandage from a Red Crescent volunteer, Halabisaz, still bleeding heavily, continued to work. Every click of the camera, the documentation of the end of so much innocence, was like a self-inflicted cut, much worse than that throbbing in his foot.

'It was the saddest moment of my career,' he recounted, 'and it pitched me into depression.'

With three stiches in his foot at the day's end, Halabisaz lay exhausted on a hospital gurney. He stared up at the fluorescent lights, which buzzed quietly above. The last year had been one of the worst, but the last three months were almost indescribable. He could not remember another time in his career when he had moved from one tragedy to another without respite or even a minute to breathe. 'Maybe some major event happens once a year,' he said, 'but not like this. It was one thing after another.' In the chaos, the fear, the disbelief and the unbelievable set of circumstances that led to that moment, all he could wonder was, '*Ma chegoone ma shodim?*' What has become of us?

While the public reeled from shock and mourning, and speculation ran rife about the cause of the disaster, senior military figures, including IRGC aerospace commander Hajizadeh, kept the truth to themselves. They did not even tell the president.

According to his own account, Hajizadeh was still in western Iran, overseeing the attack on the Iraqi bases, when he received a call from Tehran suggesting the Ukrainian plane had been shot down, likely by an officer under his command. In that moment, Hajizadeh recounted, 'I wished I was dead.'[69]

A small group of senior military figures, from both the IRGC and the army, agreed to keep the news from the rank and file, believing that if they told the soldiers, 'the ranks would be suspicious of everything' and would second guess themselves, compromising national security.[70]

By nightfall that Wednesday, barely twelve hours after the plane disaster, the IRGC's investigation concluded without doubt that 'the plane crashed because of human errors.' As the commander of the IRGC, General Hossein Salami, later revealed, 'I have never been so ashamed in my life.'[71]

But even then, no one told the president. Government officials with no knowledge of the truth fronted press conferences, denying the growing reports, including those citing US and Canadian intelligence, that suggested a missile had struck the plane. A senior military spokesperson, Brigadier General Abolfazl Shekarchi, called the reports 'pure lies'.[72]

Qasem Biniaz, spokesperson for Iran's Ministry of Roads and Urban Development, contended that authorities believed one of the plane's engines had caught on fire due to a mechanical fault.[73] The minster for roads and urban development himself, Mohammad Eslami, echoed that statement, suggesting witness accounts of the plane on fire supported the theory.

It was not until Friday morning that top military commanders called a meeting and told Rouhani what they knew. The president was apoplectic. Even then, according to reports, they did not want the truth to come out. Military commanders, with thoughts of the November fuel protests, were concerned that a public admission of culpability could lead to further destabilisation. But Rouhani pushed back and threatened to resign if the public was kept in the dark any longer. The Supreme Leader intervened and ordered the government to draft a statement immediately.[74]

For members of the Rouhani administration who had become the face of the public denials, the truth was devastating. Government spokesperson Ali Rabiei had only the night before fronted a press conference and called reports of a missile strike 'a big lie'. He and other members of the government had spent that day frantically calling different officials to try to ascertain why foreign intelligence was pointing to a missile strike. Everyone to whom Rabiei had spoken assured him that the reports were false. According to his own recollection, he had concluded that in all likelihood, the reports were part of a campaign of 'widespread American psychological war', intended to take advantage of an already tenuous situation.[75]

On Saturday morning, 11 January, a Joint Armed Forces statement acknowledged the plane had accidentally been shot down.

It also promised to prosecute those accountable, but Rouhani pushed further. The president called the missile strikes an 'unforgivable mistake' and demanded a wider investigation into the chain of decisions that led to the catastrophe, rather than just the prosecution of the man who pulled the trigger.[76]

The attempted cover-up revealed a number of unsettling truths about the Republic, including how easy it was for unelected officials, including the IRGC, to undermine the government.

As Rabiei himself recounted, 'procrastination and a lack of information [provided to the government] inflicted blows and irreparable damage on the social capital of all of us.'[77] Abbas Abdi, a prominent reformist, told *The New York Times* that when he spoke to Rabiei after the latter had learned the truth, 'he was distraught and crying.' Abdi relates that Rabiei said, 'The whole thing is a lie. What should I do? My honor is gone.'[78]

Rouhani's chief advisor, Hesamodin Ashna, also stated, 'What we thought was news was a lie. What we thought was a lie was news. We were deceived. Beware of cover-ups.'[79]

For most, the disaster provoked anger and anguish. It also triggered a memory for those old enough to remember 3 July 1988 and Iran Air 655. The Ukraine plane disaster stirred memories of a time when war, frayed nerves and the height of crisis led to catastrophic mistakes and bad decisions—the so-called 'fog of war'. Those Iranians who remembered, like Sadegh Zibakalam, looked back three decades and saw history repeat itself. But to him, there was one depressing discrepancy:

> The situation in which the Ukrainian plane was targeted was not dissimilar to the situation of our Airbus [Flight 655]. The only difference is that the Americans immediately acknowledged their tragic mistake. But we lied to the world and people for three days, and our propagandists delivered a series of conspiracy theories to the people.[80]

Others went further, including one of Iran's most popular actresses, Taraneh Alidoosti, star of lauded films such as *Darbaraye*

Elly (About Elly) in 2009 and Asghar Farhadi's Oscar-winning *Forooshande* (The Salesman) in 2016. Alidoosti, who two years earlier had refused to travel to the Academy Awards in protest of Trump's upcoming 'racist' Muslim ban, posted a black picture on her Instagram account next to the words, 'I struggled with this idea for a long time and I did not want to accept it: We are not citizens. We never were. We are captives, millions of captives.'[81]

* * *

Two and a half months later, Iran was preparing for Norooz, the Persian New Year. The arrival of spring, marked by the equinox, was the most treasured time in Iranian life and lore. Norooz, literally meaning 'new day', predated Islam and transcended earthly politics.

Signs of ritual could be seen in every alley, street or dead-end. Freshly washed Persian carpets dried in the sun; others had been slung over walls while their owners beat them with wooden brooms in a rhythmic exorcism of dust. Flowery chador-clad women, trousers rolled up to their knees, washed down pathways and paved yards. Inside homes, walls were scrubbed from ceiling to floor, while expert hands washed windows, from which dribbled little rivers of the city's black grimy breath. It was the time of *khan-e tekani*, literally 'shaking the house'—an Iranian version of spring cleaning.

The ritual of *khan-e tekani* is to shake away the stains, both literally and figuratively, of the passing year, to renew spaces and bring forth new life. New clothes, new flowers, a new year. It was a tradition that the forebearers of this land had passed down for millennia. And beyond Iran's borders, millions of others whose ancestors had once belonged to the old empire practiced it too.

But that Norooz, no amount of scrubbing or cleaning could wash away the traumas that had led them there.

Halabisaz, the photographer, was planning to spend his holidays with his parents on the Caspian Sea, like millions of others.

He desperately needed to clear his head of the seemingly endless tragedies he had witnessed. Since the plane disaster he had found it difficult to work with the same type of detachment he usually relied on to do his job.

'I used to be a calm person,' the soft-spoken Mashhadi man recounted. 'People around me always told me it was as though I was connected to a source of peace. But for the first time, I could feel the weight of the stress in my life.'

But a new disease was beginning to spread, like the poisonous tentacles of an octopus, and those plans evaporated.

The new coronavirus was first officially detected in China's Wuhan city in December 2019, before it quickly spread across the world.[82] By the end of February 2021, Covid-19 had infected more than 100 million people across the world and caused more than 2.5 million deaths, and counting.[83]

In Iran, the first reported fatalities were in the seminary city of Qom.[84] Attracting millions of visitors from across the region, including Iraq and Afghanistan, as well as those from other areas of Iran, the city was an important religious destination. But the close human contact, the prevalence of hands grasping at or kissing the tomb of Fatemeh Masoumeh and the many sweaty foreheads pressed against the metal, as breath mingled in the air in prayer, provided the perfect incubator for an outbreak.

Before long, the virus had spread to the capital.

As Iranians prepared for the New Year, the government implored people, in particular Tehranis, to abandon the traditional exodus from the capital to the country's northern provinces.

While millions complied, millions of others ignored the advice and headed to the Caspian Sea, taking Covid-19 with them. And by the time the government imposed restrictions on movement a month later, it was too late.[85]

Coronavirus had travelled the length and breadth of Iran. It was not only average citizens who fell ill; many swathes of officials did too, including at least twenty-three MPs, Vice President Masoumeh Ebtekar, Ali Larijani, Assembly of Experts member Ayatollah Hashem Bathaie Golpayegani and foreign affairs advisor Hossein Sheikholeslam.[86] Golpayegani and Sheikholeslam died soon after.

In Tehran, Halabisaz had resolved to stay home and not go out to take pictures. 'After a few days though,' he said, 'I went out. I had to. It was my job. So, I just took pictures around Tehran.'[87]

It was a strange landscape, which seemed caught somewhere between life and death. And even with the comfort of his heavy camera, clicking at the half-empty city and its remaining residents, he was struggling. 'I was trying to control the accumulated stress of the past months,' he remembered. He spoke slowly, choosing his words with the same attention with which he framed his photographs. 'But I live alone, so I couldn't talk to anyone.'

Even though the government lockdown only lasted a month, nothing had returned to normal. Cases were still rising; so too were deaths. And the North of Iran, where so many Tehranis had gone for Norooz, had become the new Iranian epicentre of the pandemic.

Rouhani had been highly criticised for not immediately locking down hotspot cities or at least shutting the shrines at the first sign of outbreak, even though the powerful seminaries opposed the idea. But there were two other realities that seemed to prevent action, according to an advisor close to the government. 'They [the government] didn't have the money to provide for people who would no longer be able to work if they were forced to stay home,' said the advisor from Tehran.[88] And only months after the violent fuel subsidy protests, the government was afraid that 'further economic disruption may cause a repeat of civil unrest. The situation was tenuous.'

Irrespective of the economic malaise, Abshenas was less forgiving. 'All in all, Rouhani's management was a disaster, and many Iranians believe that this is the worst administration Iran has faced in a century. His management decisions in the coronavirus pandemic weren't much better than those his government made in other areas.'

With the virus detected in all provinces, the focus turned to fighting Covid-19, for which there was not yet a vaccine or a cure. But again, conditions for this were not ideal.

According to the EU's foreign policy chief Josep Borrell, who took over from Federica Mogherini in December 2019, 'the problem is the capacity of Iran to have the capital ... to buy, to pay for the resources they need in order to fight against the coronavirus. ... They have needs they cannot fulfil due to the fact that they don't have the capital required.'[89]

And so, for the first time in nearly six decades, Iran applied for a five-billion-dollar emergency loan from the IMF, as part of the Fund's Rapid Financing Initiative.[90] But even in a time of global pandemic, with deaths in Iran mounting and the virus having spread to neighbouring countries like Afghanistan with devastating effect, the Trump administration was unrelenting.[91]

Rouhani was emphatic. 'All members agreed but America does not allow the payment of this loan [which will be used] for providing medicine, vaccines, and health services [to Iranians]. ... The White House today has no sense of humanity.'[92]

Three months after the beginning of the outbreak, Halabisaz left the capital and took in his first breaths of clean air in a long while amid the forests and mountains of Mazandaran Province. As he drove along its twisting roads, a little cemetery emerged. There beside a freshly dug grave, a man dressed in a suit cried with an unearthly anguish. His wife had died of Covid-19. Instead of keeping his distance, as was protocol at Covid-19 funerals, the man gripped the white shroud that wrapped his beloved wife's body and lowered her into the earth himself.

It would be the third funeral Halabisaz witnessed that day. Nearby he watched the volunteer cleric, who had performed the funeral rites in protective clothing, head to his car. As the man removed his gloves and mask and opened the trunk, Halabisaz could see more medical clothing inside. The cleric was just one of hundreds if not thousands across the country who had volunteered to help both the bereaved and the departed. And in those terrible times, his days were full.

Behind the mortuary temple, the grave diggers too were exhausted. One, dressed head to toe in a plastic suit, rested against a wall. No-one in these northern villages could remember a time when the cemetery was so busy.

But as the photojournalist went to leave, he noticed a scene playing out only metres away in a clearing in the adjoining forest. 'People were picnicking, barbecuing and drinking, as though the distance between life and death was nothing,' he recalled. It was in many ways the epitome of the modern Iranian experience, where life seems to be lived, sometimes too comfortably, right alongside tragedy.

* * *

As Covid-19 cases continued to rise, with hundreds of thousands in Iran infected and tens of thousands dead, the country's economic fortunes dropped again.[93] Iran's foreign currencies reserves reportedly slipped by $19 billion to $85 billion in 2020, and without a positive trade balance, the IMF predicted reserves would slip another $16 billion the following year.[94]

The president revealed, 'Even more importantly [than the IMF loan] we have so-called friendly countries that have our money deposited in their banks and they do not unfreeze these assets because they say America is applying pressure and threatening them.'[95]

In the very south of the country, in the Persian Gulf, déjà vu had become quite common. As oil embargoes in 1951 and 2012 had made a prisoner of Iran's most vital asset, Trump's sanctions, a global oil glut and the coronavirus had done the same in 2020. Iranian oil production reached its lowest level since the war, while global energy tracker Kpler estimated exports dropped to as low as 100,000 barrels per day in May 2020—a mere fraction of the more than 2.5 million barrels per day it had tracked in April 2018.[96] With nowhere to go, the Republic was once again having to store oil onshore and in floating tankers off the coast of Bandar Abbas. One estimate showed storage numbers had swollen from 15 million barrels in January 2020 to 63 million barrels by June.[97]

And while some commodities could not leave Iran, others could not enter.

As the pandemic forced airlines to cancel flights, one of the key avenues for imports, including unofficial or black-market goods, diminished. In better times, smugglers had fuelled the so-called grey economy, using Iran's many seaports, or working as *kolbars*—Kurdish porters—and travelling over the mountains from Iraq. They brought with them all manner of goods, from the illicit to the mundane. This included medicines, making smugglers a lifeline for millions of people, including Neda Anisi.

Since the Obama sanctions days, Anisi and other muscular dystrophy sufferers had relied on these unofficial imports. Sometimes the smugglers could get the medicines into Iranian pharmacies or marketplaces, like those on Nasser Khosrow; other times friends, family members and contacts had been able to bring them in from overseas trips. But as the Iranian rial sank further against the US dollar, many Iranians could no longer afford to travel outside the country, not even to countries in the region, like Turkey or the UAE. Less travel meant less opportunity for unofficial imports. And then, coronavirus meant no travel at all.

Without stable access to the drugs necessary to counter some of the effects of muscular dystrophy, Neda Anisi had no options left but to watch her health deteriorate. Smugglers were still managing to bring in goods over the border, but Deflazacort was not on the list. Its already high foreign price, coupled with the astronomical smuggler's tax, meant there were few Iranians able to afford it even if they could get it. A pack of twenty pills cost 2 million rial (US$47), or 100,000 rial (US$2) per tablet. And given patients usually take between three and five pills per day, it was an expensive drug for urban Iranians, who earned on average around 35,833,333 rial per month—around US$850, depending on the exchange rate.[98]

According to the head of Iran's Muscular Dystrophy Association, Ramak Heydari, the Ministry of Health itself had not tried to purchase the drug 'under the pretext it is not sufficiently effective, even though fifty countries have already approved this drug' and patients inside Iran, including Anisi, had shown benefits from its use.[99] Heydari said that the real reason was its cost; the government, like the rest of the country's citizens, couldn't afford it, especially as Covid-19 was forcing the Ministry of Health to prioritise its budget to help hospitals cope.

This was how Anisi went from trying to ration medication, in the era of Obama's sanctions, to not being able to take it at all. By September 2020, Anisi had not been able to find Deflazacort for twelve months.

As she explained, 'In order to import this, we [Iran] need to have trade with a supplying country, but because of US and Trump sanctions, the situation has worsened. From the beginning, it was being smuggled in, but now because of the decrease in passenger traffic and the coronavirus outbreak, it can't be found anywhere.'

With a compromised immune system and alternative drugs posing too many side effects, including osteoporosis and obesity, Anisi's life was in peril—not just because of dystrophy, but also because of Covid-19. By the time Iranian officials began warning of a third wave of coronavirus, the young woman, who was already imprisoned by her own body, was forced to lock herself within the four walls of her home. The fear of an illness she had had to live with all her life was finally matched by the fear of a new one.

* * *

Given the year of perpetual crisis, it was no surprise that the 2020 parliamentary elections were essentially a formality.

Unlike in 2016, there was no enthusiasm for these elections, not simply because of the overwhelming atmosphere of hopelessness that had overtaken many people, or even because of Covid-19, but because the Guardian Council had disqualified a large percentage of reformists, including at least eighty sitting MPs. Even stalwarts like Ali Motahari were banned from running. In an atmosphere of maximum external pressure, where it was easy to accept that the US and Iran were at war, the Guardian Council effectively ended political debate in Iran's oldest democratic institution. This was why the major reformist blocs didn't even bother to pretend that the election would be competitive, or even fair, and refused to endorse anyone in at least twenty-two of Iran's thirty-one provinces, including the capital.[100]

As a result, hardliners, including a dozen Ahmadinejad allies, swept the parliament. Barely twenty reformist or moderate MPs remained. Voter turnout was the lowest in the history of the Islamic Republic, lower even than the years when Iraqi bombs were falling. According to the interior ministry, only 42.57 per cent of eligible voters turned out. In Tehran, that number was predictably much less, at 26.2 per cent.[101] The national turnout was a significant drop compared to four years before, when 61.64 per cent of eligible voters had gone to the polls, many emboldened by Rouhani's success with the JCPOA.[102]

But as maximum pressure increased from the outside, the security establishment closed down around civil society, according to prominent supporters of reform like Zibakalam and Laylaz. The militarisation that Rouhani had rallied against in 2013 had seemingly returned, and so too did foreign sabotage.

* * *

The colours of spring, with its new white buds and whispered breeze, dissipated slowly into the hot breath of summer. The cool evenings warmed, and mornings brightened once again. But with Covid-19, it was a strange time. Even in an era of economic crisis and bourgeoning war, the evening abandonment of restless youth, fun, *ab talebi*, melted ice-cream and sticky *lavashak*-stained fingers had been a mainstay in Tehran's neighbourhoods. From the long roads of Jordan Street and Valiye Asr, to Gisha in the west and Nirooye Havaee in the east, summer nights in the capital were for the living.

On one such night, just before 9 p.m., Tajrish Square was buzzing. Despite the pandemic, enough people were out to at least give off the illusion of normalcy. Many of those who dragged shopping carts behind them, or lazily sipped on *khak-e shir* as they window-shopped, wore masks or gloves. But as the last rays of the summer sun dipped behind the mountains, a huge explosion sent shoppers reeling. Inside the small, colourful, winding Tajrish Bazaar, known for its fresh vegetables and crushed spices, people stopped dead in their tracks to listen. In the deepest recesses of minds, thoughts prickled with fears of war. A bombing or missile strike. Many of the lazy shoppers outside had seen it—an explosion not far away at the Sina Medical Clinic on Shariati Street, which sent a huge orange fire-ball and an array of sparks as red as lava into the sky. The heat was so intense that metal started to melt. By the time firefighters managed to put out the blaze two hours later, at least nineteen people, mostly doctors and nurses, were dead.[103]

Fire investigators quickly pronounced that the explosion and resulting fire were caused by a leaking gas tank, but conspiracy theories started to spread, given that only a week earlier a similar explosion, also blamed on a gas tank, had rocked the extremely sensitive Parchin military site in East Tehran.[104] And those fears of sabotage only increased over the next month, as a series of mysterious explosions or fires rippled across the country.

Between 26 June and the end of July 2020, an unusual number of incidents occurred at important infrastructure or defence sites, including explosions at power stations in Ahvaz, Shiraz, Tehran and Esfahan, which caused blackouts; a fire in a shipyard in Bushehr; a chlorine gas leak at a petrochemical plant in Mahshahr, which sickened seventy workers; and, perhaps most interestingly of all, a large explosion on 2 July at the sensitive Natanz uranium enrichment facility, which operated under the oversight of the IAEA.[105]

Some of the incidents were likely the result of aging infrastructure, or, in the case of the hospital fire, negligence, but at Natanz, investigators immediately suspected sabotage. Although civil defence chief Gholamreza Jalali revealed a cyber-attack, multiple reports later suggested the explosion was the result of a bomb planted by Israeli agents.[106]

In an unusually frank assessment, Behrouz Kamalvandi, spokesman for the Atomic Energy Organization of Iran, revealed the damage had the ability to 'slow down the development and expansion of advanced centrifuges.'[107]

Iran had been down that road before more than a decade earlier, when tensions between Iran and the Obama administration had reached crisis point. Between 2009 and 2012, explosions at refineries and gas pipelines in Iran increased fivefold; meanwhile, progress at Natanz had been crippled by the Stuxnet computer virus—dubbed the world's first digital weapon—which was believed to have been coordinated by the US and Israel.[108] At the same time, a massive blast at an IRGC missile facility near Tehran in November 2011 had killed seventeen soldiers, including Hassan Tehrani Moqadam, the much-lauded architect of the country's ballistic missile programme.[109] He was one of half a dozen figures related to Iran's defence or nuclear programmes who had either been assassinated by Israel or died in mysterious circumstances.[110]

A decade later, during another era of out-of-control military escalation, catastrophe and economic warfare, many again smelled sabotage. But although state news agency IRNA speculated otherwise, it was likely that many of the mysterious incidents were not the result of anything nefarious. And yet, the widespread suspicions were proof that perception in a time of psychological warfare was almost as important as reality. Public perception of strangulation, of an enemy abroad and an invisible one at home, increased.

According to Foad Shams, the damage was not limited to infrastructure—it also extended to civil reform. As hardliners increased their hold under the guise of national security, reformists retreated.

'The fact is, the election of Trump directly increased the power of one faction in Iran. But the shadow of war and sanctions is what weakened Iranian civil society,' argued Shams.[111] And reform—Rouhani's long-promised civil rights charter, as well as the release of Green Movement leaders Mousavi and Karroubi and other political prisoners, like human rights defenders Narges Mohammadi and Nasrin Sotoudeh—ended up as collateral damage.

'These issues do not seem to be a priority for Mr. Rouhani and his government,' Shams believed. 'Living conditions have become more difficult, sanctions have become more erosive and people's savings have run out. These problems have become so severe that the issue of political prisoners is no longer considered.'

Civil progress was apparently a luxury for another time.

From the States, Trita Parsi too saw the correlation between internal failures and external pressure. 'You cannot go forward, after having raised people's expectations about a brighter future, and then impose sanctions as the Trump administration has done ... and think that that type of a country would be able to move in the direction of greater political openness,' he contended. 'We just don't have any examples of that in history, anywhere, in which a country [progresses] in a short period of time under massive international sanctions and isolation.'[112]

In the end, hardliners in both Washington and Tehran had won. Although Rouhani's movement of hope and prudence had made progress and offered, even for a brief few years, a reprieve, the administration was damaged beyond repair. He was the 'unluckiest man in Iran', said journalist Rohollah Faghihi. Trump's conduct vindicated hardliners who had long contended the United States was inherently opposed to Iran, no matter what it does. And that was a stick with which they would beat moderates and reformists for the foreseeable future.

Ironically, Parsi suggested, it was hardliners alone who now had the ability to change the status quo:

> The mere notion of striking a deal with the United States is a political nonstarter for someone from the reform camp at the moment ... but I think elements of the right, because of their sheer power, assuming they have the parliament, judiciary and the presidency in 2021, is such that perhaps they will have a greater degree of confidence to do it, because there won't be much opposition to check and balance them.

One person who benefitted from the raised stakes was the former mayor of Tehran, Mohammad Baqer Qalibaf. His self-reinvention as a hardliner was complete, and in May 2020 he was overwhelmingly voted speaker of parliament.[113]

But in the words of one Iranian analyst, Qalibaf was a 'politically ambitious chameleon'. Although he bragged about using violence as Tehran's police chief in 1999—telling a group of Basij in 2013, 'There's a picture of me carrying a stick on a 1000cc motorcycle. I was with [Basij militiaman] Hossein Khaleghi. ... We were there to wipe the streets clean [of student protesters]. We were part of the club wielders and proud of it'—very few people actually believed that he was a true ideological radical.[114]

Faghihi backed this up. 'His actual policy can be seen in his first election win,' he contended. 'His comments actually angered the establishment and he was labelled a liberal. But after the events of 2009, he tried to change his image. In 2012, he was a conservative moderate. In 2017, he was completely conservative, and right now he's acting like a hardliner.'

Regardless of his real political leaning, as speaker, Qalibaf was leading Iran's most hardline parliament since the aftermath of the revolution.[115]

Perhaps it is no surprise that with escalating external pressure, in a break with precedent and tradition, the Iranian parliament's focus was now foreign policy rather than domestic affairs. And even though the legislature has no say in the country's foreign policy—which is the remit of the executive and the SNSC—parliament had become an echo chamber of protest against the JCPOA, the Rouhani administration and talks with the US.

As hardline MP Ahmad Naderi put it, 'Some easily deceived people are talking of talks with the US and its disgraceful president ... as if they have not seen the bitter experience with the JCPOA and have forgotten the tragic incident at the Baghdad Airport,' a reference to Soleimani's assassination. He added that 'negotiating with the murderer of Qasem Soleimani will bring nothing but eternal shame, and members of parliament will never let this happen.'[116]

In March 2019, Ebrahim Raisi had replaced Sadeq Larijani as Iran's chief justice. With parliament becoming a hardline bastion, Rouhani's opponents now headed two more branches of the establishment in the last year of his presidency. However, while Qalibaf had transformed himself into a hardliner, Raisi proved to be much more politically shrewd.

In 2017, Raisi was seen as a hardliner's hardliner and an establishment favourite, who espoused, rather proudly, views that many would consider extreme. During that year's election, Rouhani supporters hated him with a particular vitriol, citing not only the expansive *bonyad* he headed as proof of the cartel-like practices of the religious elite, but also his human rights abuses. The anti-Rouhani protests emanating from Mashhad further lent credence to the belief that Raisi was leading a radical wave against the government and more moderate elements of society, and that once appointed to the head of the judiciary, he would go on to extend this wave by enforcing crackdowns on the press and arrests.

However, 'Since Raisi became head of the judiciary, not one newspaper has been closed down,' said Faghihi in September 2020. 'He has attempted to soften the judiciary's image and is mindful of his own reputation.'[117]

Raisi also continued his election focus on corruption, which remained a hot-button issue among the public. And although part of his focus was the government, which Rouhani claimed was a ploy to undermine his administration, it garnered quite a lot of support from the public. As Foad Shams put it, where once the hardliners had been damaged by Rouhani's ascent and long tarnished with accusations of corruption, 'all political factions have now been discredited.'

But in a time of massive upheaval, pre-dated by years of dashed expectations, for the average Iranians who had had to deal with one tragedy after another, it had become too much.

Rohollah Faghihi celebrated his thirtieth birthday in the midst of this crisis. Born after the Iran–Iraq War and a year after the death of the Republic's founder, Ayatollah Khomeini, Faghihi was part of a generation that was supposed to inherit a new Iran. A brighter future, of peace and opportunity. A new country that hundreds of men and women had died struggling to create, and hundreds of thousands more died to defend.

Instead, the usually optimistic and laid-back journalist had fallen sullen. His voice cracked with frustration, listing the international pressures that he believed had strangled his country and his own existence.

'This is collective punishment,' he said. 'I'm starting to experience it and sense it better in a way that it is hurting me. For example, ten years ago, I couldn't sense the pressure, but right now I'm starting to sense how it's effecting our minds, our hope. A lot of my generation are getting hopeless and it is very difficult to revive this hope. The US government, Obama, Trump, all of them committed an atrocity. They destroyed the youth of Iran. And they destroyed the chance of reform. If Trump hadn't withdrawn from the JCPOA, reformists would have still had time and a chance to advance their plans. After that withdrawal, they had nothing. Nothing.'

Even pilot Hooshang Shahbazi, from a generation known for its resilience, sounded defeated. 'No, no, no,' he emphatically stated, rejecting the idea that the prospects of Iranians might improve, somehow. 'The world doesn't like the politics of Iran. It makes no difference in America who it is, Trump, Biden or Obama. It makes no difference. Trump is not important to us.'

The retired captain contended that while the US was violating international law and conventions with its 'illegal' sanctions campaign, politicians in Tehran also had a lot to answer for. 'Our future will not be optimistic, and nothing will be repaired until we change our politics. Everything is in disarray here. Our biggest problem is us.'

This hopelessness had forced some, like the graduate Mehdi Taremi, to consider leaving the country, even though it was a prospect fraught with problems and anguish. 'The process of getting a [European] visa is humiliating. I can't describe what it's like visiting one of the embassies here and how we [Iranians] are treated,' he relayed with frustration. 'And even if I could get accepted to one of their universities, how would I pay for it with a banking ban?'

Taremi would prefer to stay in Iran, because nothing could replicate a life lived amidst one's own culture, language and people. Those streets and sidewalks, no matter how worn or cracked, were as familiar as the lines on a beloved's face. The sights, sounds and scents, even when startling, were as enveloping as a father's heavy arms. And to hold the earth of home in one's hands, even though it stains fingers and seeps under nails, was to hold one's own history, both good and bad.

When the beloved late Iranian filmmaker Abbas Kiarostami was asked why he chose to live with restrictions in Iran rather than leave his homeland like hundreds of other artists, he likened himself to a tree that was rooted in the ground: '[If you] transfer it from one place to another, the tree will no longer bear fruit. ... If I had left my country, I would be the same as the tree.'[118]

As for the photojournalist Halabisaz, he said, 'We are all just waiting. Waiting to see what comes next.'[119] Whether that was the speculated return of former president Khatami to politics, or even an IRGC figure, like former defence minister Brigadier General Hossein Dehghan, to the presidency, nobody knew. Still, Halabisaz said, raising his eyebrows in thought, 'It could be something hopeful. After all, these are very strange times.'

And even in the crooked alleyways that twist Iranian life one way then the next, Shams agrees. He could still see a sliver of light. 'Certainly, human beings live for hope, and history has shown that Iranians will, in the end, get through difficult times. ... Relying on the strength of its people, Iran has survived worse days than these.'[120]

NOTES

PREFACE

1. 'Report on Iran's Nuclear Programme Sent to UN Security Council', IAEA, https://www.iaea.org/newscenter/news/report-irans-nuclear-programme-sent-un-security-council, last accessed 20 May 2020; 'UN Security Council Resolutions on Iran', Arms Control Association, https://www.armscontrol.org/factsheets/Security-Council-Resolutions-on-Iran, last accessed 5 Mar. 21.

2. 'Recent Media Report on Iran', IAEA, https://www.iaea.org/newscenter/mediaadvisories/recent-media-report-iran, last accessed 20 May 2020.

3. 'The undeclared war on Iran's nuclear program', *The Globe and Mail*, https://www.theglobeandmail.com/news/world/the-undeclared-war-on-irans-nuclear-program/article4210032/, last accessed 30 June 2020; 'Israel behind assassinations of Iran nuclear scientists, Ya'alon hints', *The Jerusalem Post*, https://www.jpost.com/Middle-East/Iran/Israel-behind-assassinations-of-Iran-nuclear-scientists-Yaalon-hints-411473, last accessed 30 June 2020; 'Mysterious explosions pose dilemma for Iranian leaders', *The Washington Post*, https://www.washingtonpost.com/world/middle_east/mysterious-explosions-pose-dilemma-for-iranian-leaders/2011/11/23/gIQA8IsSvN_story.html, last accessed 4 Mar. 2021.

4. Mahmoud Ahmadinejad, as quoted by Reuters, 11 June 2010.

5. Anoushiravan Ehteshami and Mahjoob Zweiri, in Anoushiravan Ehteshami and Mahjoob Zweiri (eds), *Iran's Foreign Policy: From Khatami to Ahmadinejad*, Reading: Ithaca Press, 2008, p. 143.

6. Seyed Hossein Mousavian, *The Iranian Nuclear Crisis: A Memoir*,

Washington, DC: Carnegie Endowment for International Peace, 2012, p. 187.

1. *DAR IN BONBAST* (IN THIS DEAD-END)

1. Author interview with Mahmoud Gomari, Tehran, 25 Oct. 2012. See also, Soraya Lennie, 'Iran's hospitals feel pain of sanctions', Al Jazeera English, https://www.aljazeera.com/video/middleeast/2012/10/201210 3182749176664.html, last accessed 4 Feb. 2020.

2. 'Why Hillary Clinton lost the election: the economy, trust and a weak message', *The Guardian*, https://www.theguardian.com/us-news/2016/nov/09/hillary-clinton-election-president-loss, last accessed 7 May 2020.

3. 'Iran's former vice president jailed for corruption', *The Guardian*, https://www.theguardian.com/world/2015/feb/16/irans-former-vice-president-jailed-for-corruption, last accessed 5 Jan. 2020; 'An Administration Plagued by Fraud and Corruption', PBS Tehran Bureau, https://www.pbs.org/wgbh/pages/frontline/tehranbureau/2010/03/ahmadinejad-and-his-men-embodiments-of-fraud-and-corruption.html, last accessed 30 June 2020; 'Corruption Verdicts Seen As Warning To Former Iranian President', Radio Free Europe Radio Liberty, https://www.rferl.org/a/iran-ahmadinejad-corruption-verdicts-warning/28650926.html, last accessed 27 June 2020.

4. 'Why Iran Pays More for Each Kilogram of European Medicine', Bourse and Bazaar, https://www.bourseandbazaar.com/articles/2019/10/3/mysterious-price-distortions-in-european-pharma-exports-to-iran, last accessed 27 June 2020.

5. 'Section 1245 of the National Defense Authorization Act for fiscal year 2012', US State Department, https://2009–2017.state.gov/documents/organization/200498.pdf, last accessed 30 June 2020.

6. 'Why Iran Pays More for Each Kilogram of European Medicine', Bourse & Bazaar, https://www.bourseandbazaar.com/articles/2019/10/3/mysterious-price-distortions-in-european-pharma-exports-to-iran, last accessed 4 Mar. 2021.

7. 'Clinton: West Wants to "Pressure" Iran Regime, but Spare Its Citizens', Haaretz, https://www.haaretz.com/1.5081715, last accessed 20 June 2020.

8. 'Sanctions, government blamed for Iran's drugs shortage', Reuters, https://www.reuters.com/article/us-iran-medicine/sanctions-government-blamed-for-irans-drugs-shortage-idUSBRE8B40NM20121205, last accessed 30 June 2020.

9. 'CNBC Transcript: Mike Pompeo, U.S. Secretary of State', CNBC, https://www.cnbc.com/2019/05/13/cnbc-transcript-mike-pompeo-us-secretary-of-state.html, last accessed 14 May 2020; 'How Europe Could Blunt U.S. Iran Sanctions Without Washington Lifting A Finger', Foreign Policy, https://foreignpolicy.com/2018/12/03/how-europe-can-blunt-u-s-iran-sanctions-without-washington-raising-a-finger-humanitarian-spv/, last accessed 17 May 2020.

10. Author interview with a Mahak Charity volunteer, Tehran, 15 Mar. 2013.

11. Kasra Naji, *Ahmadinejad: The Secret History of Iran's Radical Leader*, London: I.B. Tauris, 2007.

12. Ibid., p. 233.

13. Saïd Amir Arjomand, *After Khomeini: Iran Under His Successors*, London: Oxford University Press, 2009, p. 160.

14. Author interview with Saeed Laylaz, Tehran, 7 Nov. 2013. See also, Soraya Lennie, 'Iran Policy Rouhani', Al Jazeera English, https://www.youtube.com/watch?v=2BwBQ9FEtPs, last accessed 8 Feb. 2020.

15. 'Riots erupt in Tehran over "stolen" election', https://www.theguardian.com/world/2009/jun/13/iran-mahmoud-ahmadinejad-riots-tehran-election, last accessed 8 Feb. 2020.

16. 'IMF Survey: Iran to Cut Oil Subsidies in Energy Reform', International Monetary Fund, https://www.imf.org/en/News/Articles/2015/09/28/04/53/soint092810a, last accessed 3 June 2020.

17. Author interview with Hossein Arooni, Tehran, 10 Mar. 2013. See also, Soraya Lennie, 'Sanctions-hit Iran suburb braces for vote', Al Jazeera English, https://www.aljazeera.com/video/middleeast/2013/03/2013314183950494485.html, last accessed 3 June 2020.

18. 'Iran's Ahmadinejad scoffs at Western sanction', Al Jazeera English, https://www.aljazeera.com/news/middleeast/2013/01/2013122164856324864.html, last accessed 3 June 2020.

19. 'Iran sacks sole female minister Dastjerdi from health post', BBC News,

https://www.bbc.com/news/world-middle-east-20853142, last accessed 6 Feb. 2020.

20. General Information, Central Bank of the Islamic Republic of Iran, https://www.cbi.ir/page/GeneralInformation.aspx, last accessed 6 Feb. 2020.

21. 'The Sacking Of Marzieh Vahid Dastjerdi And The State Of The Opposition In Iran', *International Business Times*, https://www.ibtimes.com/sacking-marzieh-vahid-dastjerdi-state-opposition-iran-977744, last accessed 6 Feb. 2020.

22. 'Iran under sanctions: no money for medicine but luxury cars aplenty', *The Guardian*, https://www.theguardian.com/world/iran-blog/2015/aug/26/iran-medicine-money-to-buy-porsche-maserati, last accessed 8 June 2020.

23. 'Iran tycoon's death sentence feeds perceptions of high-level corruption', Reuters, https://www.reuters.com/article/us-iran-economy-zanjani-insight/iran-tycoons-death-sentence-feeds-perceptions-of-high-level-corruption-idUSKCN0WJ1KM, last accessed 7 June 2020.

24. 'Tussle over Iran central bank governor', *Financial Times*, https://www.ft.com/content/436c960e-63d7-11e2-af8c-00144feab49a, last accessed 20 Jan. 2020.

25. *Aghazadeh* is a pejorative term for the children of rich establishment officials.

26. 'Millionaire Mullahs', Forbes, https://www.forbes.com/global/2003/0721/024.html#7c9c89454108, last accessed 9 Feb. 2020.

27. 'The Battle of Dubai: The United Arab Emirates and the U.S.-Iran Cold War', Carnegie Endowment for International Peace, https://carnegieendowment.org/files/dubai_iran.pdf, last accessed 8 Mar. 2020. 'Tourism Performance Report', Dubai Tourism, https://www.visitdubai.com/en/tourism-performance-report, last accessed 8 June 2020.

28. Author interview with Narges Tehrani, Tehran, 2013.

29. 'Addressing the impact of economic sanctions on Iranian drug shortages in the joint comprehensive plan of action: promoting access to medicines and health diplomacy', United States National Library of Medicine, https://www.ncbi.nlm.nih.gov/pmc/articles/PMC4897941/, last accessed 11 Nov. 2019.

30. 'Access to cancer medicine in Iran', *The Lancet*, https://www.thelancet.com/journals/lanonc/article/PIIS1470–2045(13)70036–6/fulltext, last accessed 9 Nov. 2019.

31. 'Sanctions and Medical Supply Shortages in Iran', Wilson Center, https://www.wilsoncenter.org/publication/sanctions-and-medical-supply-shortages-iran, last accessed 9 Nov. 2019.

32. As of February 2021, Namazi is in an Iranian prison serving a ten-year sentence for espionage. The charges are widely considered politically motivated and are rejected by the Namazi family; 'Sanctions and Medical Supply Shortages in Iran', Wilson Center, https://www.wilsoncenter.org/publication/sanctions-and-medical-supply-shortages-iran, last accessed 9 Nov. 2019.

33. 'Iran Producing 97% of Medicines It Needs Domestically', Iran Front Page News, https://ifpnews.com/iran-producing-97-of-medicines-it-needs-domestically, last accessed 9 Nov. 2019.

34. Ibid.

35. 'Working group set up to tackle medicine imports problem', *Tehran Times*, https://www.tehrantimes.com/news/426839/Working-group-set-up-to-tackle-medicine-imports-problem, last accessed 9 Nov. 2019.

36. Reporter notes, Iran 2012–2014. This was a widespread complaint of doctors and pharmacists during this time.

37. 'Millionaire Mullahs', Forbes, https://www.forbes.com/global/2003/0721/024.html#7c9c89454108, last accessed 30 June 2020.

38. 'Son of Iran's former president gets 15 years in jail', *The Guardian*, https://www.theguardian.com/world/2015/mar/15/son-of-irans-former-president-gets-15-years-in-jail, last accessed 9 May 2020.

39. 'WHO Model List of Essential Medicines', World Health Organization, http://whqlibdoc.who.int/hq/2011/a95053_eng.pdf, last accessed 30 June 2020.

40. 'United Nations Security Council Resolution 1929 (2010)', UNSC, https://www.iaea.org/sites/default/files/unsc_res1929–2010.pdf, last accessed 22 Apr. 2020.

41. Interview with Fatemeh Hashemi, Tehran, 25 Oct 2012. See also, Soraya Lennie, 'Iran's hospitals feel pain of sanctions', Al Jazeera English, https://www.aljazeera.com/video/middleeast/2012/10/20121 03182749176664.html, last accessed 22. Apr. 2020.

42. 'Ahmadinejad UN General Assembly Speech Full Transcript (26 September 2012)', http://www.europarl.europa.eu/meetdocs/2009_ 2014/documents/d-ir/dv/ahmadinejad_un_sep_20/ahmadinejad_un_ sep_2012.pdf, last accessed 30 June 2020.

43. 'In Iran, sanctions take toll on the sick', *The Washington Post*, https:// www.washingtonpost.com/world/middle_east/sanctions-take-toll-on-irans-sick/2012/09/04/ce07ee2c-f6b2–11e1–8253–3f495ae70650_story. html, last accessed 30 Apr. 2020.

44. 'Obama to UN: "Time Is Not Unlimited" On Dealing With Iran Diplomatically', Business Insider, https://www.businessinsider.com. au/obama-un-speech-general-assembly-2012–9, last accessed 11 Nov. 2020.

45. Reporter notes, Sept. 2012.

46. Author interview with Hooshang Shahbazi, by phone, 9 Sept. 2020.

47. 'Executive Order 12959—Prohibiting Certain Transactions With Respect to Iran', Federal Register, Vol. 60. No. 89, https://www.treasury.gov/resource-center/sanctions/Documents/12959.pdf, last accessed 30 June 2020.

48. 'Iran's Aging Airliner Fleet Seen as Faltering Under U.S. Sanctions', *The New York Times*, https://www.nytimes.com/2012/07/14/world/ middleeast/irans-airliners-falter-under-sanctions.html, last accessed 4 Mar. 2021.

49. 'Hero pilot rewarded with ban for safely landing plane', *The Independent*, https://www.independent.co.uk/news/world/europe/hero-pilot-rewarded-with-ban-for-safely-landing-plane-6255861.html, last accessed 27 Feb. 2020.

50. 'Office of Foreign Assets Control, Specially Designated Nationals List Update', US Department of The Treasury, https://ofac-sdn-list-removal.com/tag/iran-air/, last accessed 26 Jan. 2021; 'Executive Order 12959—Prohibiting Certain Transactions With Respect to Iran', Federal Register, Vol. 60. No. 89, https://www.treasury.gov/resource-center/sanctions/Documents/12959.pdf, last accessed 30 June 2020.

51. 'Commission Regulation (EU) No 590/2010 of 5 July 2010 amending Regulation (EC) No 474/2006', Official Journal of the European Union, http://eur-lex.europa.eu/LexUriServ/LexUriServ.do?uri=OJ:L:2010: 170:0009:0030:EN:PDF, last accessed 30 June 2020.

52. 'The Universal Declaration of Human Rights', United Nations, https://www.un.org/en/universal-declaration-human-rights/, last accessed 4 June 2020.
53. *Tahrim*, Hooshang Shahbazi, https://www.youtube.com/watch?v=uOQZX5cuvdc&t=18s, last accessed 22 Sep. 2019.
54. 'Gozaresh nahiye barresi sanhe morkhe 88/4/24', The Islamic Republic of Iran Civil Aviation Organization, https://www.cao.ir/web/accidents/reports?p_p_id=NetFormGetFile_WAR_NetForm&p_p_lifecycle=2&p_p_resource_id=getFile&_NetFormGetFile_WAR_NetForm_file=U1lNY0JWR0QyU1dRV0tEWW9waC91SjVCQXZKSzl2RGt ZVlBDNnVFV0d2d0tYOFhGbkFkMmVzYSs2ajN3STBvWWJwRk9TZ0JxbEpkLwpnYlBSZi9LUk5nPT0=.pdf, last accessed 3 Sept. 2019.
55. 'Analysis: How Iran's aerospace dream began and ended with the licence-built IrAn-140', Flight Global, https://www.flightglobal.com/news/articles/analysis-how-iran39s-aerospace-dream-began-and-ended-with-the-licence-built-406044/, last accessed 5 Feb. 2020.
56. 'National Aspiration International Cooperation', *Iran International Magazine*, http://www.iraninternationalmagazine.com/issue_15/text/hesa.htm, last accessed 16 June 2020.
57. Ibid.
58. 'Vezir rah va tarabri: 14 farvand hayapeymaee Iran 140 amade parvaz ast', Islamic Republic News Agency, https://web.archive.org/web/20120316174512/http://www.irna.ir/NewsShow.aspx?NID=30066195, last accessed 9 June 2020.
59. 'Aircraft Accident Investigation Final Report', Islamic Republic of Iran Civil Aviation Organization, https://reports.aviation-safety.net/2014/20140810–0_A140_EP-GPA.pdf, last accessed 4 Mar. 2021.
60. Ibid.
61. 'National Aspiration International Cooperation', *Iran International Magazine*, http://www.iraninternationalmagazine.com/issue_15/text/hesa.htm, last accessed 16 June 2020.

2. THE WAR WITHIN

1. 'Organisation of Islamic Cooperation suspends Syria', Reuters, https://www.reuters.com/article/us-syria-crisis-islamic-summit/organisation-

of-islamic-cooperation-suspends-syria-idUSBRE87E19F20120815, last accessed 20 Mar. 2020.

2. Author interview with Behnam Sayfi, East Azerbaijan, Iran, 13 Aug. 2012. See also, Soraya Lennie, 'Iran's quake survivors struggle while waiting for aid', Al Jazeera English, https://www.youtube.com/ watch?v=ao2oM1zT99w, last accessed 5 Jan. 2020.

3. 'Vakansh namayande majles be amlakard television-e Iran dar mored zelzele', BBC Persian, https://www.bbc.com/persian/iran/2012/08/ 120813_l39_earthquake_television_majlis.shtml, last accessed 21 Jan. 2020.

4. Mohammad Reza Ali Payam Facebook page: https://www.facebook. com/mrhalloo/posts/377287785674856/, last accessed 21 Jan. 2020. Translated from Persian by Soraya Lennie.

5. 'Ahmadinejad arrives in Saudi for Islamic summit', AFP, https://your-middleeast.com/2012/08/13/ahmadinejad-arrives-in-saudi-for-islamic-summit/, last accessed 12 Jan. 2020.

6. Author interview with Asghar Rasouli, Iranian Red Crescent, East Azerbaijan, 13 Aug. 2012. See also, Soraya Lennie, 'Iran's quake survivors struggle while waiting for aid', Al Jazeera English, https://www. youtube.com/watch?v=ao2oM1zT99w, last accessed 22 Jan. 2020.

7. Reporter notes, Ahar, 12 Aug. 2012.

8. Author interview with Agha Reyhani, East Azerbaijan, 14 Aug. 2012. See also, Soraya Lennie, 'Iran earthquake: Two more survivors found', Al Jazeera English, https://www.youtube.com/watch?v=zIBU4ZEsVPI, last accessed 10 Jan. 2020.

9. 'Earthquakes Iran (Tabriz, Ahar, Varzghan, Heris area)—Update 27/08 Red Cross relief action', https://earthquake-report.com/2012/08/11/ extremely-dangerous-shallow-earthquake-in-the-greater-tabriz-iran-area/, last accessed 10 Jan. 2020.

10. Interview with Javad Behjat, East Azerbaijan, 14 Aug. 2012. See also, Soraya Lennie, 'Iran earthquake: Two more survivors found', Al Jazeera English, https://www.youtube.com/watch?v=zIBU4ZEsVPI, last accessed 10 Jan. 2020.

11. 'Ahmadinejad "invited" to Mecca summit', Al Jazeera English, https:// www.aljazeera.com/news/middleeast/2012/08/201285112432709886. html, last accessed 12 Jan. 2020.

12. 'Saudi King Abdullah and senior princes on Saudi policy towards Iraq', Wikileaks, https://wikileaks.org/plusd/cables/08RIYADH649_a.html, last accessed 2 Feb. 2020.

13. 'WikiLeaks and Iran', *Chicago Tribune*, https://www.chicagotribune. com/opinion/ct-xpm-2010-11-29-ct-edit-wiki-20101129-story.html, last accessed 2 Feb. 2020.

14. Abbas Fallah Babajan phone interview with Masih Alinejad, https:// soundcloud.com/frl-journalist/masih-alinejad, last accessed 23 Jan. 2020.

15. '2005 Presidential Election results', Iran Data Portal, http://irandata-portal.syr.edu/2005-presidential-election, last accessed 4 Feb. 2020. Mehr Alizadeh won the province in the first round of the 2005 election. In the second-round runoff between Ahmadinejad and Hashemi Rafsanjani, Ahmadinejad garnered the highest vote.

16. 'EU Embargo on Iran Oil Takes Effect', *Wall Street Journal*, https:// www.wsj.com/articles/SB10001424052702303649504577496463851879258, last accessed 4 Mar. 2020.

17. 'Iran: New EU sanctions target sources of finance for nuclear programme', Council of the European Union, http://www.consilium. europa.eu/uedocs/cms_Data/docs/pressdata/EN/foraff/127444.pdf, last accessed 4 Mar. 2020.

18. 'Council Regulation (EU) No 267/2012 of 23 March 2012 concerning restrictive measures against Iran and repealing Regulation (EU) No 961/2010', Official Journal of the European Union, http://eur-lex. europa.eu/LexUriServ/LexUriServ.do?uri=OJ:L:2012:088:0001:0112 :EN:PDF, last accessed 6 Mar. 2020.

19. 'SWIFT instructed to disconnect sanctioned Iranian banks following EU Council decision', SWIFT, https://www.swift.com/insights/press-releases/swift-instructed-to-disconnect-sanctioned-iranian-banks-following-eu-council-decision, last accessed 8 Mar. 2020.

20. 'Under sanctions, Iran's crude oil exports have nearly halved in three years', US Energy Information Administration, https://www.eia.gov/todayinenergy/detail.php?id=21792, last accessed 30 June 2020.

21. 'EU begins boycott of Iranian oil', Deutsche Welle, https://www. dw.com/en/eu-begins-boycott-of-iranian-oil/a-16064179, last accessed 30 June 2020.

22. 'Executive Order—Authorizing Additional Sanctions With Respect To Iran', The White House, https://obamawhitehouse.archives.gov/the-press-office/2012/07/31/executive-order-authorizing-additional-sanctions-respect-iran, last accessed 30 June 2020.

23. Mahmoud Ahmadinejad, as quoted in, 'Iran hit by oil embargo and "mismanagement"', Al Jazeera English, https://www.youtube.com/watch?time_continue=4&v=oAibzkz7tvw&feature=emb_title, last accessed 11 May 2020.

24. Reporter notes, Tehran, July 2012: See also, Soraya Lennie, 'Iran hit by oil embargo and "mismanagement"', Al Jazeera English, https://www.youtube.com/watch?time_continue=4&v=oAibzkz7tvw&feature=emb_title, last accessed 11 May 2020.

25. Author interview with Foad Izadi, Tehran, 31 July 2012. See also, Soraya Lennie, 'Iran hit by oil embargo and "mismanagement"', Al Jazeera English, https://www.youtube.com/watch?time_continue=4&v=oAibzkz7tvw&feature=emb_title, last accessed 11 May 2020.

26. Reporter notes, Tehran, August 2012.

27. History of the Non-Aligned Movement, https://mnoal.org/nam-history/, last accessed 15 Mar. 2020.

28. Ervand Abrahamian, *The Coup: 1953, the CIA, and the Roots of Modern U.S.-Iranian Relations*, New York: The New Press, 2013; '6th Summit Conference of Heads of State or Government of the Non-Aligned Movement', http://cns.miis.edu/nam/documents/Official_Document/6th_Summit_FD_Havana_Declaration_1979_Whole.pdf, last accessed 23 June 2020.

29. Sadegh Zibakalam, Tehran, Aug. 2012. See also, Al Jazeera English, 'Did the NAM summit backfire on Iran?', https://www.aljazeera.com/programmes/insidestory/2012/08/201283183424802737.html, last accessed 20 June 2020

30. Mehdi Khalaji, Aug. 2012. See also, Al Jazeera English, 'Did the NAM summit backfire on Iran?', Al Jazeera English, https://www.aljazeera.com/programmes/insidestory/2012/08/201283183424802737.html, last accessed 20 June 2020.

31. Author interview with anonymous witness, by phone, 31 May 2020.

32. 'Iran's Khamenei rebuffs U.S. offer of direct talks', Reuters, https://

www.reuters.com/article/us-iran-usa-talks/irans-khamenei-rebuffs-u-s-offer-of-direct-talks-idUSBRE9160BR20130207, last accessed 22 Mar. 2020.

33. Reporter notes, Tehran, November 2012. 'Panetta: "All options" on the table for Iran', The Iran Primer, https://iranprimer.usip.org/blog/2012/aug/02/panetta-%E2%80%9Call-options%E2%80%9D-table-iran, last accessed 14 June 2020.

34. Author interview with Iranian diplomat, on the condition of anonymity, 2015.

35. Ervand Abrahamian, *The Coup*.

36. Stephen Kinzer, *All The Shah's Men: An American Coup and the Roots of Middle East Terror*, New York: Wiley, 2003.

37. Ronald W. Ferrier, *The History of the British Petroleum Company, Vol. 1: The Developing Years, 1901–1932*, New York; Cambridge, U.K.: Cambridge University Press, 1982.

38. 'BP and Iran: The Forgotten History', CBS News, https://www.cbsnews.com/news/bp-and-iran-the-forgotten-history/, last accessed 7 Mar. 2020.

39. Ervand Abrahamian, *The Coup*, p. 28.

40. Ibid., p. 29.

41. Manucher Mirza Farman Farmaian and Roxane Farmanfarmaian, *Blood and Oil: Memoirs of a Persian Prince*, London: Random House, 1997, p. 184–185.

42. Ibid., p. 184–185.

43. Ervand Abrahamian, *The Coup*, p. 74.

44. Ibid., p. 79.

45. Stephen Kinzer, *All The Shah's Men*, p.110.

46. Ibid.; 'CIA Confirms Role in 1953 Iran Coup', The National Security Archives, https://nsarchive2.gwu.edu/NSAEBB/NSAEBB435/, last accessed 30 June 2020.

47. 'Shah Leaves Rome to Fly to Teheran', *The New York Times*, https://archive.nytimes.com/www.nytimes.com/library/world/mideast/082153iran-rome.html, last accessed 25 June 2020.

48. Reporter notes, Tehran, 2012.

49. 'Oil Backed Up, Iranians Put It on Idled Ships', *The New York Times*,

https://www.nytimes.com/2012/07/05/world/middleeast/oil-embargo-leads-iran-to-disguise-tankers.html, last accessed 25 June 2020.

50. 'Iran's Oil and Gas Management', Revenue Watch Institute, https://resourcegovernance.org/sites/default/files/rwi_bp_iran2.pdf, last accessed 23 June 2020.

51. 'Iran Economic Monitor', World Bank, http://documents.worldbank.org/curated/en/741891483046725613/pdf/111462-WP-P162048-PUBLIC-IranEcoMonitor-12-22-2016.pdf, last accessed 5 June 2020.

52. Author interview with Mohammad Hamiat, East Azerbaijan Province, Dec. 2012. See also, Soraya Lennie, 'Quake-hit Iranians facing harsh winter', Al Jazeera English, https://www.aljazeera.com/indepth/features/2012/12/201212119338578615.html, last accessed 4 June 2020.

53. 'Iran Economic Monitor', World Bank, http://documents.worldbank.org/curated/en/741891483046725613/pdf/111462-WP-P162048-PUBLIC-IranEcoMonitor-12-22-2016.pdf, last accessed 5 June 2020.

54. 'Iran's parliament dismisses another Ahmadinejad minister', *The Washington Post*, https://www.washingtonpost.com/world/middle_east/irans-parliament-sacks-another-ahmadinejad-minister/2013/02/03/190a8c2a-6e24-11e2-b35a-0ee56f0518d2_story.html, last accessed 7 May 2020.

55. Ibid.

56. Some Iranians derisively termed Ahmadinejad's picks the 'rise of the non-intellectuals'—a departure from the Khatami years, when no fewer than seven ministers in his first cabinet held PhDs.

57. 'Killer images', *The Guardian*, https://www.theguardian.com/the-guardian/2005/nov/19/weekend7.weekend3, last accessed 25 June 2020; 'Former Intelligence Minister: "We knew Zahra Kazemi was no Spy"', Iran Wire, https://iranwire.com/en/features/5194, last accessed 25 June 2020.

58. 'Parliamentary report on Kahrizak incidents released', *Tehran Times*, https://www.tehrantimes.com/news/211884/Parliamentary-report-on-Kahrizak-incidents-released, last accessed 25 June 2020; 'Iran's parliament exposes abuse of opposition prisoners at Tehran jail', *The Guardian*, https://www.theguardian.com/world/2010/jan/10/iran-prisoners-abuse-jail, last accessed 25 June 2020.

59. 'Iran's parliament exposes abuse of opposition prisoners at Tehran jail', *The Guardian*, https://www.theguardian.com/world/2010/jan/10/iran-prisoners-abuse-jail, last accessed 25 June 2020.

60. Reporter notes, Tehran, Feb. 2012. See also, Soraya Lennie, 'Corruption allegation causes stir in Iran', Al Jazeera English, https://www.aljazeera.com/video/middleeast/2013/02/201324185550285428.html, last accessed 26 June 2020.

61. 'Iran's parliament dismisses another Ahmadinejad minister', *The Washington Post*, https://www.washingtonpost.com/world/middle_east/irans-parliament-sacks-another-ahmadinejad-minister/2013/02/03/190a8c2a-6e24-11e2-b35a-0ee56f0518d2_story.html, last accessed 7 May 2020.

62. 'Ahmadinejad's Ally Arrested as Fight With Political Family Grows', *The New York Times*, https://www.nytimes.com/2013/02/06/world/middleeast/ahmadinejad-ally-arrested-as-fight-with-family-grows.html, last accessed 7 May 2020.

63. Reporter notes, Tehran, Feb. 2013. See also, Soraya Lennie, 'Iranian president ally appears in court', Al Jazeera English, https://www.aljazeera.com/video/middleeast/2013/02/201322722948871982.html, last accessed 8 June 2020.

64. 'Mokomat Mortezavi be do saal hebs taaziri', Iranian Students' News Agency, https://www.isna.ir/news/96090502697/, last accessed 30 June 2020; 'Saeed Mortezavi dastgir shod', Iranian Students' News Agency, https://www.isna.ir/news/97020200801/, last accessed 30 June 2020.

65. 'Mokomat Mortezavi be do saal hebs taaziri', Iranian Students' News Agency, https://www.isna.ir/news/96090502697/, last accessed 30 June 2020.

66. 'Notorious Iranian Prosecutor Behind Bars ... For Now', Human Rights Watch, https://www.hrw.org/news/2018/04/24/notorious-iranian-prosecutor-behind-bars-now, last accessed 30 June 2020.

3. ROMANTIC REVOLUTIONARIES

1. '1979 hostage crisis still shapes America's hostility towards Iran, says former White House aide', CBC News, https://www.cbc.ca/radio/the-sundayedition/the-sunday-edition-for-february-17-20191.5017

616/1979-hostage-crisis-still-shapes-america-s-hostility-towards-iran-says-former-white-house-aide-1.5020910, last accessed 7 Oct. 2019.

2. Reporter notes, Tehran, November 2013.

3. 'Troops kill five students in Iran riot', UPI, https://www.upi.com/Archives/1978/11/04/Troops-kill-five-students-in-Iran-riot/47528 10306743/, last accessed 12 Oct. 2019.

4. 'Shah Undergoing Cancer Tests in Hospital in N.Y.', *The Washington Post*, https://www.washingtonpost.com/archive/politics/1979/10/24/shah-undergoing-cancer-tests-in-hospital-in-ny/e781c9d4–400e-412f-91cc-a01769319f68/, last accessed 20 Oct. 2019.

5. 'Shah Flees Iran After Move To Dismiss Mossadegh Fails; MOSSA-DEGH OUSTER FAILING, SHAH FLEES Victors Over Reported Coup in Iran', The New York Times, https://www.nytimes.com/1953/08/17/archives/shah-flees-iran-after-move-to-dismiss-mossadegh-fails-mossadegh.html, last accessed 19 Oct. 2019.

6. Mirdamadi led a 13 January 2004 parliamentary sit-in amid a bitter stand-off with hardliners, in protest of the decision to bar a large number of reformists from parliamentary elections.

7. Author interview with Ebrahim Asgharzadeh, Tehran, 10 Feb 2014. See also, Soraya Lennie, 'Q&A: Iran's hostage taker-turned-reformist', Al Jazeera English, https://www.aljazeera.com/indepth/features/2014/02/qa-iran-hostage-taker-turned-reformist-2014210 195439905328.html, last accessed 29 June 2020.

8. Author interview with Mohsen Kadivar, by phone, 25 Feb. 2020.

9. 'Iran "Breaks World Record" For Intelligence- and Security-Related Work', Radio Free Europe Radio Liberty, https://www.rferl.org/a/Iran_Breaks_World_Record_For_Intelligence_and_Security_Related_Work/2054351.htm, last accessed 17 Jan. 2020; Dr Mirdamadi Facebook page, https://www.facebook.com/pg/drmirdamadi/about/?ref=page_internal, last accessed 17 Jan. 2020.

10. The Guardian Council is a twelve-member council of jurists, half of whom are experts in Islamic law and appointed directly by the Republic's Supreme Leader, and the other half of whom are elected by parliament from among the chief justice's nominees. As well as vetting legislation passed by parliament to ensure compliance with the constitution and

Islam, the Guardian Council is constitutionally charged with supervising elections and must approve candidates running for office in Iran's democratically elected institutions: the presidency, parliament and the Assembly of Experts—the body empowered to elect and dismiss the Supreme Leader.

11. 'Iran's Revolutionary Grandchildren', *The New Yorker*, https://www.newyorker.com/news/news-desk/irans-revolutionary-grandchildren, last accessed 29 June 2020.

12. 'Dolat-e Rouhani fashl ast', http://www.mostaghelnewspaper.ir/paper/post/25630/, last accessed 29 June 2020.

13. 'Rafsanjani's daughter urges Iran to separate religion, politics', Agencia EFE, https://www.efe.com/efe/english/world/rafsanjani-s-daughter-urges-iran-to-separate-religion-politics/50000262–3894207, last accessed 12 Feb. 2020.

14. Reporter notes, Tehran 2014.

15. Ervand Abrahamian, *The Iranian Mojahedin*, New Haven: Yale University Press, 1989, p. 38.

16. Ervand Abrahamian, *Tortured Confessions: Prisons and Public Recantations in Modern Iran*, Berkeley: University of California Press, 1999, p. 106.

17. 'Mohammed Ali Rajai, 47 hard-line President of Iran', *The New York Times*, https://www.nytimes.com/1981/08/31/obituaries/mohammed-ali-rajai-47-hard-line-president-of-iran.html, last accessed 17 June 2020.

18. 'Riots erupt in Tehran over 'stolen' election', *The Guardian*, https://www.theguardian.com/world/2009/jun/13/iran-mahmoud-ahmadinejad-riots-tehran-election, last accessed 16 Jan. 2020.

19. Source: Ministry of Interior of the Islamic Republic of Iran.

20. Author interview with Saeed Laylaz, 8 Nov. 2013. See also, Soraya Lennie, 'Rouhani's Iran slowly changing', Al Jazeera English, https://www.aljazeera.com/video/middleeast/2013/11/rouhani-iran-slowly-changing-201311973629451855.html, last accessed 17 Jan. 2020.

21. Ervand Abrahamian, *Khomeinism: Essays on the Islamic Republic*, Berkeley: University of California Press. 1993. p. 3.

22. Ibid., p. 7.

23. Ibid.

24. Baqer Moin, *Khomeini: Life of the Ayatollah*, London: St. Martin's Press, 2000, p. 262.

25. Ibid., p. 262.

26. 'Ezzatollah Sahabi obituary', *The Guardian*, https://www.theguardian.com/world/2011/jun/30/ezzatollah-sahabi-obituary, last accessed 25 May 2020. Sahabi, the son of prominent revolutionary figure and Mossadegh associate Yadollah Sahabi, was an advisor to Khomeini before the revolution. He later served as a parliamentarian. As a revolutionary and then a liberal reformist, he spent fifteen years in prison, including five years under the Shah and four under the Islamic Republic.

27. Ervand Abrahamian, *Tortured Confessions*, p. 210.

28. 'The Good Ayatollah', *Foreign Policy*, https://foreignpolicy.com/2010/02/11/the-good-ayatollah/, last accessed 22 May 2020.

29. 'Montazeri's Letters,' *Cheshmandaz*, No. 6, Summer 1989, pp. 35–37, as quoted in Ervand Abrahamian, *Tortured Confessions*, p. 220.

30. 'Blood Soaked Secrets', Amnesty International, https://www.amnesty.org/download/Documents/MDE1394212018ENGLISH.PDF, last accessed 12 May 2020.

31. 'Grand Ayatollah Montazeri's Fatwa', PBS Tehran Bureau, https://www.pbs.org/wgbh/pages/frontline/tehranbureau/2009/07/grand-ayatollah-montazeris-fatwa.html, last accessed 15 May 2020. Mohsen Kadivar, '*Dar mahzr faghi azadeh, Ostad Hossein Ali Montazeri Najafabadi*', http://kadivar.com/wp-content/uploads/2014/02/%D8%AF% D8%B1-%D9%85%D8%AD%D8%B6% D8%B1-%D9%81%D9%82% DB%8C%D9%87-%D8%A7%D9%93%D8% B2%D8%A7%D8% AF%D9%87-%DB%B3.pdf, last accessed 30 June 2020.

32. 'Grand Ayatollah Montazeri's Fatwa', PBS Tehran Bureau, https://www.pbs.org/wgbh/pages/frontline/tehranbureau/2009/07/grand-ayatollah-montazeris-fatwa.html, last accessed 15 May 2020.

33. 'Crowds gather to mourn reformist Iran cleric Montazeri', BBC News, http://news.bbc.co.uk/2/hi/middle_east/8423319.stm, last accessed 20 June 2020.

34. 'Grand Ayatollah on the Deteriorating State of Affairs in Iran', PBS Tehran Bureau, https://www.pbs.org/wgbh/pages/frontline/tehranbureau/2011/10/dastgheib-and-mahdavi-kani.html, last accessed 22 June 2020.

35. Ibid.

36. Saïd Amir Arjomand, *After Khomeini: Iran Under His Successors*, London: Oxford University Press, 2009, p. 187.

37. Author interview with shopkeeper Agha Reza, Tehran, 2013.

38. Author interview with Iranian journalist, on the condition of anonymity, Tehran, 2013.

39. Kasra Naji, *Ahmadinejad: The Secret History of Iran's Radical Leader*, London: I.B. Tauris, 2007.

4. HOPE RETURNS

1. Ali Larijani, quoted in Abbas William Samii, 'The Iranian Nuclear Issue and Informal Networks', *Naval War College Review*, Vol. 59, No. 1, 2006.

2. 'Is Ahmadinejad making a comeback?', Al-Monitor, https://www.al-monitor.com/pulse/originals/2014/11/iran-mahmoud-ahmadinejad-mashai-election.html, last accessed 4 Mar. 2021.

3. Author interview with Simin Siadat, Tehran, 8 June 2013. See also, Soraya Lennie, 'Presidential race shows new face of Iran', Al Jazeera English, https://www.youtube.com/watch?time_continue=36&v=gIOc jpBKKAg&feature=emb_logo, last accessed 26 Sept. 2020.

4. Author interview with Ali Moqaddasianfar, Kashan, 12 June 2013. See also, Soraya Lennie, https://www.aljazeera.com/economy/2013/06/13/iranian-youth-struggle-with-unemployment/, last accessed 24 Sept. 2020.

5. Author interview with Javad Jamalpour, Kashan, 12 June 2013. See also, Soraya Lennie, https://www.aljazeera.com/economy/2013/06/13/iranian-youth-struggle-with-unemployment/, last accessed 24 Sept. 2020.

6. Author interview with Masoud Rezakhani, Kashan, 12 June 2013. See also, Soraya Lennie, https://www.aljazeera.com/economy/2013/06/13/iranian-youth-struggle-with-unemployment/, last accessed 24 Sept. 2020.

7. Author interview with Hamed Heydari, Varamin, 9 June 2013. See also, Soraya Lennie, 'Economy high on Iran election agenda', Al Jazeera English, https://www.aljazeera.com/news/2013/06/10/economy-high-on-iran-election-agenda/, last accessed 13 Sept. 2020.

8. Author interview with Bijan Ghorbani, Varamin, 9 June 2013. See also, Soraya Lennie, 'Economy high on Iran election agenda', Al Jazeera English, https://www.aljazeera.com/news/2013/06/10/economy-high-on-iran-election-agenda/, last accessed 13 Sept. 2020.
9. Reporter notes, Tehran, 7 June 2013.

5. MR FEREYDOUN

1. 'Hassan Rohani In His Own Words', Radio Free Europe Radio Liberty, https://www.rferl.org/a/rohani-quotes-iran-president-election/25018448.html, last accessed 3 July 2020.
2. 'Voting extended in Iran presidential election', Al Jazeera English, https://www.aljazeera.com/news/middleeast/2013/06/20136142274 2470418.html, last accessed 22 June 2020.
3. A candidate needs 50% +1 vote in order to claim victory and avoid a second-round run-off.
4. According to the interior ministry, in 2009 Ahmadinejad won 62 per cent of the vote. But the results are widely disputed and are thus not considered an accurate representation for the purposes of comparison. Further, to avoid accusations of another rigged vote, an election commission was created in 2013 to oversee the interior ministry's conduct.
5. Reporter notes, Tehran, 14–15 June 2013.
6. Reporter notes, Tehran, 15 June 2013.
7. 'Polls close in Iran's presidential election', Al Jazeera English, https://www.aljazeera.com/news/middleeast/2013/06/2013614184157112307.html, last accessed 3 July 2020.
8. 'Iranians bask in Rouhani victory', Al Jazeera English, https://www.aljazeera.com/blogs/middleeast/2013/06/76466.html, last accessed 3 July 2020.
9. Reporter notes, Sorkheh, 21 June 2013.
10. Author interview with Mohammad Reza Salaami, Sorkheh, 21 June 2013. See also, Soraya Lennie, 'Iran's president-elect's hometown shows influence', Al Jazeera English, https://www.youtube.com/watch?v=rxn WHFdD5bI, last accessed 5 July 2020.
11. *Khatirat-e Doktor Hassan Rouhani, Enqelab-e Eslami, 1341–1357*, Markaz-e Asnad-Enqelab-e Eslami, 2009.

12. Hassan Rouhani interview on IRIB 1's *On Camera* programme, 28 May 2013.

13. Sakineh Peivandi, interview with *Shargh* newspaper, as republished by Tabnak News https://www.tabnak.ir/fa/news/486274/, last accessed 3 July 2020.

14. *Khatirat-e Doktor Hassan Rouhani, Enqelab-e Eslami, 1341–1357*, Markaz-e Asnad-Enqelab-e Eslami, 2009.

15. Reporter notes, Sorkheh, 21 June 2013.

16. Trita Parsi, *A Single Roll of the Dice*, New Haven: Yale University Press, 2012, p. 169.

17. 'Iran names new envoy to IAEA, extending makeover of nuclear team', Reuters, https://www.reuters.com/article/us-iran-nuclear/iran-names-new-envoy-to-iaea-extending-makeover-of-nuclear-team-idUS-BRE97Q0OD20130827, last accessed 3 July 2020.

18. Wendy Sherman, as quoted by Trita Parsi, *A Single Roll of the Dice*, New Haven: Yale University Press, 2012, p. 180.

19. Ibid.

20. Reporter notes, June 2013.

21. Ibid.

22. Author interview with Iranian political strategist, Tehran, Oct. 2013.

23. Ayatollah Ali Khamenei speech, 17 Sept. 2013.

24. Author interview with Siamak More Sedgh, Tehran, 29 Nov. 2013.

25. Author interview with Davoud Hermidas-Bavand, Tehran, Sept. 2013.

26. Author interview with Sadegh Zibakalam, Tehran, Sept. 2013.

27. Barack Obama speech to the UNGA, New York, Sept. 2013.

28. Hassan Rouhani speech to the UNGA, New York, Sept. 2013.

29. Reporter notes, Tehran, Sept. 2013.

30. 'Iranians react to US-Iran meeting at UN', Al Jazeera English, https://www.aljazeera.com/video/middleeast/2013/09/iranians-react-us-iran-meeting-at-un-201392713586327505.html, last accessed 3 July 2020.

31. Reporter notes, Tehran, Sept. 2013.

32. Author interview with Hassan Hanizadeh, Tehran, 10 Feb. 2014. See also, Soraya Lennie, 'Iran rallies to mark 35 years of revolution', Al Jazeera English, https://www.youtube.com/watch?v=IJiwbTJdjBg, last accessed 3 July 2020.

33. 'Iran's Message: There Is A Way Forward', Mohammad Javad Zarif, https://www.youtube.com/watch?v=Ao2WH6GDWz4&feature=emb_title, last accessed 3 July 2020.

34. 'Joint Plan of Action', https://www.treasury.gov/resource-center/sanctions/Programs/Documents/jpoa.pdf, last accessed 3 July 2020.

35. Author interview with Emad Abshenas, by phone, 10 Sept. 2020.

36. Reporter notes, 24–25 Nov. 2013.

37. 'Iran nuclear: Tehran crowds cheer negotiators', BBC News, https://www.bbc.com/news/av/world-middle-east-25083803/iran-nuclear-tehran-crowds-cheer-negotiators, last accessed 2 July 2020.

38. Author interview with Amir Mousavi, Tehran, 20 Jan. 2014. See also, Soraya Lennie, 'Analysis: The impact of the Iran nuclear deal', Al Jazeera English, https://www.aljazeera.com/indepth/features/2014/01/analysis-impact-iran-nuclear-deal-2014119191934456789.html, last accessed 3 July 2020.

39. Author interview with Masoud Daneshmand, Tehran, 19 Jan. 2014. See also, Soraya Lennie, 'Analysis: The impact of the Iran nuclear deal', Al Jazeera English, https://www.aljazeera.com/indepth/features/2014/01/analysis-impact-iran-nuclear-deal-2014119191934456789.html, last accessed 3 July 2020.

40. Reporter notes, Tehran, Jan. 2014.

41. Author interview with Foad Shams, Tehran, 8 Nov. 2013. See also, Soraya Lennie, 'Rouhani's Iran slowly changing', Al Jazeera English, https://www.aljazeera.com/video/middleeast/2013/11/rouhani-iran-slowly-changing-201311973629451855.html, last accessed 3 July 2020.

42. 'Nokia-Siemens Rues Iran Crackdown Role', Bloomberg, https://www.bloomberg.com/news/articles/2010–06–03/nokia-siemens-rues-iran-crackdown-role, last accessed 2 July 2020.

43. Reporter notes and author interview with witness, on the condition of anonymity, 2015.

44. Mehdi Moslem, *Factional Politics in Post-Khomeini Iran*, New York: Syracuse University Press, 2002.

45. Reporter notes, Tehran, Sept. 2013.

46. Reporter notes, Tehran, Feb. 2014.

47. Author interview with Sadegh Zibakalam, Tehran, 11 Feb. 2014.

48. Reporter notes, Tehran, 11. Feb. 2014. See also, Soraya Lennie, 'Iran celebrates revolution's 35 anniversary', Al Jazeera English, https://www. youtube.com/watch?v=b9jmytcNw88, last accessed 2 July 2020.

49. Hassan Rouhani Q & A at Sharif University, 29 May 2013, YouTube, https://www.youtube.com/watch?feature=player_embedded&v= hYwM4Na1HIQ, last accessed 14 July 2020.

6. DELIVERANCE

1. Reporter notes, Dec. 2013.

2. Author interview with Shapour Ehsanirad, Tehran, Nov. 2013. See also, Soraya Lennie, 'Iran economy hampered by sanctions', Al Jazeera English, https://www.aljazeera.com/video/middleeast/2013/11/iran-economy-hampered-sanctions-2013111052729646304.html, last accessed 14 July 2020.

3. Reporter notes, Tehran, Feb. 2014.

4. Author interview with Ramin Rabii, Tehran, Feb. 2014. See also, Soraya Lennie, 'Iran's economy open for business', Al Jazeera English, https:// www.dailymotion.com/video/x1bm0no, last accessed 4 Mar. 21.

5. Author interview with Mohammad Reza Najafi, Tehran, 23 Dec. 2013.

6. Author interview with Ramak Heydari, Tehran, 7 Jan. 2014. See also, Soraya Lennie, 'Iran's medical patients want sanctions eased', Al Jazeera English, https://www.aljazeera.com/news/2014/01/09/irans-medical-patients-want-sanctions-eased/, last accessed 20 Sept. 2020.

7. Author interview with Neda Anisi, Tehran, 7 Jan. 2014. See also, Soraya Lennie, 'Iran's medical patients want sanctions eased', Al Jazeera English, https://www.aljazeera.com/news/2014/01/09/irans-medical-patients-want-sanctions-eased/, last accessed 20 Sept. 2020.

8. 'Could Tehran (Yes, Tehran) Be the Next Aspen?', *Vogue Magazine*, https://www.vogue.com/article/skiing-in-tehran-iran, last accessed 8 July 2020.

9. Author interview with Baqer Kalhor, Dizin, 28 Dec. 2013. See also, Soraya Lennie, 'Iran hopes to unlock tourism potential', Al Jazeera English, https://www.aljazeera.com/video/middleeast/2013/12/iran-tourism-2013122913728490845.html, last accessed 8 July 2020.

10. As of 9 July 2020. 'Properties inscribed on the World Heritage List',

UNESCO, https://whc.unesco.org/en/statesparties/IR, last accessed 14 July 2020.

11. Author interview with Shafi Khani, Tehran, 1 Sept. 2013. See also, Soraya Lennie, 'New hopes for Tehran tourism', Al Jazeera English, https://www.youtube.com/watch?v=CV3PpWjfM6w, last accessed 14 July 2020.

12. Author interview with Morteza Rahmani Movahed, Tehran, 1 Sept. 2013. See also, Soraya Lennie, 'New hopes for Tehran tourism', Al Jazeera English, https://www.youtube.com/watch?v=CV3PpWjfM6w, last accessed 14 July 2020.

13. Kaveh Madani, Amir AghaKouchak and Ali Mirchi, 'Iran's Socio-economic Drought: Challenges of a Water-Bankrupt Nation', *Iranian Studies*, Vol. 49, No. 6 (2016), pp. 997–1016, http://amir.eng.uci.edu/publications/16_IR_Socio_Economic_Drought.pdf, last accessed 23 Sept. 2020.

14. Reporter notes, Esfahan, 2006 and 2013–2014.

15. Author interview with Haidar Ali Taqizadeh, Lake Urumiyeh, 17 Mar. 2014. See also, Soraya Lennie, 'Iran scrambles to save Lake Orumiyeh', Al Jazeera English, https://www.aljazeera.com/news/2014/03/22/iran-scrambles-to-save-lake-orumiyeh/, last accessed 20 Sept. 2020.

16. Author interview with Omid Bonabi, Lake Urumiyeh, 17 Mar. 2014.

17. Author interview with Mohsen Roozbani, Tehran, 15 Mar. 2014.

18. 'Iran's Rouhani rolls back on dam projects', *Financial Times*, https://www.ft.com/content/56704462-ccb7-11e4-b5a5-00144feab7de, last accessed 23 Sept. 2020.

19. Kaveh Madani, Amir AghaKouchak and Ali Mirchi, 'Iran's Socio-economic Drought: Challenges of a Water-Bankrupt Nation', *Iranian Studies*, Vol. 49, No. 6 (2016), pp. 997–1016, http://amir.eng.uci.edu/publications/16_IR_Socio_Economic_Drought.pdf, last accessed 23 Sept. 2020.

20. 'Water Management Demands New Strategy', *Financial Tribune*, https://financialtribune.com/articles/people/3022/water-management-demands-new-strategy, last accessed 4 Mar. 21.

21. Soraya Lennie, 'Iran scrambles to save Lake Orumiyeh', Al Jazeera English, https://www.aljazeera.com/news/2014/03/22/iran-scrambles-to-save-lake-orumiyeh/, last accessed 20 Sept. 2020.

22. Kaveh Madani, Amir AghaKouchak and Ali Mirchi, 'Iran's Socio-economic Drought: Challenges of a Water-Bankrupt Nation', *Iranian Studies*, Vol. 49, No. 6 (2016), pp. 997–1016, http://amir.eng.uci.edu/publications/16_IR_Socio_Economic_Drought.pdf, last accessed 23 Sept. 2020.

23. Reporter notes, Tehran, 2014.

24. 'Iran Inflation Rate (1936–2018)', *Financial Tribune*, https://financialtribune.com/tags/rate-of-inflation-in-iran, last accessed 14 July 2020. The Central Bank of Iran had halved the value of subsidised currency in July 2013 from IR12,260 per USD to IR24,779 per USD.

25. 'GE says U.S. approved overhaul of 18 aircraft engines for Iran', Reuters, https://www.reuters.com/article/us-generalelectric-iran-engines/ge-says-u-s-approved-overhaul-of-18-aircraft-engines-for-iran-idUS-BREA331YR20140404, last accessed 6 July 2020; 'US allows Boeing plane component sales to Iran', BBC News, https://www.bbc.com/news/world-us-canada-26896983, last accessed 6 July 2020.

26. 'German exports to Iran surge after easing of sanctions', Reuters, https://in.reuters.com/article/germany-economy-iran/german-exports-to-iran-surge-after-easing-of-sanctions-idINL6N0SU20220141104, last accessed 6 July 2020.

27. Author interview with diplomat, on the condition of anonymity, Tehran, May 2014.

28. 'In Speech To Congress, Netanyahu Blasts 'A Very Bad Deal' With Iran', NPR, https://www.npr.org/sections/thetwo-way/2015/03/03/390250986/netanyahu-to-outline-iran-threats-in-much-anticipated-speech-to-congress, last accessed 14 July 2020.

29. 'Israel's Netanyahu draws rebuke from Obama over Iran speech to Congress', Reuters, https://www.reuters.com/article/us-usa-israel/israels-netanyahu-draws-rebuke-from-obama-over-iran-speech-to-congress-idUSKBN0LZ0BS20150303, last accessed 14 July 2020.

30. 'GOP senators explain why Iran can't trust America in open letter', VOX News, https://www.vox.com/2015/3/9/8173681/iran-letter-senate, last accessed 14 July 2020.

31. Author interview with Trita Parsi, by phone, 21 Sept. 2020.

32. 'Top Iranian pol: "What the U.S. Congress did was really amateur-

ish"', *Politico*, https://www.politico.com/story/2015/03/tom-cotton-letter-ali-larijani-iran-lawmaker-116104, last accessed 12 July 2020.

33. 'Iran's Khamenei: GOP Letter Points to U.S. "Disintegration"', Haaretz, https://www.haaretz.com/khamenei-gop-letter-points-to-u-s-disin-tegration-1.5336016, last accessed 10 July 2020.

34. 'Iran Calls GOP Letter "Propaganda Ploy," Offers To "Enlighten" Authors', NPR, https://www.npr.org/sections/thetwo-way/2015/03/10/392067866/iran-calls-gop-letter-propaganda-ploy-offers-to-enlighten-authors, last accessed 14 July 2020/

35. Reporter notes from Vienna, June–July 2015.

36. 'Iran nuclear talks could go either way, says John Kerry', *The Guardian*, https://www.theguardian.com/world/2015/jul/05/iran-nuclear-talks-could-go-either-way-john-kerry, last accessed 14 July 2020; 'John Kerry breaks leg in cycling accident and scraps rest of four-stop Europe trip', *The Guardian*, https://www.theguardian.com/us-news/2015/may/31/john-kerry-injured-cycling-accident-france, last accessed 13 July 2020.

37. 'Iranian President: We will stick to our promises on nuclear deal', CNN, https://edition.cnn.com/2015/04/03/middleeast/iran-israel-nuclear/, last accessed 14 July 2020.

38. 'Iran's Zarif, EU say nuclear deal is new chapter of hope', Reuters, https://www.reuters.com/article/us-nuclear-iran-deal-idUSKC-N0PO0UV20150714, last accessed 14 July 2020.

39. Ibid.

40. Joint Comprehensive Plan of Action, https://www.europarl.europa.eu/cmsdata/122460/full-text-of-the-iran-nuclear-deal.pdf, last accessed 10 July 2020.

41. UNSC Resolution 2231 (2015) terminated resolutions 1696 (2006), 1737 (2006), 1747 (2007), 1803 (2008), 1835 (2008), 1929 (2010) and 2224 (2015).

42. 'Resolution 2231 (2015) on Iran Nuclear Issue Background', United Nations, https://www.un.org/securitycouncil/content/2231/background, last accessed 10 July 2020.

43. 'Democrats Hand Victory to Obama on Iran Nuclear Deal', *The New York Times*, https://www.nytimes.com/2015/09/11/us/politics/iran-nuclear-deal-senate.html, last accessed 10 July 2020.

44. 'Parliamentarians Threaten Negotiators with Death', Iran Wire, https://iranwire.com/en/features/1391, last accessed 10 July 2020; 'Jaziat dahdidat ruz gozashte Hosseinian dar gooftegoo 'entekhab' ba yek shahed aani', Entekhab, https://www.entekhab.ir/fa/news/229873/, last accessed 14 July 2020. Salehi was referring to MP Rohollah Hosseinian, a former security advisor to Ahmadinejad and deputy to controversial former intelligence chief Ali Fallahian.

45. 'Parliamentary Drama In Tehran', Lobe Log, http://lobelog.com/parliamentary-drama-in-tehran/, last accessed 14 July 2020.

46. 'Iranian lawmakers approve JCPOA details', Iranian Students' News Agency, http://isna.ir/en/news/94072113595/Iranian-lawmakers-approve-JCPOA-details, last accessed 14 July 2020.

47. 'Guardian Council approves JCPOA amid stormy Majlis session', Islamic Republic News Agency, https://en.irna.ir/news/81801135/Guardian-Council-approves-JCPOA-amid-stormy-Majlis-session, 14 July 2020.

48. 'Zarif, Obama shake hands in New York', Press TV, https://www.presstv.com/Detail/2015/09/29/431217/Iran-Zarif-US-Obama-UN-Rouhani, last accessed 14 July 2020.

49. 'Kousari: Zarif bayad esteezah shod', Mashregh News, https://www.mashreghnews.ir/news/476098/, last accessed 11 July 2020.

50. 'ANALYSIS: Political heckling gone too far in Iran', Middle East Eye, https://www.middleeasteye.net/news/analysis-political-heckling-gone-too-far-iran, last accessed 11 July 2020.

51. Author interview with Emad Abshenas, by phone, 10 Sept. 2020.

52. Author interview with Rohollah Faghihi, by phone, 4 Sept. 2020.

53. 'Iran offers flexible oil contracts to attract foreign investors', *Financial Times*, https://www.ft.com/content/b2f6bf58-95b2-11e5-95c7-d47aa298f769, last accessed 12 July 2020.

54. 'Iran says Peugeot would pay compensation for withdrawal during sanctions', Reuters, https://www.reuters.com/article/us-iran-trade-peugeot/iran-says-peugeot-would-pay-compensation-for-withdrawal-during-sanctions-idUSKCN0VF0F3, last accessed 14 July 2020.

55. 'Iran says Peugeot to pay $446 million compensation for sanctions move', Reuters, https://www.reuters.com/article/us-iran-trade-peugeot-idUSKCN0VG10V, last accessed 14 July 2020.

56. Campaign posters, Majlis Monitor, Twitter, https://twitter.com/MajlisMonitor/status/702229512059113472, last accessed 14 July 2020.

57. 'Hemayate Hashemi az list-e omid', Islamic Republic News Agency, https://www.irna.ir/news/81975406/, last accessed 14 July 2020.

58. 'Davat-e Sayed Mohammad Khatami baraye rey dadan be 'tamami afrad' list-e omid,' https://www.youtube.com/watch?v=lcSYNfNpDZw, last accessed 13 July 2020.

59. 'Hemayate honarmand az liste eslah taleban va hamiyan dolat', Aftab News, https://aftabnews.ir/fa/news/350776/, last accessed 13 July 2020.

60. Ibid.

61. '2016 Assembly of Experts Election', Iran Data Portal, https://iran-dataportal.syr.edu/assembly-of-experts-elections/2016-assembly-of-experts-election, last accessed 14 July 2020.

62. 'Esme 290 namayande majles dahom ba garayesh siasi shan', Khabar Online, http://khabaronline.ir/%28X%281%29S%28gir3jkgiutacpag5xyfhzrof%29%29/detail/531930/Politics/election, last accessed 15 July 2020.

63. 'Hassan Rouhani and The Hope for More Freedom in Iran', Committee to Protect Journalists, https://cpj.org/2014/02/attacks-on-the-press-iran/, last accessed 13 Aug. 2020.

64. Author interview with Foad Shams, by phone, 3 Sept. 2020.

65. Reporter notes, 17 June 2013.

66. 'UN condemns 16-year jail sentence for Iranian activist Narges Mohammadi', The Guardian, https://www.theguardian.com/global-development/2016/may/24/narges-mohammadi-iranian-activist-un-condemns-10-year-jail-sentence, last accessed 16 July 2020.

67. 'Rouhani clashes with Iranian police over undercover hijab agents', Reuters, https://www.reuters.com/article/us-iran-rights-rouhani/rouhani-clashes-with-iranian-police-over-undercover-hijab-agents-idUSKCN0XH0WH, last accessed 16 July 2020.

68. 'In Iran, Gender Segregation Threatens to Reshape Public Life', Iran Wire, http://en.iranwire.com/features/6001/, last accessed 6 July 2020.

69. 'Rouhani deputy slams Tehran's gender segregation plan', The Iran Project, https://theiranproject.com/blog/2014/08/08/rouhani-deputy-slams-tehrans-gender-segregation-plan/, last accessed 17 July 2020.

70. 'Nameh vezarate kar be shardari baraye logho bakhshname akhir fazaee kar mardan va zanan', Khabar Online, https://www.khabaronline.ir/news/367360/, last accessed 17 July 2020.
71. Reporter notes, Tehran, 2014.
72. 'Iran's Gender Double Standards', Iran Wire, http://en.iranwire.com/features/6085/, last accessed 6 July 2020; 'Nam-e hamsar aval ba samt rasmi ezdevaje dovom az shenasname hezf mishavad', Khabar Online, http://khabaronline.ir/detail/376862/society/family, last accessed 6 July 2020.
73. Reporter notes, Tehran, 2014.

7. SABOTAGE

1. 'Why Republican voters decided on Trump', FiveThirtyEight, https://fivethirtyeight.com/features/why-republican-voters-decided-on-trump/, last accessed 15 July 2020.
2. 'Read Donald Trump's Speech to AIPAC', Time, https://time.com/4267058/donald-trump-aipac-speech-transcript/, last accessed 15 July 2020.
3. 'Az hamle mogul be in soo feshari mesl emrooz be Iran vared nashode ast', Aftab News, https://aftabnews.ir/fa/news/659276/, last accessed 15 July 2020.
4. Author interview with Iranian official, on the condition of anonymity, 2016.
5. 'Donald Trump Wins the 2016 Election', Time, https://time.com/4563685/donald-trump-wins/, last accessed 17 July 2020.
6. 'Transcript: Donald Trump's Victory Speech', The New York Times, https://www.nytimes.com/2016/11/10/us/politics/trump-speech-transcript.html, last accessed 17 July 2020.
7. Hamid Aboutalebi, Twitter, https://twitter.com/DrAboutalebi/status/796267655695101952.
8. 'The outcome of the US election has no bearing on the policies of the Islamic Republic of Iran', Iranian Students' News Agency, http://www.isna.ir/news/95081913693/, last accessed 15 July 2020.
9. 'Foreign Minister Zarif of Iran pays a visit to Turkey', Turkish Ministry of Foreign Affairs, http://www.mfa.gov.tr/foreign-minister-zarif-of-

iran-pays-a-visit-to-turkey.en.mfa, last accessed 2 Aug. 2020; 'Meeting with Foreign Minister of Iran Mohammad Javad Zarif', Kremlin press release, http://en.kremlin.ru/events/president/news/page/415, last accessed 2 Aug. 2020.

10. 'US Must Fulfil JCPOA Commitments: Iran's FM Says after Trump Victory', Tasnim News Agency, https://www.tasnimnews.com/en/news/2016/11/09/1235850/us-must-fulfil-jcpoa-commitments-irans-fm-says-after-trump-victory, last accessed 15 July 2020; 'Trump on latest iteration of Muslim ban: "You could say it's an expansion"', CNN, https://edition.cnn.com/2016/07/24/politics/donald-trump-muslim-ban-election-2016/index.html, last accessed 17 July 2020.

11. 'Iran signs $16.6 billion deal for 80 Boeing planes: IRNA', Islamic Republic News Agency, https://www.reuters.com/article/us-iran-boeing-idUSKBN1400CR, last accessed 20 July 2020; 'Iran signs $16bn deal to buy 80 Boeing aircraft', BBC News, https://www.bbc.com/news/business-38280724, last accessed 20 July 2020.

12. 'Minister: Iran Needs over 500 Airplanes in Ten Years', Fars News, https://en.farsnews.ir/newstext.aspx?nn=13950402001358, last accessed 20 July 2020.

13. Author interview with Hooshang Shahbazi, by phone, 9 Sept. 2020.

14. 'Boeing, Iran Air Announce Agreement for 80 Airplanes', Boeing, https://boeing.mediaroom.com/2016-12-11-Boeing-Iran-Air-Announce-Agreement-for-80-Airplanes, last accessed 20 July 2020.

15. 'Airbus seals deal with Iran for sale of 100 aircraft', Reuters, https://www.reuters.com/article/us-iran-aircraft/airbus-seals-deal-with-iran-for-sale-of-100-aircraft-idUSKBN14B1H9, last accessed 20 July 2020.

16. 'ATR signs a major agreement with Iran Air for 40 ATR 72–600s', ATR, http://www.ataircraft.com/newsroom/atr-signs-a-major-agreement-with-iran-air-for-40-atr-72-600s-1377-en.html, last accessed 20 July 2020.

17. 'Iran welcomes Airbus as first post-sanctions airliner', BBC News, https://www.bbc.com/news/world-middle-east-38601510, last accessed 4 Aug. 2020.

18. 'Farood nakhastin Airbus rooye farsh-e ghermez', Hamshahri Online, https://www.hamshahrionline.ir/news/358584/, last accessed 4 Aug. 2020.

19. Author interview with Rohollah Faghihi, by phone, 4 Sept. 2020.

20. Author interview with Emad Abshenas, by phone, 10 Sept. 2020.

21. Author interview with Neda Anisi, by phone, 12 Sept. 2020.

22. 'Hassan Rouhani and The Hope for More Freedom in Iran', Committee to Protect Journalists, https://cpj.org/2014/02/attacks-on-the-press-iran/, last accessed 15 July 2020.

23. 'Iran Accuses Thomson Reuters Charity Official of Sedition', *The New York Times*, https://www.nytimes.com/2016/06/16/world/middleeast/iran-accuses-thomson-reuters-official-of-sedition.html, last accessed 22 July 2020.

24. 'Iranian official calls jailed Washington Post journalist "good reporter" but offers few details on detainment', PBS, https://www.pbs.org/newshour/world/iranian-official-on-jailed-reporter, last accessed 22 July 2020.

25. Author interview with Trita Parsi, by phone, 21 Sept. 2020.

26. 'Martin Baron statement on conclusion of Jason Rezaian's trial in Iran', *The Washington Post*, https://www.washingtonpost.com/pr/wp/2015/08/10/martin-baron-statement-on-conclusion-of-jason-rezaians-trial-in-iran/, last accessed 22 July 2020.

27. 'Iran releases Washington Post journalist Jason Rezaian in prisoner swap with US', *The Guardian*, https://www.theguardian.com/world/2016/jan/16/iran-releases-washington-post-journalist-jason-rezaian, last accessed 22 July 2020.

28. Reporter notes, January 2017.

29. 'Hazoor sarlashgar Soleimani dar Hosseiniye Jamaran, Tasnim News Agency, https://www.tasnimnews.com/fa/news/1395/10/19/1291525/, last accessed 4 Aug. 2020.

30. 'Death of Iran's Rafsanjani Removes Influential Voice Against Hard-Liners', *The New York Times*, https://www.nytimes.com/2017/01/08/world/middleeast/iran-ali-akbar-hashemi-rafsanjani-dies.html, last accessed 4 Aug. 2020.

31. 'Iran's former president Rafsanjani dies aged 82', *The Guardian*, https://www.theguardian.com/world/2017/jan/08/iran-former-president-rafsanjani-dies-aged-82, last accessed 4 Aug. 2020.

32. 'Tashiyeh peygar Hashemi; bozorgtarin tashiyeh pas az rahlet Imam',

Asr Iran, https://www.asriran.com/fa/news/516763/, last accessed 4 Aug. 2020.

33. 'Hazoor 2.5 million nafari mardom dar tashiyeh Hashemi', Bartarinha News, https://www.bartarinha.ir/fa/news/458737/, last accessed 31 July 2020.

34. Data from the Institute for Research and Planning in Higher Education, https://irphe.ac.ir/, last accessed 4 Aug. 2020.

35. 'Rafsanjani Visits Saudi Arabia', Associated Press, https://apnews.com/77430abcda25f8ce15f9d6e9368b4ae0, last accessed 31 July 2020.

36. Reporter notes, Jan. 2017.

37. 'Two Labor Rights Activist Sentenced to 11 Years in Prison for Peaceful Activism', Center for Human Rights in Iran, https://www.iranhumanrights.org/2016/10/jafar-azimzadeh-and-shapour-ehsani-rad/, last accessed 23 July 2020.

38. Author interview with Shapour Ehsanirad, Tehran, Nov. 2013.

39. 'Tycoon Babak Zanjani receives death penalty', Mehr News, https://en.mehrnews.com/news/115017/Tycoon-Babak-Zanjani-receives-death-penalty, last accessed 23 July 2020.

40. 'Pasokh Rouhani be sohbathaye Qalibaf darbareye jame'e 4 darsadi', Entekhab, https://www.entekhab.ir/fa/news/340730/, last accessed 4 Aug. 2020.

41. 'Iran names head of country's wealthiest foundation', Al-Monitor, https://www.al-monitor.com/pulse/originals/2016/03/tabasi-endowment-imam-reza-astan-quds-razavi.html, last accessed 24 July 2020.

42. 'The surprising rise of the head of Iran's most influential charity', Al-Monitor, https://www.al-monitor.com/pulse/originals/2017/03/iran-ebrahim-raisi-presidential-candidate-quds-razavi.html, last accessed 24 July 2020.

43. 'A Deep Dive Into Bonyads and How They Work', Double Think Institute, https://doublethink.institute/report/bonyad-findings/, last accessed 24 July 2020.

44. 'Chera ostane qods, setada jariee farman Imam va bangae haye eghtesadi niroohaye mesleh maliat nemidahand?', Aftab News, https://aftabnews.ir/fa/news/380530/, last accessed 28 July 2020.

45. 'No Tripling of Cash Subsidies', *Financial Tribune*, https://financial-tribune.com/articles/economy-business-and-markets/63783/no-tri-pling-of-cash-subsidies, last accessed 23 July 2020.

46. 'Majles hezf 24 milion yarane begir ra nahiyee kard', Iran Online, http://www.ion.ir/News/68555.html, last accessed 29 July 2020.

47. Pre-election National Opinion Polls, conducted 11–14 April 2017, https://static1.squarespace.com/static/5525d831e4b09596848428 f2/t/58f4035b5016e1718c7b5acf/1492386653025/IranPoll+pre-election+results+2017-4-16.pdf.

48. Tasnim News Agency, Twitter, https://twitter.com/Tasnimnews_Fa/status/863017305114120197, last accessed 4 Aug. 2020.

49. 'The Race: Third Presidential Debate', The Iran Primer, https://iranprimer.usip.org/blog/2017/may/15/race-final-presidential-debate, last accessed 28 July 2020.

50. 'The IRGC Commercial and Financial Institutions: Khatam-al-Anbiya Construction Headquarters', Iran Wire, https://iranwire.com/en/features/5741, last accessed 28 July 2020.

51. 'Taboo-breaking election is test of how much dissent Iran can handle', The Christian Science Monitor, https://www.csmonitor.com/World/Middle-East/2017/0518/Taboo-breaking-election-is-test-of-how-much-dissent-Iran-can-handle, last accessed 28 July 2020.

52. 'Shoma dom az azadi nazanid ke azadi khejalat mi keshad', *Etemad*, http://www.etemadnewspaper.ir/fa/main/detail/74468/, last accessed 4 Aug. 2020.

53. 'Iran's Politics Color Ramadan Prayer Dispute', Radio Free Europe Radio Liberty, https://www.rferl.org/a/iran-ramadan-prayer-shajar-ian-politics-rohani/28516858.html, last accessed 29 July 2020.

54. 'Salam azadi be Rouhani', Iranian Labour News Agency, https://www.ilna.news/fa/tiny/news-488992, last accessed 4 Aug. 2020.

55. IPPO Poll, conducted 17 May 2017, http://ippogroup.com/poll/, last accessed 4 Aug. 2020.

56. 'Pishtazi Hassan Rouhani dar davozdahomin dore entekhabat reyasat jomhori', Iranian Labour News Agency, https://www.ilna.news/fa/tiny/news-490915, last accessed 4 Aug. 2020.

57. 'Enteshar natije tafsili entekhabat reyasat jomhori be tafkil ostan va

shahrestan va nakaat jalebe an', Islamic Republic News Agency, https://www.irna.ir/news/82561684/, last accessed 29 July 2020.
58. Ibid.

8. HARDENING HEARTS

1. 'Sunni rebels declare new "Islamic caliphate"', Al Jazeera English, https://www.aljazeera.com/news/middleeast/2014/06/isil-declares-new-islamic-caliphate-201462917326669749.html, last accessed 14 Aug. 2020.
2. Author interview with Imam Hamour Omar Halil, Mosul, June 2017. See also, Soraya Lennie, 'The Fight for Mosul: The imam who once led Mosul's Great Al Nuri Mosque is alive', TRT World, https://www.youtube.com/watch?v=6Nn1csLOndU, last accessed 14 Aug. 2020.
3. Reporter notes, June 2014.
4. 'How Iraq's "ghost soldiers" helped ISIL', Al Jazeera English, https://www.aljazeera.com/news/middleeast/2014/12/how-iraq-ghost-soldiers-helped-isil-2014121072749979252.html, last accessed 12 Aug. 2020.
5. 'Iran Deploys Forces to Fight al Qaeda-Inspired Militants in Iraq', Wall Street Journal, https://www.wsj.com/articles/iran-deploys-forces-to-fight-al-qaeda-inspired-militants-in-iraq-iranian-security-sources-1402592470, last accessed 10 Aug. 2020.
6. 'Iran sends troops into Iraq to aid fight against Isis militants', The Guardian, https://www.theguardian.com/world/2014/jun/14/iran-iraq-isis-fight-militants-nouri-maliki, last accessed 20 Aug. 2020.
7. 'Dargozasht baradar shahidan Shamkhani, nemad parhiz az tajmol gerayee', Tabnak, https://www.tabnak.ir/fa/news/826928/, last accessed 11 Aug. 2020.
8. 'Obama Authorizes "Targeted" Airstrikes Against ISIS in Iraq', NBC News, https://www.nbcnews.com/storyline/iraq-turmoil/obama-authorizes-targeted-airstrikes-against-isis-iraq-n175201, last accessed 19 Aug. 2020.
9. 'Profile: New Security Council Chief', The Iran Primer, http://iranprimer.usip.org/blog/2013/sep/10/profile-new-security-council-chief, last accessed 12 Aug. 2020.
10. 'Qassem Suleimani: the Iranian general "secretly running" Iraq', The

Guardian, https://www.theguardian.com/world/2011/jul/28/Qasem-suleimani-iran-iraq-influence, last accessed 21 Aug. 2020. Author interview with former IRGC member, on the condition of anonymity, by phone, 2015.

11. 'The Shadow Commander', *The New Yorker*, http://www.newyorker.com/magazine/2013/09/30/the-shadow-commander, last accessed 20 Aug. 2020.

12. Mohsen Momeni, *Rishe dar aseman*, Kerman: Sepah-e Pasdaran Enghelab-e Eslami (IRGC), 2009.

13. 'Iran's Military Doctrine', The Iran Primer, http://iranprimer.usip.org/resource/irans-military-doctrine, last accessed 20 Aug. 2020.

14. Excerpt from, 'Bakhshaye khandani "Hajj Qasem"', Young Journalists Club, https://www.yjc.ir/fa/news/5415423/, last accessed 30 Sept. 2020.

15. 'The Canny General: Quds Force Commander Qasem Soleimani', PBS, https://www.pbs.org/wgbh/pages/frontline/tehranbureau/2011/12/profile-the-canny-general-quds-force-commander-Qasem-soleimani.html, last accessed 9 Sept. 2020.

16. 'Qasem Soleimani; zendegi name farmande Quds Sepah', BBC Persian, https://www.bbc.com/persian/iran-features-50979973, last accessed 30 Sept. 2020.

17. Hossein Ardestani, *Rouzshomar-e Jang-e Iran va Iraq*, Tehran: Sepah-e Pasdaran Enghelab-e Eslami (IRGC), 2003, p. 257.

18. 'Iran's new Quds-connected envoy to Iraq arrives in Baghdad', Rudaw, https://www.rudaw.net/english/middleeast/iraq/190420173-amp, last accessed 20 Aug. 2020.

19. Author interview with Fawas Gerges, by phone, June 2014. See also, Soraya Lennie, 'Analysis: Iran's double game in Iraq', Al Jazeera English, http://www.aljazeera.com/news/middleeast/2014/06/analysis-iran-double-game-iraq-201462694820573703.html, last accessed 20 Aug. 2020.

20. 'France funding Syrian rebels in new push to oust Assad', *The Guardian*, https://www.theguardian.com/world/2012/dec/07/france-funding-syrian-rebels, last accessed 14 Aug. 2020; 'Kurdish leader: No to arming the Syrian opposition', *Foreign Policy*, https://foreignpolicy.com/2012/04/05/kurdish-leader-no-to-arming-the-syrian-opposition/,

last accessed 11 Aug. 2020; 'Obama authorizes secret support for Syrian rebels', Reuters, https://www.reuters.com/article/us-usa-syria-obama-order/obama-authorizes-secret-support-for-syrian-rebels-idUS-BRE8701OK20120802, last accessed 12 Aug. 2020; Author interview with KRG official, Erbil, April 2018.

21. 'Dr. Zarif Speech & Q&A at the European Parliament Committee on Foreign Affairs. 16 Feb. 2016', https://www.youtube.com/watch?v=z FE8RmPrxq4, last accessed 12 Aug. 2020.

22. 'Kurdistan's Prime Minister: We Warned U.S. About ISIS in Iraq Months Ago', NBC News, https://www.nbcnews.com/storyline/iraq-turmoil/kurdistans-prime-minister-we-warned-u-s-about-isis-iraq-n137686, last accessed 10 Aug. 2020; 'Sunni Discontent Fuels Growing Violence In Iraq's Anbar Province', NPR, https://www.npr.org/sec-tions/parallels/2014/04/18/304187407/sunni-discontent-fuels-grow-ing-violence-in-iraqs-anbar-province, last accessed 14 Aug. 2020.

23. US Department of Defense, Information Report, http://www.judi-cialwatch.org/wp-content/uploads/2015/05/Pg.-291-Pgs.-287-293-JW-v-DOD-and-State-14-812-DOD-Release-2015-04-10-final-version11.pdf?D=1, last accessed 12 Aug. 2020.

24. The brazen assassination of Russia's ambassador to Turkey, Andrei Karlov, three years later, proved as much. A Turkish police officer, incensed by the situation in Aleppo, had shouted, 'Don't forget about Aleppo, don't forget about Syria', after firing a volley of shots at the diplomat, who was speaking at an art exhibition in Ankara in December 2016.

25. 'The Rise of ISIS in Lebanon', Atlantic Council, https://www.atlan-ticcouncil.org/blogs/menasource/the-rise-of-isis-in-lebanon/, last acces-sed 11 Aug. 2020.

26. 'Suicide bombings kill 23 near Iran embassy in Beirut', Reuters, https://www.reuters.com/article/us-lebanon-blast/suicide-bombings-kill-23-near-iran-embassy-in-beirut-idUSBRE9AI08G20131119, last acces-sed 11 Aug. 2020.

27. 'With Beirut bombing, Iran takes direct hit for helping Assad', The Christian Science Monitor, https://www.csmonitor.com/World/Security-Watch/2013/1119/With-Beirut-bombing-Iran-takes-direct-hit-for-helping-Assad, last accessed 11 Aug. 2020.

28. 'Isis: world leaders give strong backing for Iraq at Paris conference—as it happened', *The Guardian*, https://www.theguardian.com/world/live/2014/sep/15/isis-leaders-hold-crisis-meeting-on-isis-in-paris-live-coverage, last accessed 16 Aug. 2020.

29. 'Iranian Foreign Minister Pledges Support for Iraq in Fight Against ISIS', Council on Foreign Relations, https://www.cfr.org/event/iranian-foreign-minister-pledges-support-iraq-fight-against-isis-0, last accessed 14 Aug. 2020.

30. 'Iranian general killed by sniper bullet in embattled Iraqi city', Reuters, https://www.reuters.com/article/us-mideast-crisis-iran/iranian-general-killed-by-sniper-bullet-in-embattled-iraqi-city-idUSKBN0K60F020141228, last accessed 19 Aug. 2020.

31. 'Shamkhani dar marasem tashiyeh peykar sardar shahid Taghavi', Farda News, https://www.fardanews.com/fa/news/389228/, last accessed 15 Aug. 2020.

32. Dilip Hiro, *A Comprehensive Dictionary of The Middle East*, Northampton, MA: Olive Branch Press, 2013.

33. Reporter notes, June 2017.

34. 'Iran IRIB2 CCTV parliament annexe building ISIL terrorist attack', IRIB Channel 2, https://www.youtube.com/watch?v=tjt0ycNCzrM&ab_channel=alijavid, last accessed 15 Aug. 2020.

35. 'Ravayethayee darbareye hamele teroristi be majles', Tabnak Azar Sharghi, http://www.tabnakazarsharghi.ir/fa/news/438658/, last accessed 21 Aug. 2020.

36. 'Ravayet fordi ke chahar saat dar hamele teroristi dar atagh mahboos bud', Iranian Students' News Agency, https://www.isna.ir/news/96032010696/, last accessed 15 Aug. 2020.

37. 'Ravayethayee darbareye hamele teroristi be majles', Tabnak Azar Sharghi, http://www.tabnakazarsharghi.ir/fa/news/438658/, last accessed 21 Aug. 2020.

38. 'Kidnapped Iran soldiers freed in Pakistan by militants', BBC News, https://www.bbc.com/news/world-asia-26888975, last accessed 14 Aug. 2020. The latter of the two groups had risen to prominence after the high-profile kidnapping of five young soldiers in 2014, all of whom were serving their two-year mandatory military service. The group exe-

cuted one of the young men, before taking the others to Pakistan. Sunni imams in Iran's Sistan-Baluchestan Province helped secure their release two months later.

39. 'Ba khanevadeh Ali Toudeh Fallah—Shahid terror', IRINN, https://www.irinn.ir/fa/news/504834/, last accessed 18 Aug. 2020.

40. 'Iranian Lawmakers Keep Calm, Take Selfies As Gunmen Attack Parliament', Radio Free Europe Radio Liberty, https://www.rferl.org/a/iran-parliament-attack-lawmakers-selfies/28533777.html, last accessed 17 Aug. 2020.

41. 'Ravayethayee darbareye hamele teroristi be majles', Tabnak Azar Sharghi, http://www.tabnakazarsharghi.ir/fa/news/438658/, last accessed 21 Aug. 2020.

42. 'Eftetah mooze yadmeman shahidee terror', Eghtesad Online, https://www.eghtesadonline.com/n/117G, last accessed 17 Aug. 2020.

43. Parliament attack video, posted on *Amaq* website, available at: https://www.aparat.com/v/Zsr8A; Claim of responsibility, posted on *Amaq* website, available at: https://www.aparat.com/v/tfIiM.

44. 'Islamic State says Iran attack will not be the last: al Furqan', Reuters, https://www.reuters.com/article/us-iran-military-attack-islamicstate/islamic-state-says-iran-attack-will-not-be-the-last-al-furqan-idUSKC-N1M62FS, last accessed 21 Aug. 2020.

45. 'Denmark Arrests Three Iranians Accused Of Spying For Saudi Arabia', Radio Farda, https://en.radiofarda.com/a/denmark-arrests-three-iranians-accused-of-spying-for-saudi-arabia/30415026.html, last accessed 21 Aug. 2020.

46. 'Gates: Saudis want to fight Iran to the last American', *Foreign Policy*, https://foreignpolicy.com/2010/12/01/gates-saudis-want-to-fight-iran-to-the-last-american/, last accessed 20 Aug. 2020.

47. Author interview with Trita Parsi, by phone, 21 Sept. 2020.

48. 'Bill Clinton, Boris Yeltsin, and U.S.-Russian Relations', US State Department, https://history.state.gov/milestones/1993–2000/clinton-yeltsin, last accessed 20 Aug. 2020; 'Trump gets elaborate welcome in Saudi Arabia as he embarks on first foreign trip', *The Washington Post*, https://www.washingtonpost.com/politics/trump-gets-elaborate-welcome-in-saudi-arabia-embarking-on-first-foreign-trip/2017/05/20/6

79f2766-3d1d-11e7-a058-ddbb23c75d82_story.html, last accessed 12 Aug. 2020.

49. 'Fanfare And Deals Dominate Trump's First Day In Saudi Arabia', NPR, https://www.npr.org/2017/05/20/529313814/fanfare-and-deals-dominate-trumps-first-day-in-saudi-arabia, last accessed 12 Aug. 2020.

50. 'Saudi Arabia Welcomes Trump With Billions of Dollars of Deals', Bloomberg, https://www.bloomberg.com/news/articles/2017–05–20/aramco-to-sign-50-billion-in-deals-with-u-s-companies-today, last accessed 12 Aug. 2020.

51. 'Fanfare And Deals Dominate Trump's First Day In Saudi Arabia', NPR, https://www.npr.org/2017/05/20/529313814/fanfare-and-deals-dominate-trumps-first-day-in-saudi-arabia, last accessed 12 Aug. 2020.

52. Author interview with Trita Parsi, by phone, 21 Sept. 2020.

53. 'Qatar embraces Wahhabism to strengthen regional influence', Middle East Online, https://middle-east-online.com/en/qatar-embraces-wah-habism-strengthen-regional-influence, last accessed 14 Aug. 2020.

54. 'Qatar: QNA hacking linked to countries boycotting Doha', Al Jazeera English, https://www.aljazeera.com/news/2017/06/qatar-qna-hack-ing-linked-countries-boycotting-doha-170620194406644.html, last accessed 12 Aug. 2020.

55. Reporter notes, Doha, June 2017.

56. Author interview with Khalid bin Mohammad al-Attiyah, Qatar Minister of Defence, Doha, June 2017.

57. 'Severing ties with Qatar not solution for regional crisis: senior Iranian official', Reuters, https://www.reuters.com/article/us-iran-qatar-gulf-idUSKBN18W0OR, last accessed 12 Aug. 2020.

58. 'Saudi FM: Iran must be punished for its interference in the region', Al Arabiya, https://english.alarabiya.net/en/News/gulf/2017/06/06/Saudi-FM-Qatar-must-change-its-policies.html, last accessed 13 Aug. 2020.

59. 'Revolutionary Guards blame Saudi Arabia for Tehran terror attack', *Financial Times*, https://www.ft.com/content/190e854e-4b58–11e7–919a-1e14ce4af89b, last accessed 12 Aug. 2020.

60. 'Powerful Saudi prince sees no chance for dialogue with Iran', Reuters, https://www.reuters.com/article/us-saudi-prince-iran-idUSK-BN17Y1FK, last accessed 13 Aug. 2020.

61. 'Zarif condemns Tehran terror attacks, implicitly points finger at Riyadh', *Tehran Times*, https://www.tehrantimes.com/news/414079/Zarif-condemns-Tehran-terror-attacks-implicitly-points-finger, last accessed 13 Aug. 2020.

62. 'The real reason Iran is pointing finger at Riyadh for IS attack', Al-Monitor, https://www.al-monitor.com/pulse/ar/contents/articles/originals/2017/06/iran-zarif-jafari-abdollahian-blame-saudi-tehran-attacks.html, last accessed 13 Aug. 2020.

63. 'The Ramification of Rouhani's Re-election', Center for International and Security Studies at Maryland (CISSM) and IranPoll, p. 5, July 2017, https://cissm.umd.edu/sites/default/files/2019–07/CISSM%20full%20Iran%20PO%20report%20-%20072717-Final2.pdf, last accessed 13 Aug. 2020.

64. 'At Least 12 Killed in Pair of Terrorist Attacks in Iran', *The New York Times*, https://www.nytimes.com/2017/06/07/world/middleeast/iran-parliament-attack-khomeini-mausoleum.html, last accessed 13 Aug. 2020.

65. Author interview with a US security advisor, on the condition of anonymity, Doha, July 2017.

66. Podesta Emails, Wikileaks, https://wikileaks.org/podesta-emails/emailid/3774, last accessed 21 Aug. 2020; 'Qatar hosts largest US military base in Mideast', CNN, https://edition.cnn.com/2017/06/05/middleeast/qatar-us-largest-base-in-mideast/index.html, last accessed 13 Aug. 2020.

67. 'In secret Goldman Sachs speech, Hillary Clinton admitted no-fly zone would "kill a lot of Syrians"', *The Intercept*, https://theintercept.com/2016/10/10/in-secret-goldman-sachs-speech-hillary-clinton-admitted-no-fly-zone-would-kill-a-lot-of-syrians/, last accessed 13 Aug. 2020.

68. US State Department Cable, Wikileaks, https://wikileaks.org/plusd/cables/09STATE131801_a.html, last accessed 20 Aug. 2020.

69. 'Behind Biden's gaffe lie real concerns about allies' role in rise of the Islamic State', *The Washington Post*, https://www.washingtonpost.com/news/worldviews/wp/2014/10/06/behind-bidens-gaffe-some-legitimate-concerns-about-americas-middle-east-allies/, last accessed 13 Aug. 2020.

70. Reporter notes, Ahvaz, 2014.

71. Mohammad Hossein Fahmideh was a thirteen-year-old volunteer who ran away from home in Qom to join the war. In the first weeks of the invasion, as Iraqi troops and tanks advanced on Khorramshahr, the volunteers, lacking heavy weapons, were cut down, unable to stop the advancing column. So, the young Fahmideh wrapped grenades around his body and threw himself under an advancing Iraqi tank. The Iraqi unit, thinking the Iranians had mined the area, retreated.

72. Mostafa Chamran was an Iranian leftist, who received degrees from Texas A&M and UC Berkeley. He abandoned life as an academic in the US to join the Iranian revolution and was appointed the new Islamic Republic's first defence minister. He founded the Irregular Warfare Headquarters during the Iran–Iraq War. He was killed in action on 20 June 1981, in Dehlaviyeh, Khuzestan Province.

73. 'Return of 175 Iranian bodies from Iraq stirs painful memories', Al-Monitor, https://www.al-monitor.com/pulse/fa/originals/2015/05/iran-175-martyrs-iran-iraq-war.html, last accessed 17 Aug. 2020.

74. Author interview with Ahmad Zangiabadi, Tehran, Feb 2013.

75. Author interview with Shahriar Khateri, Tehran, Feb. 2013.

76. UNSC Report S17911—Investigation into allegation of chemical weapons use, UNSC, http://www.securitycouncilreport.org/atf/cf/%7B65BF CF9B-6D27-4E9C-8CD3-CF6E4FF96FF9%7D/Disarm%20S17911.pdf, last accessed 20 Aug. 2020.

77. 'Iraq use of chemical weapons', US Department of State declassified internal memorandum, https://nsarchive2.gwu.edu/NSAEBB/NSAE BB82/iraq24.pdf, last accessed 20 Aug. 2020; 'Chemical Weapons: Meeting with Iraqi Charge', NSA declassified dispatch, https://nsar-chive2.gwu.edu/NSAEBB/NSAEBB82/iraq54.pdf, last accessed 20 Aug. 2020.

78. 'Iraq use of chemical weapons', US Department of State declassified internal memorandum, https://nsarchive2.gwu.edu/NSAEBB/NSAE BB82/iraq24.pdf, last accessed 20 Aug. 2020.

79. 'Letter dated 30 July 2002 from the Chargé d'affaires a.i. of the Permanent Mission of the Islamic Republic of Iran to the United Nations addressed to the Secretary-General', available at: http://www.

iranwatch.org/international/UNSC/unsc-s2002860-irancomm-080202.
pdf, last accessed 20 Aug. 2020.

80. 'Seeking answers for Iran's chemical weapons victims—before time runs out', *Science*, https://www.sciencemag.org/news/2018/01/seeking-answers-iran-s-chemical-weapons-victims-time-runs-out, last accessed 18 Aug. 2020.

81. '1988: Thousands die in Halabja gas attack', BBC News, http://news.bbc.co.uk/onthisday/hi/dates/stories/march/16/newsid_4304000/4304853.stm, last accessed 19 Aug. 2020.

82. 'Saddam's "Dutch link"', BBC News, http://news.bbc.co.uk/2/hi/middle_east/4358741.stm, last accessed 21 Aug. 2020; 'Iraqi Kurds sue French companies for Halabja chemical attack', RFI, https://www.rfi.fr/en/france/20130611-iraqi-kurds-sue-french-companies-halabja-chemical-attack, last accessed 21 Aug. 2020; 'The long road to war: The arming of Iraq', PBS, https://www.pbs.org/wgbh/pages/frontline/shows/longroad/etc/arming.html, last accessed 21 Aug. 2020; 'Britain's dirty secret', *The Guardian*, https://www.theguardian.com/politics/2003/mar/06/uk.iraq, last accessed 21 Aug. 2020; 'Leaked report says German and US firms supplied arms to Saddam', *The Independent*, https://www.independent.co.uk/news/world/politics/leaked-report-says-german-and-us-firms-supplied-arms-to-saddam-136466.html, last accessed 21 Aug. 2020.

83. 'Iran's Message: We Can Make History', Mohammad Javad Zarif, https://www.youtube.com/watch?v=16VIQ6LJCt8&feature=emb_title, last accessed 21 Aug. 2020.

84. Reporter notes, April 2017.

85. 'IRGC Commanders' Letter to Khatami', Iran Data Portal, https://irandataportal.syr.edu/irgc-commanders-letter-to-khatami, last accessed 12 July 2020.

86. Author interview with Rohollah Faghihi, by phone, 4 Sept. 2020.

87. 'The Shadow Commander', *The New Yorker*, http://www.newyorker.com/magazine/2013/09/30/the-shadow-commander, last accessed 20 Aug. 2020.

88. 'Major General Qasem Soleimani', *Time*, https://time.com/collection/2017-time-100/4736337/qasem-soleimani/, last accessed 20 Aug. 2020.

89. 'Hajj Qassem Soleimani kist?', Asr Iran, https://www.asriran.com/000mx2, last accessed 9 Sept. 2020.

9. *MA CHEGOONE MA SHODIM?* (WHAT HAS BECOME OF US?)

1. 'War in Europe reaches end', UPI, https://www.upi.com/Archives/1945/05/08/War-in-Europe-reaches-end/7236411013416/, last accessed 31 Aug. 2020.

2. 'Remarks by President Trump on the Joint Comprehensive Plan of Action', White House, https://www.whitehouse.gov/briefings-statements/remarks-president-trump-joint-comprehensive-plan-action/, last accessed 31 Aug. 2020.

3. 'John Kerry: "[Trump] has taken a situation where there was no crisis, and created crisis", MSNBC, https://www.msnbc.com/deadline-whitehouse/watch/john-kerry-trump-has-taken-a-situation-where-there-was-no-crisis-and-created-crisis-1228479555505, last accessed 1 Sept. 2020.

4. 'Trump fires Rex Tillerson as secretary of state', BBC News, https://www.bbc.com/news/world-us-canada-43388723, last accessed 31 Aug. 2020.

5. 'Press Briefing by National Security Advisor John Bolton on Iran', White House Press Briefing, https://www.whitehouse.gov/briefings-statements/press-briefing-national-security-advisor-john-bolton-iran/, last accessed 1 Sept. 2020.

6. 'John Kerry: "[Trump] has taken a situation where there was no crisis, and created crisis"', MSNBC, https://www.msnbc.com/deadline-whitehouse/watch/john-kerry-trump-has-taken-a-situation-where-there-was-no-crisis-and-created-crisis-1228479555505, last accessed 1 Sept. 2020.

7. 'Iran nuclear deal: Trump pulls US out in break with Europe allies', BBC News, https://www.bbc.com/news/world-us-canada-44045957, last accessed 1 Sept. 2020.

8. 'Nucléaire iranien: pour Hollande, "la stratégie de la séduction ne pouvait marcher sur Trump"', Europe 1, https://www.europe1.fr/politique/nucleaire-iranien-pour-francois-hollande-la-strategie-de-la-seduction-ne-pouvait-marcher-sur-trump-3647996, last accessed 1 Sept. 2020.

9. 'Updated Blocking Statute in support of Iran nuclear deal enters into force', European Commission Press Release, https://ec.europa.eu/commission/presscorner/detail/en/IP_18_4805, last accessed 2 Sept. 2020.

10. 'French carmaker PSA to leave Iran over risk of US sanctions', France 24, https://www.france24.com/en/20180605-business-iran-usa-france-carmaker-psa-peugeot-citroen-leave-over-risk-us-sanctions, last accessed 1 Sept. 2020

11. 'Iran: Total signs heads of agreement to develop Phase 11 of the giant South Pars Gas Field', Total press release, https://www.total.com/media/news/press-releases/iran-total-signs-heads-agreement-develop-phase-11-giant-south-pars-gas-field, last accessed 1 Sept. 2020; 'Total tells Iran it's quitting South Pars gas project', Reuters, https://www.reuters.com/article/us-iran-france-total-gas/total-tells-iran-its-quit-ting-south-pars-gas-project-idUSKCN1L51LH, last accessed 1 Sept. 2020.

12. 'Iran urges EU to press Washington on Airbus deliveries: ISNA', Reuters, https://www.reuters.com/article/us-iran-airbus/iran-urges-eu-to-press-washington-on-airbus-deliveries-isna-idUSKBN1OG19X, last accessed 1 Sept. 2020.

13. Author interview with Hooshang Shahbazi, by phone, 9 Sept. 2020.

14. Author interview with Trita Parsi, by phone, 21 Sept. 2020.

15. 'Treasury Sanctions Companies for Enabling the Shipment and Sale of Iranian Petrochemicals', US Department of the Treasury, https://home.treasury.gov/news/press-releases/sm1114, last accessed 4 Sept. 2020.

16. 'Treasury Targets Iran's Billion Dollar Metals Industry and Senior Regime Officials', US Department of the Treasury, https://home.treasury.gov/news/press-releases/sm870, last accessed 4 Sept. 2020.

17. 'After the Deal: A New Iran Strategy', US State Department, https://www.state.gov/after-the-deal-a-new-iran-strategy/, last accessed 31 Aug. 2020.

18. 'Iranian leaders shun "chalice of poison"', The Christian Science Monitor, https://www.csmonitor.com/World/Middle-East/2019/0628/Iranian-leaders-shun-chalice-of-poison, last accessed 31 Aug. 2020.

19. 'SWIFT says suspending some Iranian banks' access to messaging sys-

tem', Reuters, https://www.reuters.com/article/us-usa-iran-sanctions-swift/swift-says-suspending-some-iranian-banks-access-to-messaging-system-idUSKCN1NA1PN, last accessed 2 Sept. 2020.

20. 'U.S. imposes record fine on BNP in sanctions warning to banks', Reuters, https://www.reuters.com/article/us-bnp-paribas-settlement/u-s-imposes-record-fine-on-bnp-in-sanctions-warning-to-banks-idUSKBN0F52HA20140701, last accessed 4 Sept. 2020.

21. 'Europe Circumvents U.S. Sanctions On Iran', Forbes, https://www.forbes.com/sites/francescoppola/2019/06/30/europe-circumvents-u-s-sanctions-on-iran/#4d7efbb32c8d, last accessed 2 Sept. 2020.

22. 'Facing Reality: Europe's Special Purpose Vehicle Will Not Challenge US Sanctions', Atlantic Council, https://www.atlanticcouncil.org/blogs/iransource/facing-reality-europe-s-special-purpose-vehicle-will-not-challenge-us-sanctions/, last accessed 2 Sept. 2020.

23. 'Salehi: Iran has fully implemented fourth step of reducing JCPOA commitment', Iranian Diplomacy, http://irdiplomacy.ir/en/news/1995351/salehi-iran-has-fully-implemented-fourth-step-of-reducing-jcpoa-commitment, last accessed 15 Sept. 2020.

24. Author interview with Emad Abshenas, by phone, 10 Sept. 2020.

25. 'Agriculture min. facing impeachment over rising prices', Mehr News, https://en.mehrnews.com/news/130647/Agriculture-min-facing-impeachment-over-rising-prices, last accessed 13 Sept. 2020; 'Dramatic Rise in Egg Prices', Financial Tribune, https://financialtribune.com/articles/economy-business-and-markets/78667/dramatic-rise-in-egg-prices, last accessed 9 Sept. 2020.

26. 'Iranians protest rising food prices,' The New York Times, https://www.nytimes.com/2017/12/28/world/middleeast/iranians-protest-rising-food-prices.html, last accessed 18 Sept. 2020.

27. Author interview with Iranian analyst, on the condition of anonymity, by phone, 9 Sept. 2020.

28. 'Iran protests: Supreme leader blames "enemies" for meddling', Associated Press, https://apnews.com/article/0337232e446e41e49211dc71a788e152, last accessed 28 Sept. 2020.

29. 'Rouhani's budget transparency stokes Iran unrest', Financial Times, https://www.ft.com/content/d3f6eebe-f9e0-11e7-a492-2c9be7f3120a, last accessed 9 Sept. 2020.

30. 'IRGC Told to Lay Off Economic Activities', *Financial Tribune*, https://financialtribune.com/articles/economy-domestic-economy/80544/irgc-told-to-lay-off-economic-activities, last accessed 9 Sept. 2020.

31. 'Khamenei Apologizes for Iran State Shortcomings Amid Discontent', Bloomberg, https://www.bloomberg.com/news/articles/2018–02–18/khamenei-extends-apology-says-iran-must-provide-more-justice, last accessed 9 Sept. 2020.

32. 'Iranians Protest Rising Food Prices,' Associated Press, https://apnews.com/article/e6d0d8af36bd4d2da759a380ed582642, last accessed 2 Mar. 2021.

33. 'Saeed Laylaz: Hadaf aterazat mardom, benzin nist; fased va nakaramadi ast', Shafaqna, https://fa.shafaqna.com/news/842798/, last accessed 15 Sept. 2020.

34. 'Iran gasoline rationing, price hikes draw street protests,' Reuters, https://uk.reuters.com/article/us-iran-gasoline-rationing/iran-gasoline-rationing-price-hikes-draw-street-protests-idUKKBN1XO2ZE, last accessed 10 Sept. 2020.

35. 'Iran's Information Minister Says Country's Internet Was Shut Down to Keep Nation Safe', *Newsweek*, https://www.newsweek.com/iran-minister-internet-shut-safety-1472470, last accessed 10 Sept. 2020.

36. 'How the Iranian Government Shut Off the Internet', Wired, https://www.wired.com/story/iran-internet-shutoff/, last accessed 10 Sept. 2020.

37. 'Iran says hundreds of banks were torched in "vast" unrest plot', Reuters, https://www.reuters.com/article/us-iran-gasoline-protests-minister-idUSKBN1Y10GY, last accessed 18 Sept. 2020.

38. 'Iran: Details released of 304 deaths during protests six months after security forces' killing spree', Amnesty International, https://www.amnesty.org/en/latest/news/2020/05/iran-details-released-of-304-deaths-during-protests-six-months-after-security-forces-killing-spree/, last accessed 15 Sept. 2020.

39. Forough Farrokhzad, in Michael C. Hillman, *A Lonely Woman: Forugh Farrokhzad and Her Poetry*, Washington, DC: Three Continents Press, 1987. Translated from Persian by Michael C. Hillman.

40. 'Japanese oil tanker owner disagrees with US military that a mine caused

blast near Iran', CNBC, https://www.cnbc.com/2019/06/14/oil-tanker-owner-disagrees-with-us-that-mine-caused-blast-near-iran.html; 'Two Major Saudi Oil Installations Hit by Drone Strike, and U.S. Blames Iran', *The New York Times*, https://www.nytimes.com/2019/09/14/world/middleeast/saudi-arabia-refineries-drone-attack.html, last accessed 29 Sept. 2020.

41. 'Iran shoots down US drone aircraft, raising tensions further in Strait of Hormuz', CNN, https://edition.cnn.com/2019/06/20/middleeast/iran-drone-claim-hnk-intl/index.html, last accessed 28 Sept. 2020.

42. 'Operation Praying Mantis', Naval History and Heritage Command, https://www.history.navy.mil/browse-by-topic/wars-conflicts-and-operations/middle-east/praying-mantis.html, last accessed 28 Sept. 2020.

43. 'Sea Of Lies', *Newsweek*, https://www.newsweek.com/sea-lies-200118, last accessed 28 Sept. 2020.

44. Ibid.

45. 'America's Flight 17', *Slate*, https://slate.com/news-and-politics/2014/07/the-vincennes-downing-of-iran-air-flight-655-the-united-states-tried-to-cover-up-its-own-destruction-of-a-passenger-plane.html, last accessed 4 Mar. 21.

46. 'Excerpts of Vice President George Bush's Remarks to U.N. Security Council', Associated Press, https://apnews.com/article/11dfc43c80db471b5980831baf676cfd, last accessed 28 Sept. 2020.

47. 'Navy Awards Medals To Vincennes Officers', Associated Press, https://apnews.com/article/fd61c6f19690534cff58995092cbe885, last accessed 28 Sept. 2020.

48. 'American Contractor Killed in Rocket Attack in Iraq', *The New York Times*, https://www.nytimes.com/2019/12/27/us/politics/american-rocket-attack-iraq.html, last accessed 28 Sept. 2020.

49. 'Kataib Hezbollah: Iraq condemns US attacks on Iran-backed militia', BBC News, https://www.bbc.com/news/world-middle-east-50951742, last accessed 15 Sept. 2020.

50. 'Iraq slams US airstrikes, warns of consequences', Deutsche Welle, https://www.dw.com/en/iraq-slams-us-airstrikes-warns-of-conse-quences/a-51840975, last accessed 28 Sept. 2020.

51. 'Protesters storm US embassy compound in Baghdad', Al Jazeera English, https://www.aljazeera.com/news/2019/12/31/protesters-storm-us-embassy-compound-in-baghdad/, last accessed 23 Sept. 2020.

52. 'Iran's Rouhani under fire over "peace time" promises', Al-Monitor, https://www.al-monitor.com/pulse/originals/2019/12/iran-rouhani-under-fire-peace-time-promises.html, last accessed 15 Sept. 2020.

53. Data and flight tracking information via https://www.flightradar24.com/data/flights/6q501#236437bb, last accessed 4 Jan. 2020.

54. 'Tracked, targeted, killed: Qassem Soleimani's final hours', Middle East Eye, https://www.middleeasteye.net/news/tracked-targeted-killed-qassem-soleimanis-final-hours, last accessed 18 Sept. 2020.

55. Babak Taghvaee, Twitter, https://twitter.com/BabakTaghvaee/status/1212908388763480071, last accessed 4 Mar. 21.

56. Author interview with Mehdi Taremi, by phone, February 2020.

57. 'Hamelate sangin moshaki sepah be paygah ain al assad', Mashregh News, https://www.mashreghnews.ir/news/1028835/, last accessed 17 Sept. 2020.

58. 'Iran missile strike: Two US-Iraq bases hit by 22 rockets in revenge attacks as crisis escalates', *The Independent*, https://www.independent.co.uk/news/world/middle-east/iran-rocket-attack-iraq-missiles-us-bases-trump-soleimani-a9274546.html, last accessed 17 Sept. 2020.

59. '"Surviving was a miracle": Iran's missile attack on Iraq base', France 24, https://www.france24.com/en/20200114-surviving-was-a-miracle-iran-s-missile-attack-on-iraq-base, last accessed 18 Sept. 2020.

60. 'Additional US service member diagnosed with brain injury from Iran attack', The Hill, https://thehill.com/policy/defense/484151-additional-us-service-member-diagnosed-with-brain-injury-from-iran-attack, last accessed 17 Sept. 2020.

61. '"Woman was worried before her plane crashed in Iran, her husband says. She called him 20 minutes before takeoff", CNN, https://edition.cnn.com/2020/01/09/middleeast/iran-plane-crash-victim-husband-speaks/index.html, last accessed 26 Feb. 2021.

62. 'Sheyda Shadkhoo, who worked in Markham, remembered as "very nice, super funny"', York Region, https://www.yorkregion.com/news-story/9806788-sheyda-shadkhoo-who-worked-in-markham-remembered-as-very-nice-super-funny-/, last accessed 19 Sept. 2020.

63. 'Mourning his wife after Iran plane crash', CBC, https://www.cbc.ca/player/play/1668407875952, last accessed 19 Sept. 2020.

64. 'Anatomy of a Lie: How Iran Covered Up the Downing of an Airliner', *The New York Times*, https://www.nytimes.com/2020/01/26/world/middleeast/iran-plane-crash-coverup.html, last accessed 17 Sept. 2020.

65. 'PS752 Accident Investigation', Civil Aviation Organization of the Islamic Republic of Iran, https://reports.aviation-safety.net/2020/2020 0108–0_B738_UR-PSR_FACTUAL.pdf, last accessed 17 Sept. 2020.

66. Ibid.

67. 'The Iranian Who Obtained The Video Of Two Missiles Striking The Ukrainian Plane Has Gone Into Hiding', Buzzfeed News, https://www.buzzfeednews.com/article/christopherm51/the-iranian-who-got-the-video-of-two-missiles-striking-the, last accessed 17 Sept. 2020.

68. Author interview with Ahmad Halabisaz, by phone, 29 Sept. 2020.

69. 'Kash mordam va shad hadse sarnegooni havapeymai ukraini nabudam', Mashregh News, https://www.mashreghnews.ir/news/1030069/, last accessed 18 Sept. 2020.

70. Ibid.

71. 'Tosihat farmande sepah dar majles darmored eshtebah padofand', Tabnak News, https://www.tabnak.ir/fa/news/951223/, last accessed 18 Sept. 2020.

72. 'Entegham ma tanha be yek sili mahdoud nemishavad', Mashregh News, https://www.mashreghnews.ir/news/1029222/, last accessed 19 Sept. 2020.

73. 'Iran Admits It Accidentally Shot Down Ukrainian Plane', *Time*, https://time.com/5761206/iran-plane-crash/, last accessed 17 Sept. 2020.

74. 'Anatomy of a Lie: How Iran Covered Up the Downing of an Airliner', *The New York Times*, https://www.nytimes.com/2020/01/26/world/middleeast/iran-plane-crash-coverup.html, last accessed 18 Sept. 2020.

75. 'Bianie heyat dolat darkhasous vaghaye akhir keshvar,' Khabaran, https://khabarban.com/a/26492453, last accessed 17 Sept. 2020.

76. Hassan Rouhani, Twitter, https://twitter.com/HassanRouhani/status/1215856679423823872.

77. 'Raviat sokhangooi dolat darbareye nahve e'tela'a dolat az dalil soghoot

havapeyma', Khabaran, https://khabarban.com/a/26495091, last accessed 17. Sept. 2020.

78. 'Anatomy of a Lie: How Iran Covered Up the Downing of an Airliner', *The New York Times*, https://www.nytimes.com/2020/01/26/world/middleeast/iran-plane-crash-coverup.html, last accessed 18 Sept. 2020.

79. 'Anche dorough mi pandashtand khabar bud', Etemad Online, https://etemadonline.com/content/376837/, last accessed 17 Sept. 2020.

80. 'Vakansh Zibakalam be khabar asabat mooshak be havapeiymai ukraini', Hamshahri Online, https://www.hamshahrionline.ir/news/477221/, last accessed 16 Sept. 2020.

81. Taraneh Alidoosti, Instagram, 15 Jan. 2020, https://www.instagram.com/p/B7TWbqOJpg7/, last accessed 18 Sept. 2020.

82. 'Pneumonia of unknown cause—China', World Health Organization, https://www.who.int/csr/don/05-january-2020-pneumonia-of-unkown-cause-china/en/, last accessed 13 Sept. 2020.

83. 'WHO Coronavirus Disease (COVID-19) Dashboard', World Health Organization, https://covid19.who.int/, last accessed 13 Sept. 2020.

84. 'Two patients suspected of coronavirus quarantined in northern Iran', Islamic Republic News Agency, https://en.irna.ir/news/83682322/Two-patients-suspected-of-coronavirus-quarantined-in-northern, last accessed 23 Sept. 2020.

85. 'Coronavirus: Iran bans internal travel to avert "second wave"', BBC News, https://www.bbc.com/news/world-middle-east-52039298, last accessed 14 Sept. 2020; 'Iran to re-impose virus restrictions if rules violated', Anadolu Agency, https://www.aa.com.tr/en/middle-east/iran-to-re-impose-virus-restrictions-if-rules-violated/1875633, last accessed 13 Sept. 2020.

86. 'Iran's Majlis speaker tests positive for coronavirus', Islamic Republic News Agency, https://en.irna.ir/news/83736684/Iran-s-Majlis-speaker-tests-positive-for-coronavirus, last accessed 13 Sept. 2020.

87. Author interview with Ahmad Halabisaz, by phone, 29 Sept. 2020.

88. Author interview with government advisor, on the condition of anonymity, by phone, 11. Aug. 2020.

89. 'EU foreign policy chief chides U.S. for blocking Iran loan', *Politico*, https://www.politico.com/news/2020/04/22/eu-foreign-policy-chief-chides-us-for-blocking-iran-loan-201724, last accessed 14 Sept. 2020.

90. 'Iran calls on IMF to defy U.S., grant it $5b loan', *Tehran Times*, https://www.tehrantimes.com/news/448909/Iran-calls-on-IMF-to-defy-U-S-grant-it-5b-loan, last accessed 14 Sept. 2020.

91. 'EU foreign policy chief chides U.S. for blocking Iran loan', *Politico*, https://www.politico.com/news/2020/04/22/eu-foreign-policy-chief-chides-us-for-blocking-iran-loan-201724, last accessed 14 Sept. 2020.

92. 'White House knows nothing about humanity: Rouhani', Mehr News, https://en.mehrnews.com/news/163407/White-House-knows-nothing-about-humanity-Rouhani, last accessed 14 Sept. 2020.

93. 'Iran (Islamic Republic of)', World Health Organization, https://covid19.who.int/region/emro/country/ir, last accessed 13 Sept. 2020.

94. 'Dollar Soars to Near Record Level in Iran', Radio Farda, https://en.radiofarda.com/a/dollar-soars-to-near-record-level-in-iran-/30829462.html, last accessed 14 Sept. 2020.

95. 'Iran on US medicine sanctions: White House has no sense of humanity', Pars Today, https://parstoday.com/en/news/iran-i126601-iran_on_us_medicine_sanctions_white_house_has_no_sense_of_humanity, last accessed 4 Mar. 21.

96. 'Iran's oil storage almost full as sanctions and pandemic weigh', Reuters, https://www.reuters.com/article/us-iran-oil-storage-idUSKBN2481M3, last accessed 24 Sept. 2020.

97. Ibid.

98. 'Hazine va daramad khanvarhayi Irani aalam shod', Iranian Students' New Agency, https://www.isna.ir/news/98060301070/, last accessed 19 Sept. 2020.

99. 'Liste darooi sazman ghaza va daroo be roui bimaran distrofi baste ast', Saalem News, http://www.saalemnews.com/news/7733/, last accessed 20 Sept. 2020.

100. 'Factbox: The outcome of Iran's 2020 parliamentary elections', Atlantic Council, https://www.atlanticcouncil.org/blogs/iransource/factbox-the-outcome-of-irans-2020-parliamentary-elections/, last accessed 14 Sept. 2020.

101. 'Masharkat 42/57 darsadi dar entekhabat', Iranian Students' News Agency, https://www.isna.ir/news/98120403161/, last accessed 14 Sept. 2020.

102. '2016 Parliamentary Election,' Iran Data Portal, https://irandataportal.syr.edu/parliamentary-elections/2016-parliamentary-election, last accessed 2 Mar. 2021.

103. 'Tasviri az dakhel kelinik Sina Athar ke dishab dochar enfejar va atash souzi shod', Khabar Online, https://www.khabaronline.ir/news/1405583/, last accessed 19 Sept. 2020.

104. 'Gas explosion at Iran medical clinic kills 19', *The Guardian*, https://www.theguardian.com/world/2020/jul/01/tehran-gas-explosion-at-iran-medical-clinic-kills-19, last accessed 19 Sept. 2020; 'Blast in East Tehran Caused by Gas Tank Explosion: Defense Ministry', Tasnim News Agency, https://www.tasnimnews.com/en/news/2020/06/26/2293768/blast-in-east-tehran-caused-by-gas-tank-explosion-defense-ministry, last accessed 5 July 2020.

105. 'Incident in one of the niches being built in Natanz complex', Atomic Energy Organization of Iran, https://aeoi.org.ir/EN/portal/home/?news/45799/69280/303760/incident-in-one-of-the-niches-being-built-in-natanz-complex, last accessed 20 Sept. 2020; 'Jaziate atashsouzi dar karkhane lanjsazi Bushehr', Tasnim News Agency, https://www.tasnimnews.com/fa/news/1399/04/25/2307438/, last accessed 20 Sept. 2020; 'Hale 70 masdoum hadase nashte kelor dar petroshimiaee Mahsahr matloub', Islamic Republic News Agency, https://www.irna.ir/news/83844163/, last accessed 20 Sept. 2020; 'Cause of Natanz's accident to be made public at appropriate time due to security considerations', Iranian Students' News Agency, https://en.isna.ir/news/99041410337/Cause-of-Natanze-s-accident-to-be-made-publice-at-appropriate, last accessed 20 Sept. 2020.

106. 'Iran Admits Serious Damage to Natanz Nuclear Site, Setting Back Program', *The New York Times*, https://www.nytimes.com/2020/07/05/world/middleeast/iran-Natanz-nuclear-damage.html, last accessed 20 Sept. 2020; 'Iran threatens retaliation after what it calls possible cyber attack on nuclear sit', Reuters, https://www.reuters.com/article/us-iran-nuclear-natanz/iran-threatens-retaliation-after-what-it-calls-possible-cyber-attack-on-nuclear-site-idUSKBN2441VY, last accessed 19 Sept. 2020.

107. 'Iran Admits Serious Damage to Natanz Nuclear Site, Setting Back

Program', *The New York Times*, https://www.nytimes.com/2020/07/05/world/middleeast/iran-Natanz-nuclear-damage.html, last accessed 20 Sept. 2020.

108. 'Mysterious explosions pose dilemma for Iranian leaders', *The Washington Post*, https://www.washingtonpost.com/world/middle_east/mysterious-explosions-pose-dilemma-for-iranian-leaders/2011/11/23/gIQA8IsSvN_story.html, last accessed 19 Sept. 2020; 'Obama Order Sped Up Wave of Cyberattacks Against Iran', *The New York Times*, https://www.nytimes.com/2012/06/01/world/middleeast/obama-ordered-wave-of-cyberattacks-against-iran.html, last accessed 26 Feb. 2021; 'An Unprecedented Look at Stuxnet, the World's First Digital Weapon', *Wired*, https://www.wired.com/2014/11/countdown-to-zero-day-stuxnet/, last accessed 20 Sept. 2020.

109. 'Blast at Revolutionary Guard base kills 17', *The Washington Post*, https://www.washingtonpost.com/world/middle_east/blast-at-revolutionary-guard-base-kills-15/2011/11/12/gIQAtML7EN_story.html, last accessed 20 Sept. 2020.

110. 'When Israel Hatched a Secret Plan to Assassinate Iranian Scientists', *Politico*, https://www.politico.com/magazine/story/2018/03/05/israel-assassination-iranian-scientists-217223, last accessed 20 Sept. 2020.

111. Author interview with Foad Shams, by phone, 3 Sept. 2020.

112. Author interview with Trita Parsi, by phone, 21 Sept. 2020.

113. 'Qalibaf elected Iran's new Parliament speaker', *Tehran Times*, https://www.tehrantimes.com/news/448288/Qalibaf-elected-Iran-s-new-Parliament-speaker, last accessed 15 Sept. 2020.

114. 'Defaye Qalibaf az kod dar paygah basij: majoz masour nezami va tirandazi dar kooye daneshgah ra man gereftam', Kaleme, https://www.kaleme.com/1392/02/25/klm-143690/?theme=fast, last accessed 19 Sept. 2020.

115. 'Iran's Majles: A Parliament Of IRGC Commanders', Radio Farda, https://en.radiofarda.com/a/iran-majles-a-parliament-of-irgc-commanders/30649083.html, last accessed 19 Sept. 2020.

116. 'Mazakare ba ghatel Hajj Qasem Soleimani chizi jaz sharm abadi nadarad', Mizan Online, https://www.mizanonline.com/fa/news/626990/, last accessed 18 Sept. 2020.

117. Author interview with Rohollah Faghihi, by phone, 4 Sept. 2020.
118. 'Landscapes of the Mind', *The Guardian*, https://www.theguardian. com/film/2005/apr/16/art, last accessed 22 July 2020.
119. Author interview with Ahmad Halabisaz, by phone, 29 Sept. 2020.
120. Author interview with Foad Shams, by phone, 3 Sept. 2020.

ACKNOWLEDGEMENTS

This book has been many years in the making, and there are countless Iranians, nameless or otherwise, who have contributed in immeasurable ways. They have shaped the pages of this book, and I am forever grateful to those who have shared even a brief moment of their lives with me.

Immeasurable gratitude goes to the team at Hurst, in particular Michael Dwyer and Farhaana Arefin for the possibility, expertise and direction. It has been a pleasure working with you all.

On a personal level, I want to thank the following people:

Abji Faranak for your loyalty and friendship, and Ahmad Halabisaz for your honesty and beautiful photographs. Thank you also to Mohsen Kadivar for sharing, with great humour, your memories, including of his eminence Grand Ayatollah Montazeri.

Thank you also to Trita Parsi, Foad Shams, Rohollah Faghihi, Neda Anisi and Hooshang Shahbazi.

I would also like to thank friends, in particular Nevin, Noosheen and Lina, for the enthusiasm when I had run out, and Judy, Jo and Irene for the years of support. David Patrikarakos for the much-needed prod, and Tanya Goudsouzian for the kindness, food and port that helped turn a long-buried frustrated idea into a possibility.

I would also like to thank my other family, Arsalan, Shy, Azi and Sia for all the love. As always, Azi, I would be adrift without you, including on this project.

ACKNOWLEDGEMENTS

Lastly, I'd like to thank my mother, father, Roya and Yasmin for the understanding, *ghormeh sabzi*, endless cups of tea and free housing. I am very lucky indeed, and none of this would have been possible without you.

INDEX

INDEX

INDEX

INDEX

INDEX

INDEX

INDEX

INDEX

INDEX

INDEX

INDEX

INDEX

INDEX

INDEX

INDEX

INDEX

INDEX

Syria, 31, 32, 36, 42, 192, 196–9, 212–13

Tajgardoon, Gholam Reza, 205
Tajrish Square, Tehran, 11, 258
Takht-e Ravanchi, Majid, 156
takht, 97
Talabani, Jalal, 195
Taleghani Park, Tehran, 90
Taliban, 123
Talwar, Puneet, 119
Taqavi, Hamid, 193, 195, 199
Taqizadeh, Haidar Ali, 147–8
Taraghi, Hamidreza, 211
Taremi, Mehdi, 239, 243, 264–5
Tasnim News Agency, 186
Tasu'a, 208
Tehran
  Ab-o-Atash Park, 90
  Azadi Square, 134, 204
  Azadi Stadium, 187
  Bagh-e Melli, 79
  Baharestan, 200–207
  Behesht-e Zahra Cemetery, 206
  Bostan-e Honarmand, 132
  British Embassy attack (2011), 126
  Darband, 95–6
  Ebrat Museum, 68–70
  Evin Prison, 31, 70, 117
  Gisha, 165
  Grand Bazaar, 13, 144, 204, 214
  Haft-e Tir, 94, 98, 118
  Hosseinieh Jamaran, 177

hostage crisis (1979–81), 57–63
  Imam Khomeini Airport, 20, 21, 41, 245
  Imam Sadiq University, 87–8
  Imam Hussein University, 218
  Iran Air 742 emergency (2011), 19–25
  ISIL attacks (2017), 200–207, 210–11, 228
  Israeli assassinations (2010–12), xv
  Jamkaran Mosque, 100
  Jewish quarter, 124
  Kahrizak Detention Center, 53, 54–5, 70
  Khomeini Mausoleum, 181, 204, 206, 207
  Khorasan, 9
  Mahak Charity bazaar, 7
  Mehrabad Airport, 19, 21, 129, 171
  Metro, 89
  NAM summit (2012), 40–42
  Nasser Khosrow Street, 13, 14, 15, 255
  Niayesh Tunnel, 89
  Parchin military site, 259
  Park-e Mellat, 89
  Peace Museum, 217
  Pol-e Tabiat, 89
  Qalibaf mayoralty (2005–17), 89, 164–5
  Sadr Expressway, 89
  Sepahan Airlines crash (2014), 26–7

INDEX

INDEX

INDEX